Design for London

Design for London

Experiments in urban thinking

Edited by

Peter Bishop and Lesley Williams

UCLPRESS

First published in 2020 by
UCL Press
University College London
Gower Street
London WC1E 6BT

Available to download free: www.uclpress.co.uk

A CIP catalogue record for this book is available from The British Library.

ISBN: 978-1-78735-896-6 (Hbk)
ISBN: 978-1-78735-895-9 (Pbk)
ISBN: 978-1-78735-894-2 (PDF)
ISBN: 978-1-78735-897-3 (epub)
ISBN: 978-1-78735-898-0 (mobi)
DOI: https://doi.org/10.14324/111.9781787358942

There is still a chance against all the odds, if we fight, that some of it will turn out well.

– Mark Brearley, Introduction to the Thames Gateway Strategy, 2004

Contents

List of figures

Notes on contributors

Isabel Allen was a member of Design for London and is Editor-in-Chief of *Citizen* magazine.

Peter Bishop was Director of Design for London from 2006 to 2011 and is currently Professor of Urban Design at The Bartlett School of Architecture, UCL, and a partner at Bishop and Williams Consultants.

Mark Brearley joined the newly established Architecture and Urbanism Unit in 2001 and was Head of Design for London from 2008 to 2013. He is now the proprietor of the London manufacturer Kaymet and Professor of Urbanism at the London Metropolitan University School of Art, Architecture and Design.

Esther Everett was a member of Design for London and is now Head of Design at the London Legacy Development Corporation.

Eleanor Fawcett was a member of Design for London and is now Head of Design at the Old Oak Common Development Corporation.

Tobias Goevert was a member of Design for London and is now City Planning and Urbanism Director at the City of Hamburg.

Eva Herr was a member of Design for London and is now Planning Director at the City of Cologne.

Lara Kinneir was a member of Design for London and is now a designer, ministerial advisor and programme leader at the London School of Architecture.

Richa Mukhia was a member of Design for London and is now a Director of M.OS Architects and Senior Lecturer at the University of Westminster.

Adam Towle was a member of Design for London and is now Principal Development Manager at the London Borough of Ealing and Design Advisor to Design South East.

Lesley Williams is a planner, writer and partner at Bishop and Williams Consultants.

Foreword: strategies for a global city

Ken Livingstone

After leaving school I had a job in the research laboratories of the Royal Marsden Hospital and for eight years I worked with a series of brilliant people, people who were driven by a curiosity for the truth and by facts, not by ideology. This was a lesson that I took into politics when I joined the Labour Party in the late 1960s. I was fortunate that this was at a time when local councils were powerful agents of government, institutions with powers and resources to change people's lives for the better. As a councillor in Lambeth I had responsibility for housing programmes. Providing decent housing for all sections of society was universally seen as one of the cornerstones of a decent society. Councils did things and politicians were judged accordingly. One of my early political influences had been Herbert Morrison, Leader of the London County Council in the 1930s. Morrison brought about real structural change in London: he unified transport under a single authority, created the metropolitan green belt and built council housing. His influence endures today. The progressive weakening of local authorities has been a sad trend that has continued from the Thatcher period to the present day. Most of today's politicians no longer work their way up through local government and as a consequence they have no experience of the business of running major public bodies. Ideology has replaced the practicalities of delivering change on the ground, where politics are applied with a high degree of pragmatism in order to build alliances and get things done. The body politic is the poorer for it.

I was elected to the Greater London Council (GLC) in 1973 and became leader in 1981. Many of the issues facing London were the same as those of today: how to provide decent housing, how to deliver efficient public transport, how to ensure a healthy environment and how to make sure that economic benefits reach all of the population. Other issues, though, are different. In the 1980s the UK economy was being forcibly restructured by the Thatcher government, with consequent catastrophic reductions in manufacturing. Climate change was still a theoretical concept and globalisation was in its infancy. There were still debates to be won in favour of the city as a sustainable place to live, against the car as the primary form of transport and about regeneration (as opposed to redevelopment) of poorer and more vulnerable communities. At the GLC we introduced the notion of 'community areas', where we combined spatial planning with social and economic programmes that were based on an inclusive dialogue with the people living in these areas. We also introduced the Fares Fair policy to ensure that public transport was accessible to all.[1] The GLC was still a major service delivery body running housing, education and transport. It was trying to deal with the real issues faced by Londoners struggling for a better life. It was completely at odds with the agenda of the Thatcher government, who abolished it in 1986 as an act of political spite, with disastrous consequences for London.

After 1986, in the absence of a democratically elected body for London (the only major city in a Western democracy without one), London had no voice, no one to make a case for investment and no mechanisms to tackle the pressing problems of growth, housing, transport and the quality of the physical environment. This was a barren time for London. During this time I was a Labour MP and campaigned on London issues. I also edited the *Socialist Economic Bulletin* with John Ross and learnt a fundamental lesson of city politics: if you want to bring forward positive change then you have to bring in investment. In this respect I have been more influenced by Keynes than by Marx. Political change can best be brought about through interventions to redress market imperfections and failures, and this requires public and private investment.

The re-establishment of a Greater London Authority (GLA) in 2000, under a mayor, was a major turning point in the city's fortunes. At this time the world had changed and so had London. The economy was dominated by the service sector, inequality had increased and there had been over a decade of underinvestment in transport and housing. Moreover, London had slipped behind other European cities in terms of its environmental quality and liveability. The GLA, though, was fundamentally different from the GLC. It was deliberately strategic and the legislation that reconstituted London government specifically excluded any responsibility for housing, social services or education. It did, however, focus significant power into the office of the mayor and I no longer had to manage internal party politics but could concentrate on setting in place the foundations for London to re-emerge as a global city. It was clear at this time that London had to attract investment and footloose talent, and was in direct competition with cities such as New York, Tokyo and Paris, as well as cities like Shanghai and Mumbai in the new emerging economies of Asia. To prosper (and therefore create the resources for redistribution to benefit all in society), London needed a strong economy, efficient public transport, a skilled workforce, good housing for all sectors of society and a broad cultural offer, and it needed to be attractive and comfortable to live in. It was also becoming increasingly clear that cities needed to be environmentally responsible and resilient.

To create these conditions, I prioritised a number of key actions. The first was to change Transport for London from a highway authority to a transportation authority. I brought in Bob Kiley from New York as transport commissioner and we set about investing in the tube, renewing the bus fleet, integrating ticketing and creating conditions to encourage walking and cycling. We invested £1.3 billion in the overground and introduced another 8,000 buses. Today, ridership is 100 per cent up from the year 2000. The next move was to rethink planning policy and produce a new London Plan. I can see no purpose in arbitrary planning restrictions such as on height or density. Higher density means that you get more good things in the same space. There are limits, of course, but the UK planning system does allow developments to be judged on their merits, and in my view good internal housing standards, restrictions on the private car and good design are far more important than random planning requirements. A case in point is Renzo Piano's Shard at London Bridge. This could not have been 'planned', but it has transformed the area. I would have been happy to see a higher building had it not been for restrictions to flightpaths coming into London City Airport.

I also brought in Richard Rogers as my architectural and urbanism advisor and supported his proposals to set up the Architecture and Urbanism Unit and then Design for London. I was interested in learning from Barcelona as well as New York, and Richard's philosophy that was to be embedded in Design for London was sympathetic to my own vision for London: namely, a city designed on a human scale, with efficient public transport, diverse and mixed neighbourhoods and decent housing for all. Public spaces and living streets are one of the cornerstones of a civilised city, where everyone should be only a short walk away from a park. In all of this vision, architects are important players. If you have good architecture, you are likely to have an inspirational city. But architecture needs to reflect the culture and history of your own city. As much as I admire parts of New York, I would never have allowed London to end up looking like parts of central Manhattan that are simply horrible. Personally, I prefer San Francisco with its lively streets, cafes and human scale.

If you are going to achieve anything as a mayor, then you have to get on top of economics. You have to create an environment where the economy can grow and people will invest. The decision to bid for the 2012 Olympics was driven by a realisation that without a major project that could capture the imagination (and financial support) of central government, the deeply entrenched social and economic problems of east London would never be tackled. The Olympics locked in the government to invest in the area, to help us acquire over 100 hectares of land, to decontaminate it, put in the infrastructure and improve transport in the area. It was also part of a wider strategy to promote London as the global capital, a place that was welcoming and open to anyone who wanted to come and achieve their ambitions.

Had I had a third term as mayor, then one of the top priorities would have been housing. I had obtained a commitment from the chancellor, Gordon Brown, to remove restrictions on the GLA building new housing, along with a pledge of £5 billion for public housing programmes. I would also have prioritised public health issues, in particular measures to improve air quality, and extended both the congestion charge zone and the low emission zone, possibly to the Greater London boundary. The partial dismantling of congestion charging and the lack of policy to tackle air quality (it is estimated that 9,500 Londoners a year die prematurely due to poor air quality) are in my view significant failures of the Boris Johnson mayoralty.

Good mayors backed by good advisors and teams of talented professionals can make a difference to cities. The issues facing our cities have not diminished – in fact some, such as inequality, shortage of affordable housing and climate change, have become significantly worse since I was mayor. Policies concerning health, public transport, housing and the creation of high-tech jobs to match a skilled and highly productive labour force would still be top of any mayoral agenda in almost any major city in the world. The design agenda has broadened to embrace environmental criteria. The link between the construction and refurbishment of buildings and measures to reduce carbon emissions *and* create new jobs must now be at the centre of urban policy. In this respect the green agenda is the next big project that could transform London – the 'next Olympics'. City governments must also be prepared to regulate and this applies as much to their economies and financial sectors as to their streets and buildings. Appropriate regulation is the hallmark of a good society. All of these ideas can be framed by city strategies that imagine what a good city might look like, how it might function and how the conditions for civic life might be enhanced.

When I set up Design for London, I challenged the team to 'think about London, what qualities made London unique as a city and how we could make it better'. I gave them licence to think, to question, to imagine and to challenge. All cities need people who can do this.

February 2020
Ken Livingstone was Mayor of London from 2000 to 2008.

Note

1 The Fares Fair programme was a manifesto commitment and reduced fares on London Transport by 32 per cent. It was successfully challenged in the courts by the (Conservative) London borough of Bromley.

Foreword: London, a city of beauty, a city for its citizens

Richard Rogers

I came to London as a six-year-old refugee, fleeing fascist Italy with my parents in 1939. While Florence, my birthplace, is a city that I love to visit again and again, I will always treasure London as my adopted home.

But for many years, apart from its wonderful parks, London was a grey and colourless place, the smogs that swirled through its streets matched by an introverted and segregated social life, where men spent their time in pubs and clubs, and women stayed home. London had great modern architects – many, like Lubetkin, also refugees – but the city of the mid twentieth century seemed suspicious of modernism in general, and modern architecture in particular.

I had studied near New York in the early 1960s and worked in Paris through the 1970s. I had read Jane Jacobs, Michael Young and Lewis Mumford – writers who brought cities, their physical structure and social networks to life. These places and these writers helped me to see a better future for our cities, an aspiration that urban planning had sought to avoid through much of the twentieth century.

When I came back to the UK and became more directly engaged in politics, it felt as though London was losing out. The gradual revival in urban living that was taking place in other big cities was slow to take off. UK government was intensely centralised – even more so when the Greater London Council and other metropolitan councils were abolished in the 1980s – and the quality of urban design, planning and architecture seemed very poor compared to cities like Barcelona, Rotterdam, Curitiba and Copenhagen.

The Reith Lectures that I delivered in 1995, and which formed the basis of *Cities for a Small Planet*,[1] looked at the role of cities through the lens of mounting concern about climate change following the 1992

Rio Earth Summit. I argued that cities – long seen as the source of all ills – would be the only sustainable way to accommodate a growing population. Only socially just cities, with the density that supports services and vitality, the transport services that can take cars off the road, and the quality of urban and architectural design to move the spirit, could answer the challenges posed by climate change.

The election of a Labour government in 1997 gave me the opportunity, as Chair of the Urban Task Force, to develop these ideas and explore how they could be implemented. The recommendations of our report, *Towards an Urban Renaissance*,[2] looked at governance and social justice, as well as planning and architecture. This changed the tone of debate about cities and led to the setting up of new organisations such as the Commission for Architecture and the Built Environment (CABE).

Tony Blair's election also enabled the election of a Mayor of London, a major step in London's revival. Ken Livingstone won – despite Tony's best efforts to prevent it – and called me in to ask me to make a test case for *Towards an Urban Renaissance*. I had been working as an advisor to Pasqual Maragall, the Mayor of Barcelona, and first discussed a role as 'City Architect' overseeing the capital's planning and regeneration programmes. This suggestion clearly cut across too many established professional hierarchies, so I settled on a different approach – a small team, which would work alongside the existing structures but have a direct line to the mayor.

Joined by Ricky Burdett, who had been pivotal in the Urban Task Force, I set about assembling a team. We took on Richard Brown to manage the team and programme, and Mark Brearley to lead the design work. The Architecture and Urbanism Unit (A+UU) initially focused on four main work areas. Internally, we worked with the mayor's planners to make sure that the London Plan reflected the principles of the Urban Task Force report (but, to avoid conflicts of interest, we agreed I would play no formal part in taking planning decisions). We also worked with Transport for London (TfL) and the London Development Agency (LDA) to make sure that their schemes were well designed, mainly through pushing them to use design competitions and other open approaches that would give a new generation of architects the opportunity to shape the city's infrastructure and regeneration schemes.

Outside the mayor's organisations, the team began to work with local authorities and partnerships to develop a masterplan-led approach to urban change – particularly in east London, where piecemeal development and ill-considered schemes risked throwing away London's biggest opportunity for growth. We also launched a 100 Public Spaces programme, modelled on the programme that Barcelona ran around the time of the 1992 Olympics.

Some elements of the programme were more successful than others. Ken Livingstone's London Plan, which has set the template for his successors, made a powerful commitment to compact city planning. It linked density and public transport, strengthened a commitment to use brownfield rather than greenfield land and included specific policies on design quality. Our masterplanning and urban strategy work in east London began to stitch together a framework for 'City East' – a new 'city within the city' that could accommodate 400,000 new homes and form one of the foundation stones for the London 2012 Olympic bid.

The public spaces programme had some successes – in Brixton, Bankside, Dalston and Acton, for example. But it was hard to maintain momentum behind some of our more radical proposals, particularly when there was a change of mayor in 2008. The biggest challenge, however, was probably in changing behaviour in TfL and the LDA, both of which were nominally under the mayor's control, but had a significant degree of independence and were used to doing things their way.

After several difficult debates, Livingstone proposed merging the A+UU (by then comprising around 10 people) with the design teams from TfL and the LDA, so that we all operated under unified direction as Design for London (DfL). Richard Brown left to lead the team setting up the London 2012 Olympic delivery organisations, and Peter Bishop, who had been leading the planning of King's Cross at the London Borough of Camden, took over as director.

DfL focused on town centres, on housing and public realm design guidance and on regional landscape strategies such as the East London Green Grid. It also continued the A+UU's focus on east London (Ricky Burdett became an advisor to the Olympic Delivery Authority) and the 100 Public Spaces programme. With 25 people in the team, we managed to accelerate and extend our reach, but Boris Johnson's election as mayor in 2008 meant a change in my role. Initially, Johnson was effusively enthusiastic about our work, but he soon started pulling the plug on schemes such as the pedestrianisation of Parliament Square (one of the 100 Public Spaces). He made me deputy chair of his design advisory group, but I am not good at sitting on committees; I prefer to work with a team on actual projects. I resigned in 2009, and DfL was shut down (as part of the LDA) in 2013.

DfL and the A+UU operated at the margins of London government, pushing for better practice in a city where the mayor's powers are heavily limited, as are those of the 33 boroughs. The team achieved some great projects, including some in previously neglected places like Barking town centre. It created drawings and ideas that changed the way we think about London – from the City East masterplan to the East London Green Grid and the mapping of London's high streets and neighbourhoods. And it brought a highly talented team of architects, planners and urban designers together. many of whom are continuing to work, as if deep under cover, in the Greater London Authority, TfL, the mayoral development corporations and the boroughs.

I still feel conscious of how much more needs to be done to make London a more civilised and humane city, but the work of the A+UU and DfL pushed design issues from the periphery of urban governance to somewhere near the centre, where they have stayed ever since. Sadiq Khan's Good Growth by Design programme and the Mayor's Design Advocates can be seen as legacies of the programmes that we operated. This book is a valuable record both of our achievements and of our frustrations. In its pages, the architects and designers who worked with me at City Hall set out the scope and significance of our experiment, its roots in urban design theory, and the contribution that it can make to the continuing debate about how we shape cities to be great places to live in.

November 2018
Richard Rogers was architecture and urbanism advisor to the Mayor of London from 2000 to 2009.

Notes

1 Richard Rogers, *Cities for a Small Planet*, London: Faber and Faber, 1995.
2 Urban Task Force, *Towards an Urban Renaissance*, London: HMSO, 1999.

Acknowledgements

With thanks to Richard Brown, Ricky Burdett, Sarah Considine, Jamie Dean, Paul Harper, Charlotte Kokken, Kieran Long and Fenna Wagenaar for their assistance. With special thanks to Jill Bowie for her copy-editing of the text.

Introduction: urban interventions in a time of rapid global change

Peter Bishop

In 2008 Design for London held an exhibition at Somerset House called London: Open City. This was a tangential look at how cities might be influenced and shaped through design strategies. One of the images (Figure 0.1) was entitled *Who Designs London?* This was not meant to explain the process of design, but instead sought to show the complex relationships between all the agencies that are involved in designing one piece of public space in London.

The drawing was intended to show how design is achieved through the brokerage of deals between agencies with the powers to change the

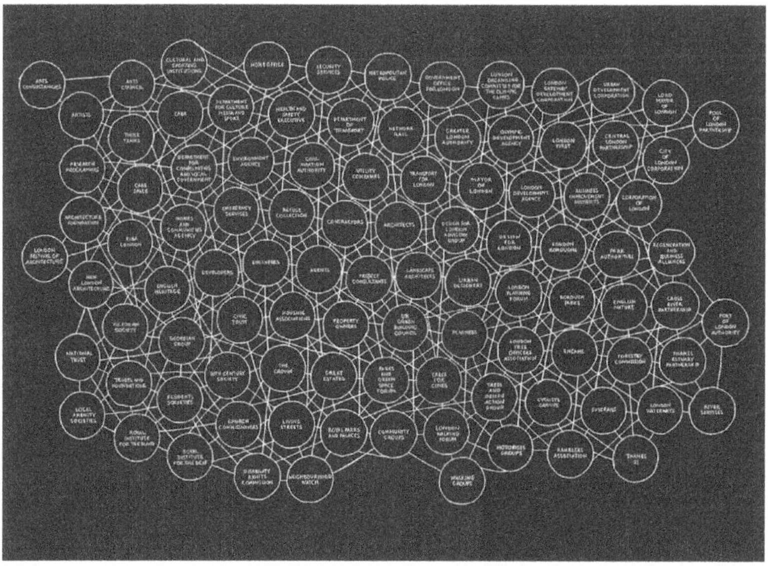

Figure 0.1 *Who Designs London?* Source: DfL/GLA.

city. In this respect, the designer is a navigator and guide. Sometimes, just sometimes, if the right agencies can be aligned then opportunities might be identified, and change might take place. And if you work hard enough, the outcome might be good. In many ways this diagram summarises the purpose of this book, which is to reflect on how it is possible to shape a city as complex as London through a series of brokered initiatives and oblique strategies. But first of all, it is important to understand the context within which designers work in the fluid city of the twenty-first century.

Over the past 30 years we have seen the collapse of communism as an ideological and geopolitical force,[1] progressive shifts of economic and political power to Asia, the development of the internet and mobile communications, and the realisation that climate change is a very real global threat. The demise of Lehman Brothers in September 2008 presaged a global economic crash and events such as the Greek sovereign debt crisis, the 'Arab Spring' and the emergence of global terrorism. At the time of writing[2] a global pandemic is causing city regions to be put into quarantine with restrictions on travel and major reductions in economic activity. All of these events have challenged any lingering notion of a stable world. At the urban scale, economic liberalisation, transnational conglomerates, global flows of capital, new and 'smart' technologies and the splintering of political allegiances have fundamentally altered the role and nature of city government. Constant change and uncertainty now prevail and seem likely to persist.

This has confronted us with a radical set of challenges. Social forms and institutions no longer have the time to solidify and act as potential models from which to extrapolate plans for an increasingly uncertain future. A different set of strategies is required for both the individual and the organisation. These involve a *tactical* approach, splicing together a series of short-term projects instead of formal long-term plans – strategies of constant adaptation. What is trustworthy and works today may be obsolete by tomorrow. Tactics are formulated, tested, utilised and abandoned as opportunities open up and close down. Success depends on a high degree of adaptability and resilience, and in consequence state and city governments need to be, above all else, *agile*.

Successful cities are responding with adaptive strategies where agility and resilience are seen as the new hallmarks of stability. The politics of persuasion are replacing the politics of direction and this poses significant structural challenges for city government. The new issues facing cities are also less tangible and discrete and far more interconnected. Economic restructuring, crime, inequality and social marginalisation, disparities in health and demographic change now dominate the agenda. Ageing and ethnically diverse populations pose far more complex questions than governments have hitherto had to deal with. So does a young and often excluded generation that has access to social media. While bureaucracies may, at times, be efficient at delivering services, they are seldom suited to dealing with the so-called 'wicked' issues – those involving great social complexity. These require completely new solutions that rely on interdisciplinary working, alliance building, brokerage and engagement.

The broadening of the urban agenda raises significant questions around the definition and scope of design in the built environment. Previous generations inevitably worked on a far narrower scope than today's practitioners. The definition of design as being primarily concerned with architectural aesthetics has widened to include social and economic issues, the regeneration of urban neighbourhoods, public health and environmental sustainability. Nevertheless design, what a place looks like and how it functions, is still vitally important. Few people would willingly opt for *poor* design, but most are hard pressed to define what *good* design looks like and, critically, how this might be achieved. At the same time the design of buildings has (rightly) embraced issues of performance and lifetime costs. Environmental impact and resilience are now recognised as central components in any design debate. The design debate sits at the heart of urban management and therefore urban politics.

The global economy rests increasingly on the interrelationships between cities that trade and exchange knowledge. These cities are in competition with one another as they vie to attract mobile capital and human talent. In a world where people and businesses have choices over location, the design of the places where people live and work matters as never before. With the urban agenda moving into areas of new complexity around health, learning, social resilience and environmental impact, there is a growing need to coordinate and reconcile spatial policy across numerous different areas and priorities. Within the city there are multiple clients and therefore any activity of designing at the metropolitan scale is inevitably a political act, requiring complex trade-offs that may tip the balance of benefit from one group to another. Many cities are still defined by their historic political boundaries, but their impact now reaches far beyond these. The relationship between cities and their hinterlands in terms of transport, commuting, supply chains and environmental management (especially water and energy management) is now raising significant new policy issues that are calling for new thinking and new alliances. Arguably, the metropolis of London now extends across most of south-east and central England,

and indeed some European cities are amalgamating across national boundaries.

Across the developed (democratic) world the traditional mechanisms of city government have come into question. The rise of the global neoliberal economy (and restrictions in public funding) have pushed governments to adopt alternative forms of partnership, procurement and service delivery (frequently involving contractual partnerships with the private and community sectors). City authorities are moving away from being service providers to becoming strategic enablers and commissioning agencies, and this is leading to new forms of governance. If the role of the state has changed then it is not surprising that the role of the professional architect and planner within government has changed as well. Design agencies, as a consequence, have had to develop new approaches and methodologies. A definition of agency is 'an action or intervention producing a particular effect'. Implicit in the notion of agency is the facilitation of (positive) change. Increasingly, governments are moving away from specific projects towards creating the conditions for change – in other words, towards *enabling*. Design agency is less about planning the city region and more about how it can be shaped through sophisticated practices and interventions. It is increasingly about the creation of the *conditions* under which positive change may take place.

Design strategies can take a number of different forms within government. They might be concerned with the creation of a suitable policy framework that can set the rules and the parameters for urban living. 'Good' city life does require a degree of regulation; policy frameworks set appropriate standards that will shape the growth of the city and the quality of the urban experience. The creation of good policy frameworks makes it possible to ensure better housing, protect open space and raise environmental standards. These in themselves are fundamental in establishing the foundations for the quality of life in the city. Design agency, though, builds on regulatory planning to add the power of imagination and produce clear visions of a better future. In today's pluralistic world, any policy needs to be based on an open and realistic dialogue between equals – government, other public and private bodies and the communities within which any project or initiative will sit. Design in itself is an interdisciplinary, alliance building, brokering and engaging tool that is required in order to continually respond to our changing world.

Regulatory frameworks might form a foundation for urban living but do not of themselves set a clear vision of a future state, articulate outcomes or map a process to get there. Design strategies that translate into projects and programmes can provide a dynamic for change. This requires a sophisticated understanding of the role of government vis-à-vis other stakeholders, of finance and of process. Design agencies can work *within* government to generate a wider debate and raise aspirations. In this respect agency might act through education, advocacy, consultancy or advice. City governments are still major landowners, funders and commissioners of services and projects. Here the role of agency is to improve the effectiveness of government as an informed and competent agent and client. Part of this role involves helping government to raise and broaden its aspirations to areas outside its core operational remit.

Another role for design strategies can be facilitating, advising and assisting external agencies and organisations. There is a legitimate role for design agencies within government to assist with advice that leads to a greater public good, especially in areas where design expertise might be lacking. There is also a role for a design agency to challenge existing practices through research into best practice, through strengthening the range of client competencies and through constructive criticism, for example through design review. All of these areas fit into the category of capacity building.

A final area is for design agencies to coordinate an exchange of ideas within government. Government is inevitably structured on a departmental basis into policy or delivery silos. Effective design agency can cut across these and facilitate broader debates outside day-to-day operational concerns; it can corral competencies and can bring together commonalities at the local level. This might resolve conflicting policies or ensure that local projects sit within a clear contextual framework and are more than the sum of their constituent parts. In executing this role, an agency can often reframe critical questions, find compromise solutions and help politicians make difficult decisions by finding alternative options.

Design agency is open-ended. Cities are always a work in progress – never finished, they are constantly adapting and evolving. Embedding design excellence is largely about making cultural changes in the way an organisation thinks. This is likely to be a gradual process. Effective agency should be concerned with opening up future opportunities, rather than closing them down. Well-established government design agencies have the advantage of cumulative experience, continuity of knowledge and the maturity of long experience. All too often these important attributes have been discarded for short-term political goals. A degree of long-term certainty is a prerequisite for an agency to be effective, as many projects may take years to come to fruition.

A key role of design agency is one of 'thought-leadership': that is, to ask the big questions such as 'How do we want to live in the future?' and then to engage government departments and the public in this debate. A design agency can create a 'space for thinking' within the heart of government. As politicians wrestle with the truly 'wicked' issues, a design agency has a key role in questioning, thinking and debating, and through this process it might possibly create new solutions to politically sensitive issues. Effective urban design is often about reframing the design debate within the broader concerns of government.

Design for London (DfL) was a design agency that was part of London government but had no formal reporting lines. The team's close relationship with Richard Rogers, who had direct access to the mayor, gave them considerable influence. Other chapters of this book describe the advantages (and problems) of this unique model within the public sector. There are other models. Most other UK cities employ architects and urban designers, but these are generally embedded in planning or regeneration departments. The closest analogy to DfL was the City of Leeds, whose 'civic architect', John Thorp, had an advisory role within Leeds government for close to 25 years. He operated with a small staff and acted as the city's design conscience and memory. He could develop long-term strategies and ensure policy continuity. Over the period of his work he was able to shape the city through subtle and long-term strategies.

Like the UK, many European countries have been wrestling with the problems of urban decline, structural economic change and shifts in urban transportation. The difference, though, was that in the 1990s other European governments were not experimenting with neoliberalism on the same scale as in the UK. The traditions of strong local government with mayors, city architect departments and locally derived tax revenues allowed cities such as Barcelona, Lyon, Turin and Bilbao to invest in their areas and reap the rewards (where these strategies were successful). Architecture and urban design were generally seen as positive drivers of change and powerful forms of expression allowing cities to promote themselves. City government was a powerful design patron and this created a market that allowed architectural practices to develop and experiment with new approaches to masterplanning, housing and public space.

Many European cities, such as Berlin, Aarhus and Dublin, continue to demonstrate design leadership through the role of a formal city architect with overall responsibility for achieving design quality for large-scale plans and projects. They and their teams work strategically across individual project boundaries to ensure there is coherency and consistency in how the city is developed. Paris has a long track record of promoting architectural projects, from the Centre Pompidou in 1977 (Rogers and Piano), to the Parc de la Villette of 1984–7 (Tschumi), the Louvre Pyramid in 1989 (Pei) and the Parc de Bercy in 1997 (Huet, Ferrand, Feugas and Leroy). These *grands projets* were championed by the city mayor, Jacques Chirac, and President François Mitterrand. They recognised that cultural institutions and architectural design could be key components in defining and celebrating the city and promoting it on the international stage. This tradition of design-led regeneration continues in Paris today. Dominique Alba, previously the director of the Pavillon de l'Arsenal, is the special advisor to the current mayor of Paris, Anne Hidalgo.

Barcelona under Mayor Pasqual Maragall was hugely influential as a model for DfL. In the 1980s the city embarked on an ambitious programme to renew its urban infrastructure, and in 1986 it was nominated as host city for the 1992 Olympic Games. Barcelona used this not just as an excuse for a series of *grands projets*, but as an opportunity to restructure key parts of the city – to reconnect the historic core to the waterfront and to create new public spaces within its dense core. Barcelona, of course, had a long tradition of innovative architecture and urbanism stretching back to Cerdà's 1856 plan for the city and continuing through to the establishment of the Laboratorio de Urbanismo de Barcelona in 1968. From the 1970s, Manuel de Solà-Morales and practices like MBM and Rafael Moneo began to experiment with new approaches to architecture at an urban scale. This agenda was further developed by Oriol Bohigas.[3] When he became head of urbanism in the city in the early 1980s, he sponsored an ambitious series of public realm improvements and new boulevards. His programmes were maintained through the 1990s by Josep Acebillo and extended to include parks and public housing. To support this urban renaissance, the city established a design studio, the Twelve Golden Pens, staffed by some of the most promising architect graduates. They also created a strategic architectural panel.

The drivers behind the restructuring of Barcelona were rooted deep in the traditions of the European city: human scale, the primacy of the urban block, civic and local public spaces and the street as a place rather than a transport corridor. Projects in different parts of the city were promoted through Beauty Commissions, and major architectural commissions were procured, particularly in the urban realm. Both Richard Rogers and Ricky Burdett were closely involved with Barcelona at this time, and its influence, especially in the use of internal design teams, can be seen in the decision to set up the Architecture and Urbanism Unit.

Copenhagen, under the influence of architect Jan Gehl, was transformed from a car-based to a pedestrian- and cycle-orientated city. His first major publication, *Life Between Buildings: Using public space* (1971),[4] was in many ways a reaction to modernism's emphasis on the city as a machine, whereby the citizen became subservient to the large-scale intervention of the architect, planner and traffic engineer (and the subsequent domination of the automobile). Gehl's theories and approach explicitly reference the influence of Jane Jacobs and represent an important train of urban thinking that focuses on the relationships between urban form and human behaviour. Gehl's work subsequently influenced many cities, including New York and Melbourne. In London it was to influence the public space programmes of the Architecture and Urbanism Unit and DfL.

A theme of London government under Ken Livingstone was its relationship with New York. The two cities saw each other as competitors but they probably had more in common with each other than with many cities in their own countries. New York had had mayoral government long before London, and the mayor appoints a set of commissioners who oversee departments in City Hall. Alex Washburn was Head of Urban Design in New York between 2007 and 2013 and reported to the planning commissioner, Amanda Burden. An architect, he had been a congressional advisor in Washington and had well-developed political and organisational skills. He established a small design team which exploited the opportunities that Burden could create through her role as planning commissioner. There are strong parallels between the approach that Washburn and his team developed and the work of DfL. Both teams were agile and opportunist and both were headed up by individuals who were able to operate in an overtly political environment. Washburn described his role as 'protecting the team from political turmoil so they could just get on and do their work'.[5] Both teams believed in the power of doing the drawings: 'we drew and drew and drew'.[6] Both teams also believed in following the opportunities as they appeared (and were prepared to gear their work programmes accordingly): 'when the window of urban design opens then you take it'.[7] Both teams looked at ideas emerging from other cities and then tailored their responses to the circumstances of their own cities. A key common element was the way in which both teams were prepared to work from the city scale to the design of the park bench. Both also believed that being open and reasonable helped to secure a place at the negotiating table.

Mayor Bloomberg of New York visited London and learnt of DfL. He then established his own team, the Office for Long-Term Planning and Sustainability (OLTPS). The existence of this team was written into the New York City Charter, which means that, unless the charter is changed, it must always exist regardless of political changes. The roles of the urban design group and the OLTPS continue in New York under the present mayor, Bill de Blasio.

Perhaps the closest agency to DfL is the Government Architect for New South Wales (GANSW). This strategic agency sits within government and has a brief to develop design policies and strategies for the state. It also advises on procurement, carries out area-based design studies and runs design reviews. The GANSW has been very effective in raising the quality of design in the Sydney metropolitan area and is generally respected within government. Unlike DfL, it is a formal part of the machinery of government. While this has the advantage of defining its role clearly, it does limit its role in campaigning and advocacy.

The DfL model has been influential in Albania through Edi Rama, who was Mayor of Tirana, the capital, from 2000 to 2013. In 2010 Rama met DfL's head, Mark Brearley, at the Rotterdam biennale and was interested to hear more about the work of DfL. In a visit to London in 2011, he made a point of meeting the DfL team, which presented its methodology of design strategies based on strong ideas and conviction. Rama had already established a reputation as a progressive mayor who was interested in using architecture and design to reshape his city. He left DfL armed with multiple copies of its strategies and publications, and established a similar model in Tirana. Underpinning the model was the establishment of a school that provided the training for those working in Tirana city government. When Rama became Prime Minister of Albania in 2013, he brought this model with him to national government, and in 2014 he established a new office called Atelier Albania. This is integrated into the Albanian Ministry of Urban Development's National Planning Office (AKPT) and directly advises the Albanian government. The office was created to be a tool and incubator to enable design-based methods to be applied to urban policy and development at a national scale. It still exists within government today, providing the space 'to think' and supporting regional city teams and city mayors with spatial thinking and urban strategies.

Although design agencies may exist in more traditional forms of city government, the office of mayor can (if the mayor is interested) give them greater weight and influence. Indeed, in some cases it is the mayor's office that is the de facto design agency. This might be the mayor and a small group of close advisors operating *above* the city administration or it might entail the establishment of a design studio through which the mayor might work. In Colombia's capital, Bogotá, Enrique Peñalosa (mayor 1998–2001 and 2016–19) instituted major programmes to restructure the city through the construction of a network of cycleways and to extend the city's parks, largely through the use of unorthodox strategies. He did, however, finish his term with the highest approval ratings of any mayor in Bogotá's history, and his thinking has influenced a number of other cities across the world. In 1989 the architect and urban planner Jaime Lerner was beginning his third (non-consecutive) term as Mayor of Curitiba in Brazil and established the Urban Planning and Research Institute (IPPUC). The idea of 'urban acupuncture'[8] that was first developed in Curitiba illustrates his belief in cities as complex organisms. Small-scale interventions at crucial points can have a positive ripple effect that benefits the city as a whole. In parallel, the city government delivered large projects focusing on the environment, transportation and civic inclusion. It also pioneered 'shared responsibility', involving citizens in the environmental management of the city. These governance strategies continue to be applied today and Curitiba is frequently cited as an international paradigm.[9]

In Asian countries the rapid pace of urbanisation is beginning to pose significant challenges that stretch beyond the limited remit of formal land use planning. Where a city's infrastructures have to be adapted and retrofitted, more subtle forms of design agency are required. The growth imperative that could be accommodated through urban planning is now being replaced by agendas concerning urban quality, resilience, social equitability and environmental sustainability. Seoul's mayor, Park Won-soon, appointed Seung H-Sang as city architect in 2014 in a move to re-establish the city's 'architectural identity' after decades of unchecked development.[10] The Seoul city architect oversees a team of architects, planners and urbanists who oversee the planning and bidding process for all public projects, as well as influencing the approval process and design criteria for private buildings. The appointment and structure of the office were modelled on European and North American cities. Seung, when interviewed on his appointment,[11] described his role as follows: 'I wish to establish Seoul's architectural identity (and) what public interest values architecture should embody.' Prior to this appointment, Seoul, a city of over ten million people, treated design as a branch of civil engineering. Although the city was engaged in many large architecture projects, responsibility was uncoordinated and it lacked any plan that could revive its identity. At the core of Seung's design philosophy are the importance of rooting urban strategies in the culture and morphology of place, the treatment of narrative as more important than image, and the celebration of 'ordinariness' – all themes that resonate with experiments in 'Western' urban thinking in the past 30 years.

Seoul is unusual and represents the experience of a maturing city, one that is beginning to address the difficulties of consolidating rapid growth. Tokyo and other Japanese cities have long traditions of urban planning but do not have any centralised roles regarding city architecture at either a political or technical level. Large-scale urban transformation projects such as the Tokyo Olympics are dealt with by special development vehicles. In Hong Kong the Architectural Services Department exists in government, but this is more of a traditional works department than a strategic design agency. The Urban Redevelopment Authority in Singapore has a broad remit around development and urban design, but is very much a government department. In Chinese cities, regeneration programmes are becoming increasingly important to address urban obsolescence from the first wave of urbanisation, but although government agencies such as the Beijing Institute of Architecture and Design may play a role in procuring or undertaking large-scale projects, there are, as yet, no examples of emerging agile and strategic design agencies in individual cities. Indeed, it is possible that this model of enquiry, debate and speculation would sit uncomfortably within the present systems of urban governance in China.

Taipei has made significant progress in addressing the problems of growth through major regeneration and transportation programmes but has not developed a specific design agency for the city. It has, however, established the Smart City Living Lab, a project office within the urban administration that looks to broker partnerships between organisations wishing to develop smart technologies at the scale of the urban region. This might be a variation on the idea of design agency that is uniquely suited to the Asian situation. Elsewhere a number of cities, including Zhuhai (China), Goyang (South Korea) and Riyadh (the capital of Saudi Arabia), have set up design advisory panels that report directly to the mayor or a government agency with a role of distilling 'big picture' strategies and advising on new projects. This represents an extension of the importance of urban design and might be the beginning of a new movement as cities in Asia and the developing world address post-growth urban issues that include identity, renewal, conservation and sustainability.

When DfL was set up, it was able to benefit from all the thinking and urban practice that had gone before – a cross-fertilisation of ideas from other cities. New team members also brought their own ideas into DfL. Some of these key ideas are examined briefly in the first chapter of this book, which looks at the theories that DfL drew on and the methodologies that were developed to exploit the opportunities of the moment. As a team we were driven by a belief that we might make the city better. At the heart of this is London itself, that wonderful anarchic, pragmatic, mysterious and constantly surprising city. We hope this book will illustrate some ideas and lessons for the next generation of city strategists and designers in London and other cities.

Notes

1 Marked spectacularly with the breach of the Berlin Wall on 9 November 1989.
2 March 2020.
3 Head of the practice MBM.
4 Gehl 2011 (first published in 1971).
5 Interview with Alex Washburn, March 2020.
6 Interview with Alex Washburn, March 2020.
7 Interview with Alex Washburn, March 2020.
8 Now a commonly used term but coined by Jaime Lerner.
9 Nicky Gavron, Deputy Mayor of London under Ken Livingstone, had visited Curitiba in the early 1990s and had been deeply influenced by Lerner's thinking. Gavron was one of the early champions of DfL.
10 Winston 2014.
11 Winston 2014.

Bibliography

Gehl, Jan, *Life Between Buildings: Using Public Space*, translated by Jo Koch, London: Island Press, 2011.

Winston, Anna, 'Seoul Names Seung H-Sang as Its First City Architect', *Dezeen*, 8 September 2014. https://www.dezeen.com/2014/09/08/seung-h-sang-first-city-architect-seoul-south-korea/ (accessed 11 July 2020).

1

London, the unique city: the establishment of the Architecture and Urbanism Unit

Peter Bishop, Lara Kinneir and Mark Brearley

This chapter examines the circumstances that led to the re-establishment of London government in 2000 and the formation of the Architecture and Urbanism Unit (A+UU) by the mayor, Ken Livingstone, and his architecture and urbanism advisor, Richard Rogers. It reviews the work and methodologies of the A+UU, which provided an important platform for the later establishment of Design for London (DfL).

Context: London, the unique city

Although London shares many of the characteristics of other European cities – neighbourhoods, parks, civic buildings and the street (as both public space and public thoroughfare) – it has some important differences. It is generally less compact and therefore less 'urban' than many European cities. It has always been a city focused on trade and commerce and therefore one open to new ideas and people – cosmopolitan and mercantile. London has also been fortunate throughout most of its history. It was able to dismantle its city walls much earlier than other European cities and thus could expand outwards, 'capturing' existing settlements. This has given it a different, less dense urban morphology and considerable physical diversity between its neighbourhoods.

Power in London has never been concentrated into the hands of an individual or small ruling clique, but has instead been dispersed and shared between corporations, businesses and individuals. The early introduction of freeholds produced a class of landowners and a model of growth and development that was reliant on private capital. The separation of government (Westminster) from commerce and trade (the City) ensured that no single all-powerful individual was able to stamp their image on the city through personal *grands projets*. When London started its first major outwards expansion at the beginning of the eighteenth century, development was largely financed by private landowners. This created not only the 'great estates' that still exist today, but also a pattern of fragmented development and fine-grained urban form that has been able to adapt and renew itself while accommodating significant changes in social organisation and technology. Finally, London's great period of expansion in the nineteenth and early twentieth centuries made it both polycentric and diverse – as was so elegantly captured in the diagram in the 1943 Abercrombie Plan (Figure 1.1). Significantly, this growth largely preceded the automobile and was based on the creation of comprehensive rail and tram routes.

The growth of London to become the largest metropolis in the world challenged notions of governance and administration. The Municipal Corporation Act 1835 started to regularise the chaos of new and largely ungoverned districts; the Metropolis Management Act 1855

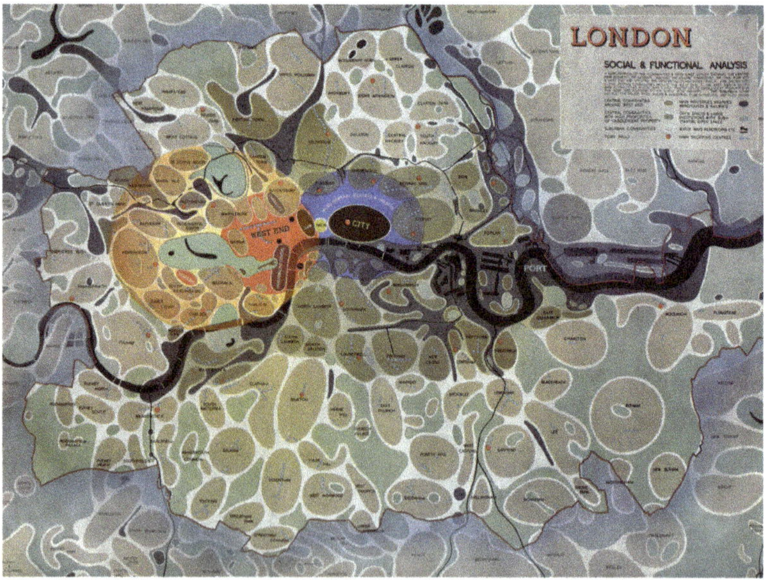

Figure 1.1 London, a city of neighbourhoods, by Abercrombie, 1943. Source: Patrick Abercrombie and John Forshaw, Greater London Plan, 1944.

tackled the need for coordinated investment in infrastructure; and the Local Government Act 1888 established the London County Council. Subsequent Local Government Acts, in 1894 and 1900, established a lower tier of government – the London boroughs. While this produced a local tier of democratic accountability and service delivery, it also dispersed power within London, a situation that was consolidated in 1965 when boroughs were amalgamated into larger units – the 33 boroughs that exist today. This form of administrative organisation was well suited to the conditions of the twentieth century where powerful state agencies were accepted as necessary in order to tackle issues of urban growth, urban renewal, postwar reconstruction, slum clearance, urban transportation and welfare provision.

By the beginning of the 1970s, the role of the state started to be questioned and was then severely shaken by the policies of the Thatcher governments from 1979 onwards. A weak national economy placed significant strains on public funding for transport, housing and urban renewal, and successive funding reductions weakened local authorities. Even before the 1979 election, the powerful technical departments that had driven large-scale urban restructuring were being dismantled. The end of the 1970s effectively spelt the end of the powerful and proactive public sector as the major participant in urban development.

The idea of a reduced state presence was manifest in reduced funding and powers for local government. This ushered in a period of protracted opposition to central government from a number of left-wing inner London boroughs. Central government prevailed and one of the casualties was the Greater London Council (GLC), which was abolished in 1986.[1] The abolition of the GLC meant that central government took direct control of London government, in effect depriving London of an independent voice. While often portrayed as an act of political spite, the abolition of the GLC was part of the trend of centralisation of political power into Westminster, at the expense of cities and the regions. Of direct benefit to London, however, was a change in UK regional policy. Postwar programmes had sought to direct investment away from London and the South East in favour of the depressed former industrial areas. This policy was abandoned in the 1980s in favour of allowing market forces to decide regional investment priorities. This change and the financial deregulation of the City meant that investment began to flow back into London.

For London, the 1990s was a period of transition. Stripped of its elected strategic level of government, it was administered by central government and a series of non-elected advisory bodies. Consequently, at a time of globalisation there was no governing body to promote the interests of the city as a whole or to develop projects or strategies on the scale of Paris, New York or Berlin (where German reunification was driving major urban change). There were, however, changes taking place. First, London's population, in line with many major cities across the world, was beginning to grow again. The population of London had been in decline[2] since the end of the Second World War due to industrial restructuring and the impact of housing renewal programmes that had displaced populations beyond the city fringe to the New Towns and elsewhere. This decline had left large areas of land derelict, particularly in east London, and had created severe pockets of unemployment and social deprivation in many other parts of the city. The government had responded by setting up the London Docklands Development Corporation, tasked with bringing forward regeneration in the east of the city. Meanwhile, the financial deregulation (the Big Bang) of the 1980s had led to a series of new commercial developments such as Broadgate and Canary Wharf.

As London emerged from the economic slump of the early 1990s, new money was injected into the economy, much of it from overseas. At this time, a new generation of architects was emerging who had been influenced by Josef Paul Kleihues' 1987 International Building Exhibition Berlin.[3] This was a seminal moment when architects and urban thinkers, including Aldo Rossi, Léon Krier and James Stirling, refashioned an urbanism based on the principles of the European city – the street, the perimeter block and the public space. This inspired architectural practice in cities like Barcelona and Paris. Cheap airfares to these and other European destinations had produced a small but influential class of 'city consumers'. Their visits to cities such as Lyon, Turin and Bilbao fuelled demands for more investment in their own cities and public spaces. The National Lottery, set up in 1994, provided new funding for heritage and 'millennium projects'. It triggered architecture-led interventions including the Tate Modern at Bankside (Herzog & de Meuron), the Great Court at the British Museum (Foster), the Millennium Bridge (Foster), the Greenwich Dome (Rogers) and the London Eye (Marks Barfield). These captured the public imagination and were undoubtedly popular. In parallel, the new confidence in the City of London stimulated a new generation of tall buildings like Foster's Swiss Re Tower. Initially derided by the Prince of Wales as 'the Gherkin', it was generally acclaimed by the public and soon became a symbol of London's new-found confidence. Slowly, London was reclaiming its urbanity, and architecture was becoming a talking point.

By the late 1990s, the Conservative governments of Margaret Thatcher and John Major were running out of steam and the Labour Party under Tony Blair was preparing a transformative agenda for government. This agenda was forward-looking and saw technology and design as some of the key strengths of 'Cool Britannia'.[4] Architecture was part of this agenda. The spirit of the time was captured by the Architecture Foundation. Established in 1991 to examine contemporary issues in architectural design and theory (and with Richard Rogers, Norman Foster, James Stirling, Alan Yentob and Nick Serota on its board), it organised a series of debates, roadshows and exhibitions to stimulate public interest in architecture and urbanism. The most influential of these were monthly debates in a packed Westminster Central Hall. One of these, in 1996, debated the future governance of London. It provided the forum for the newly elected leader of the opposition, Tony Blair, to formally pledge to re-establish London government in the event of a Labour election victory.

Tony Blair won a landslide victory in May 1997, and in April 1998 Richard Rogers was asked to set up and chair the Urban Task Force to rethink urban policy. John Prescott, the deputy prime minister, set out the need for this rethinking:

> Over the past few decades many of our urban areas have suffered neglect and decline with an exodus from the inner cities, driven by a lack of confidence in schools, fear of crime, an unhealthy environment, and poor housing. This is bad for our people, bad for quality of life, bad for our economy and bad for our society.[5]

The Urban Task Force brought together leading practitioners, representatives of government institutions, academia and the development sector, and gathered evidence from many experts in fields from architecture to engineering to environmental sustainability. It looked at examples of best practice in the UK, the rest of Europe and America, and from these it derived the concept of the city as a sustainable place to live, a city built on a human scale and a city built around the individual citizen. The subsequent report, *Towards an Urban Renaissance*,[6] set out a framework for urban thinking that included concepts like the compact city, the reuse of 'brownfield land', the city based on walking and cycling and the city that recognises the importance of public spaces. It set the foundations for planning and design in London when Ken Livingstone was elected mayor in 2000. It celebrated the role of the city in human culture and marked a major shift in thinking and practice in urban policy. It led to the production and publication of the government's *Urban White Paper* in 2000[7] and, in 2005, to an updated report of the Urban Task Force's research, *Towards a Strong Urban Renaissance*.[8]

Mayoral government in London: in the court of the Medicis

The new Labour government held a referendum on the principle of re-establishing metropolitan government in London presided over by an elected mayor. Subsequently, the 1999 London Government Act paved the way for the establishment of the Greater London Authority (GLA). Its principal purpose was to promote the economic and social development and the environmental improvement of Greater London. Ken Livingstone, the last leader of the GLC, was elected as London's first mayor in 2000.[9] Livingstone's agenda was both strategic and pragmatic. Despite his left-wing reputation, he recognised that London's future would depend on being a major player on the world stage and that a strong economy and inward investment were vital in order to support programmes around public transport, improved housing and environmental quality. While still an important global city, London had slipped well behind New York in terms of its economic power, cultural offer and influence. With the arrival of the new century, London looked outwards again and redefined itself as the major trading centre in the global economy.

Livingstone's advisor on planning, Nicky Gavron, fully embraced the ideas in the Urban Task Force report and was keen to incorporate these into a new London Plan. For Livingstone they resonated with his vision of a global city that could outperform New York economically, be environmentally responsible and socially equitable, and create the conditions of urban life that would attract both global investment and footloose global talent. Underpinning this vision was a city that was diverse, cosmopolitan, confident and open. In retrospect, this vision does not appear to be radical, but at the time it articulated London's role in the emerging global liberal economy in a way that had not been done before. This vision still provides the basis of London's urban policies and has survived subsequent changes in political leadership.

The ideas of the Urban Task Force were translated into planning policies through a new London Plan. These included the idea of the compact city (dense rather than sprawling), the reuse of brownfield land (rather than building on green space) and development focused on public transport (involving restraint on private car use). Transport for London (TfL) was transformed from a highway agency into a transport authority, and budgets were redirected towards public transport, walking and cycling. Tall buildings were encouraged, partly to densify the city but also partly to symbolise London's new confidence. The regeneration of east London was prioritised (ultimately leading to the successful bid for the 2012 Olympics) and the London Development Agency (LDA) was tasked with land acquisition and decontamination. Critically development, responsibly controlled, was seen as a source of growth and future prosperity rather than a threat to communities. In parallel, programmes were established to channel funds into employment and training schemes to facilitate the wider distribution of London's new wealth.

The restoration of London government under an elected mayor produced an entirely new form of political administration – one without precedent or established practices. The mayor was supposed to exercise executive power under the scrutiny of a number of committees that theoretically could hold him to account. In practice they were weak and their role was constrained. That said, the London Government Act of 1999 had deliberately sought to limit the GLA to a strategic remit. The Blair government did not want a return to the days of the GLC where strategic control and service delivery sat alongside one another in a large and unwieldy body.

The new mayor did take over control of transport (through TfL) and economic development (through the LDA). These two bodies came with significant powers and money as well as traditions of organisational independence. London government had been re-established, but it was organised in silos and the only point of intersection was the office of the mayor. Livingstone worked through close political allies who became portfolio holders and advisors – in effect a non-elected cabinet. This modus operandi clearly suited Livingstone, whose skills combined strategic thinking with attention to detail and a highly developed political acumen. The GLA was young, unfettered by institutional history and in campaigning mode to wrest greater powers and money from central government. The fluidity of the structure, combined with an absence of service delivery responsibilities (apart from running TfL), was perfectly set up for an experienced political operator like Livingstone. Early in its establishment, Deputy Mayor Nicky Gavron described it enthusiastically as being 'like working in the court of the Medicis'.[10]

The creation of the Architecture and Urbanism Unit (A+UU)

Ken Livingstone asked Richard Rogers to investigate how London could deliver on the recommendations in the Urban Task Force report. The structure of city government in London lacked the role of a city architect, a position that many European cities had established. The role was offered to Richard Rogers on a part-time basis at a considerable salary. Rogers accepted on condition that he would be an advisor (not city architect) and that the salary would be reduced to one pound with the balance being used to build a design team to support him. This led to the creation of the Architecture and Urbanism Unit (A+UU).

The A+UU was set up within the GLA. Initially, it included a seconded member of the mayor's private office (Richard Brown) alongside Richard Rogers in his role as chief advisor to the mayor.[11] They reviewed the existing regeneration services within the mayor's family of organisations – the GLA, the LDA and TfL – to consider how existing resources could be restructured in light of the Urban Task Force's recommendations. This review established new connections between people and projects across the different organisations and set the foundation for collaboration on regeneration projects across the GLA. Mark Brearley, a partner at the architecture practice East, was appointed as the first head of the unit. By the end of 2002 the team employed five staff members: a unit manager from the mayor's private office, an urban design manager, a public space project manager, an architectural assistant and an administrator. Architecturally trained professionals held two of these positions.[12] The creation of the A+UU was a key step in developing new design thinking on London. Its focus on contemporary urban theory was an important innovation introduced by Rogers and his close collaborator Professor Ricky Burdett from the London School of Economics.

Although the A+UU sat alongside the GLA planning teams, its reporting lines were ambiguous. Initially, it reported to the mayor through Richard Rogers and it had no formal statutory role in London government. This was both a strength and a weakness. Without formal power or spending budgets, the team could be strategic and agile – and could think outside the constraints that often limit government employees. The success of this arrangement relied heavily on the use of 'soft power' and political influence. This works as long as the mayor is in power and is willing to support the arrangement. If the mayor or the relationship changes, then life can become uncomfortable very quickly.

This theme recurs in the next chapter concerning the A+UU's successor body Design for London (DfL).

The A+UU and its influences

The A+UU had the rare privilege of being able to fashion a new work approach that was tailored specifically to London. Its thinking was shaped by a wide range of influences that were then central to European urbanism. These included the importance of mixed-use neighbourhoods and the primary position of the street as civic space – ideas that stretched back to Jane Jacobs and the Internationale Bauausstellung (IBA Berlin), which first brought forward the concept of 'careful urban renewal'. The concept of mixed zones is now well established in UK and European planning. Single-use zones might be efficient in terms of industrial-style economies of scale but are ill-suited to the new economy which is based on intense exchange of ideas. Here proximity and interconnectivity are the keys. The idea of an urban paradigm based on synergies and a degree of tolerated disorder sits comfortably with the concept of 'everyday urbanism' introduced by John Chase, Margaret Crawford and John Kaliski in 1999.[13] Influenced by the thinking of Lefebvre, it explicitly rejects the aesthetics of 'new urbanism' in favour of an empirical approach of studying and recording the activities of everyday life. Inherent in this approach is an appreciation of the fine grain of the city. 'Everyday spaces' are defined by Crawford as 'a diffuse landscape of banal, repetitive and "non-design" locations'[14] – a city's public spaces, markets and streets.

This approach also begins to develop thinking about the temporal nature of the city where changes such as the appropriation of space for different activities and by different groups is part of the urban dynamic. This in turn opens the door to new forms of urbanism that develop from activism to embrace a shift in power towards active community participation. Here the architect becomes a 'player' and design moves beyond mere speculation on form to become involved in the realisation, curation and management of urban space. As a result, the city can be viewed as a series of temporary events and this contributes a new dynamic to urban planning and design, a perspective that extends urban thinking further into the field of experience. This is explored by Bishop and Williams in their book *The Temporary City*.[15]

Brearley had been influenced by the thinking of British urbanists and architects, most notably Alison and Peter Smithson, and the anarchist social observer Colin Ward. He drew on a peculiarly British strand of urban thinking that recognised and celebrated all the 'stuff' of cities – a wider range of elements than the conventional building blocks of many mainstream European urban theorists. These included components as disparate as industrial areas, housing estates, motorways, derelict land, retail sheds, football pitches and cemeteries, together with what goes on in such settings. Brearley recognised the primacy of the street and the significance of both formal and informal urban spaces, and took close interest in the 'found' elements of the urban fabric and the activity it hosted, which the city shaper could choose to work with rather than obliterate. Deeply embedded in this thinking was an antithesis towards planning as a mechanism for pursuing 'neatness'.

At Cambridge, Brearley's contact with Peter Salter (ex-Smithsons) and Peter Carl had reinforced the idea of the value of first-hand experience and the power of urban narratives. He also encountered Josep Lluís Mateo's work through *Quaderns* and Hans Kollhoff (who had worked with Oswald Ungers and Wim Wenders on the concept of the 'green archipelago' in Berlin).[16] Before joining the A+UU, Brearley had been a partner with Julian Lewis in the architecture firm East. Their work was propositional and challenging. For instance, the River Places project considered the area around Rainham village and the marshes on either side of the Thames and reimagined them as a part-wild pleasure garden that spanned the river. Harnessed to this was a particular form of British activism which challenged conventional planning strategies from within the process. Earlier in his career Brearley had been involved with a People's Plan for the Royal Docks and was an advisor to one of the more successful City Challenge programmes in Stratford. This experience brought with it a deep scepticism of conventional planning and a desire to shape new ways of working.

The resulting approach to urbanism was grounded in a careful examination of the ways in which the city functions. It stressed the importance of survey, mapping and documentation as well as a thorough understanding of urban form and function. From this emerged an urbanism based on small adjustments rather than grand interventions. These interventions were to be framed by the structure of the city, by its big roads and its high streets, its suburbs and its infrastructures. This was perhaps the essential element that UK thinking brought to the understanding of cities and urban form. This was an urbanism of negotiation, of understanding that process was a key part of design and that the perfect plan was always likely to be sidelined by the reality of the situation. It was not incompatible with European mainstream thinking at the time, but it did add a dose of healthy pragmatism.

The development of a methodology

The approach of the A+UU owed much to the thinking emerging from places such as the Architecture Association (AA). Brearley's time at the AA in the 1990s had brought him into contact with like-minded practitioners such as Tony Fretton and Peter St John. Their thinking explored the gaps in the planning system that might be filled with new design strategies – to create a 'culture of the ordinary'.[17] A number of practitioners had come together at the AA in the 90s and these contacts would be a strong thread through the work of both the A+UU and DfL. These people, who included Peter Beard, Liza Fior and Julian Lewis, were to form a London network of practices that blended design agency with conviction. In particular, the notion of 'bottom-up' urbanism would be developed into an operational methodology that would fuse design with activism. Underlying this was a deep-seated belief that urban design was about the 'carefulness of urban change' and about the designer being an agent of change in the city. Design was not a matter of neutrality or a debate about the aesthetics of architecture. As a group they were interested in the potential of urban planning as a vehicle for radical change.

This background gave the A+UU a sense of curiosity, but one based on serious empirical research. The city might be open to new forms of experimentation, but these should not be frivolous. In this there was a fundamental difference in approach from that of the Commission for Architecture and the Built Environment. Design was not about being a commentator, it was about active involvement; and while design review might make a scheme better, it would never act as a powerful change agent in the city. The designer should be prepared to take a position. In Mark Brearley's words, 'Design is where you make drawings to work out what you are going to do before *you do it*.'[18]

As a new team, the A+UU had the advantage of starting from a clean slate. Without any specific powers or funding, they used their knowledge of London to grow a portfolio of regeneration projects developed in cooperation with TfL and the LDA. These mayoral bodies both owned land and had the budgets for urban infrastructure that the A+UU lacked. This 'catch and steer' approach was opportunistic. It relied on the fact that there was so much happening in London that any form of comprehensive involvement would be impossible. In any event, the team did not have any powers or control. Collaboration, on the other hand, allowed the team to influence projects and to deflect them into better outcomes.

Richard Rogers had highlighted this cross-organisational, collaborative, site-specific and evidence-based approach as the key missing ingredient in the implementation of regeneration frameworks. However, the A+UU's involvement was not statutory and was reliant on good working relationships with the various clients, stakeholders, landowners and funders. This was challenging since the role and value of design was frequently questioned by other stakeholders who often held contradictory views on value within the regeneration context. While the A+UU sometimes met with hostility, it could offer strategic knowledge-gathering, an overview of initiatives across London government and fresh ideas. As a result, it gained credibility and some of the decision-makers started to appreciate the benefits of well-designed regeneration and were willing to give the team a role at the table.

The A+UU identified and addressed London-wide strategic issues such as the lack of good civic spaces and the role of strategic landscapes. From this thinking emerged a public space programme: 100 Public Spaces and the East London Green Grid. The team also began working in challenging areas for regeneration, such as Barking, Dagenham and the wider Thames Gateway. Here the mayor owned significant areas of land, and strategic design thinking was much needed. These localities had been largely neglected by planning, and the A+UU's involvement in the place-shaping process was more readily accepted by the boroughs and the LDA. These were also places where new ideas could be piloted. The team's approach of research, local knowledge-gathering and collaborative working and its appreciation of the intrinsic value of 'found' assets resulted in its methods being trusted and understood. In almost all collaborations with the boroughs, additional projects were subsequently developed and, with these, long-term associations with the places.

This methodology encouraged new conversations between the mayor's separate regeneration teams, especially in the more deprived areas of the city. Achieving tangible change on the ground in these areas was entirely consistent with the mayor's desire to address social deprivation in the capital. The A+UU's most significant work was delivered through 'conceptual masterplanning'. The City East project (see below) was an enquiry into the nature of London's future growth into the Thames Gateway and posed questions as to why growth and investment were not happening in an area with available land, proximity to the central area and good transport infrastructure. This work focused on the brand and identity of City East and the need for collective dialogue across the mayor's family of organisations and with other stakeholders.

This approach was later developed by DfL into the Green Enterprise District (see Chapter 2) and the Royal Docks Regeneration Strategy (see Chapter 6).

This deliberately pragmatic and opportunistic approach had both negative and positive results. The loose and ad hoc nature of the A+UU's involvement and the services and skills it offered allowed for tactical targeting of projects. But for the outsider, a lack of clarity on its role, combined with a lack of understanding of its approach, created mistrust and tension. Its perceived 'special relationship' with the mayor through Richard Rogers also caused a degree of envy and mistrust.

The approach developed by the A+UU is summarised below under a series of subheadings.[19]

'Big ideas – small actions'

The A+UU recognised that it had to operate strategically and seek to influence rather than dictate. Consequently, a series of programmes were put together that could operate on a metropolitan scale, capturing the imagination of Londoners, but would also allow incremental implementation (Figure 1.2). Implementation was often opportunistic through a series of small-scale projects. These might be funded and managed by different public and private agencies and could be implemented in almost any sequence as funding became available. Individually they had little impact, but collectively they could transform places and lives.

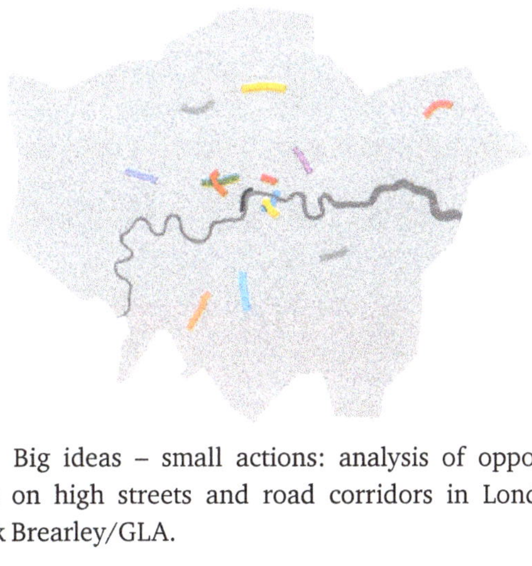

Figure 1.2 Big ideas – small actions: analysis of opportunities for intervention on high streets and road corridors in London. Source: A+UU/Mark Brearley/GLA.

'Catch and steer'

'Catch and steer' linked the idea of making small adjustments to the city to the political reality of a relatively weak institution of London government. Too many different agencies, all of them considerably more powerful than the A+UU, were involved in projects. It would have been impossible to influence more than a fraction of the projects generated within London government. It was also considered somewhat futile to produce an objective matrix of criteria that might assess which projects were or were not worth consideration. Government was not that logical and in any case the A+UU did not have the power automatically to intervene, especially as many agencies jealously guarded their turf. 'Catch and steer' was essentially opportunistic. The team would pick up projects and try and mould them into more effective configurations. To achieve this, it focused on building working relationships with organisations and individuals that were sympathetic to its aims and wanted to cooperate with it. 'Catch and steer' can be traced back to East's contribution to the 1996 Future Southwark exhibition[20] and was succinctly described by Brearley as 'defining selective strategies for change, making the difficult jumps between desire to save and willingness to erase, and embracing the diversity of what determines place'.[21]

'Mapping and understanding'

Some of the early conceptual plans produced by the A+UU set out its approach to spatial thinking on a metropolitan scale (Figure 1.3). This was clearly influenced by new public spaces in Barcelona, as well as Jan Gehl's thinking about the public realm. It also recognised the London context of streets as places rather than simply connectors. The dual focus on places and streets was a theme that carried through into the work of DfL. It fused Continental European and British thinking on the nature of place, but the projects that flowed from this idea also illustrate the divergence of British and European urban thinking. Inherent in this thinking is the important idea that the city is essentially a 'messy place'. This reflected the ideas of Christopher Alexander: that the 'natural' city does not conform to formal geometries or constructs but comprises a rich mix of different but essentially organic elements.[22] The approach fitted both the urban condition of London and its political realities. Formal notions of design were expanded to include

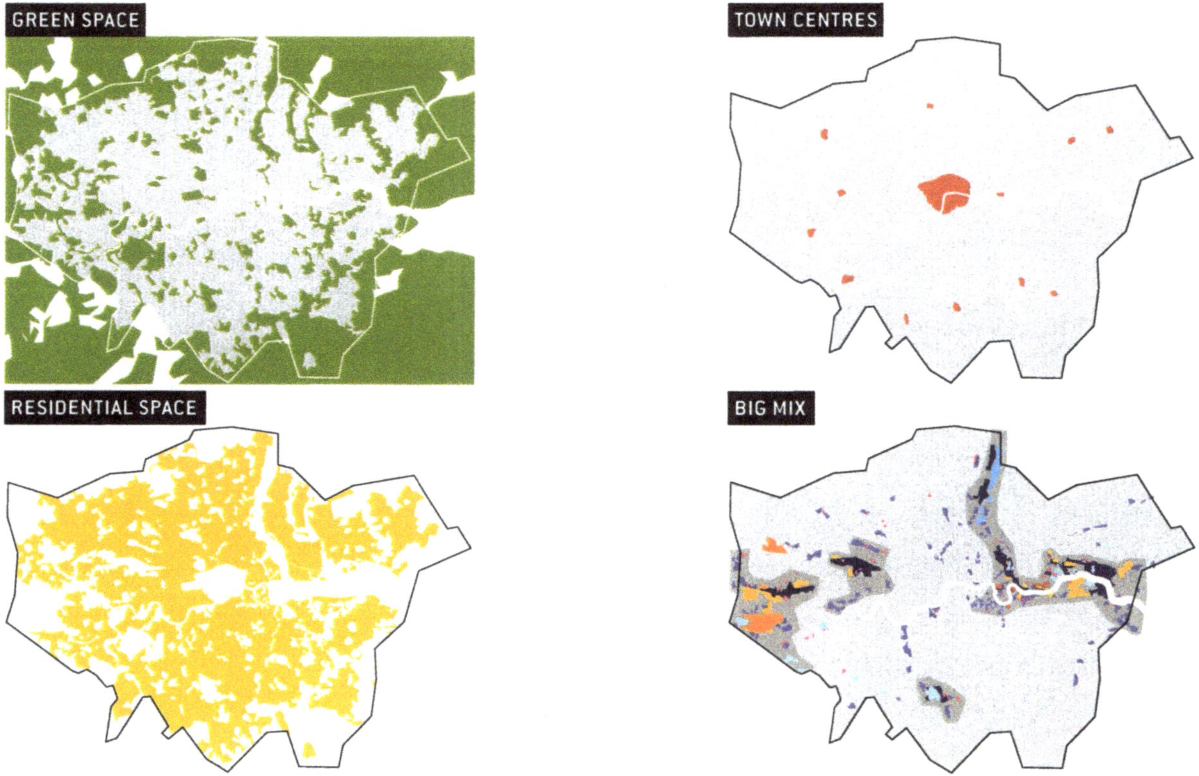

Figure 1.3 Mapping and masterplanning: A+UU studies of London. Source: A+UU/Mark Brearley/GLA.

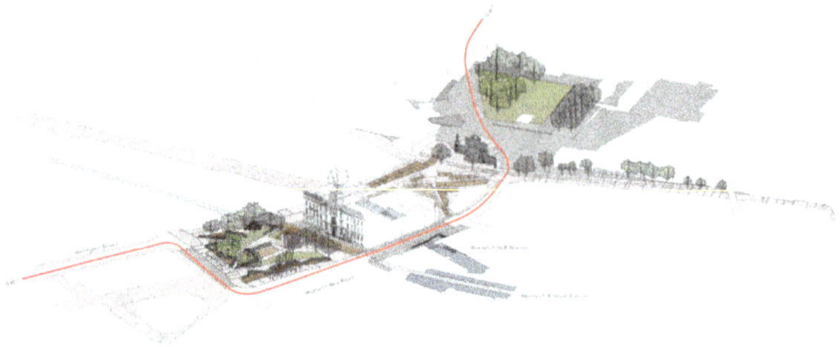

Figure 1.4 Woolwich town centre masterplan. Source: A+UU/GLA/Witherford Watson Mann.

the messy realities of roads, industrial areas, wastelands and suburbs. Design interventions were also fashioned around the social condition of neighbourhoods to address poverty and deprivation. To be relevant, urbanism had to engage.

'Do the drawings, win the argument'

The A+UU's work was strategic, deliberately propositional and backed by research and analysis. It could change scale from the metropolis to the neighbourhood, from the conceptual to the design of the street block or the quality of finish of street paving. The common element was the use of drawings (Figure 1.4) and 'minted phrases' to communicate ideas, capture imagination and garner support. In this respect its work was the very opposite of the norm for a public agency.

Continuity through relationships

From the start there was a clear realisation that the A+UU's work would be time-limited. Urban change on the scale that was required would only be possible by working through others, agencies that would almost certainly outlast the team itself. Partnerships were based on building trust. What the A+UU could offer was knowledge of London, the ability to make connections and the luxury of being able to think, research and develop new perspectives. This was a fragile opportunity, but influence was possible if the team could embed itself in organisations and communities and 'become the locals'.

Working within political structures

The A+UU's approach was specifically shaped by the political realities of working in Livingstone's 'court of the Medicis'. The power rested with the mayor. There was no formal relationship between the mayor and his advisors, and business therefore had to be conducted through informal conversations, social networks and ad hoc meetings. This worked well enough for advisors who were prepared to spend time in the mayoral suite of offices on the top floor of City Hall, but it posed difficulties for Rogers, who as a part-time specialist advisor was also running a major architectural practice. Although he had the respect of the mayor, he was not part of the inner circle of advisors or policy-makers. Initially, within such a young and evolving government institution, this did not matter too much. Rogers and the team had regular meetings with the mayor and decisions were made to develop ideas and programmes. There was no formal process for these decisions to be put into practice other than the fact that the mayor had agreed them. In the early days this was an advantage as the team was developing ideas and the mayor's backing was sufficient to make other agencies cooperate. But later the mayoral advisors entrenched their positions and protected their turf and the mayoral agencies developed their own programmes and funding streams. The A+UU worked within this environment by influencing and shaping but was always aware of the political and organisational tensions. In order to avoid creating a threatening profile, it eschewed any notion of authorship or ownership of ideas. Instead, it sought to seed ideas in other organisations such as TfL and the boroughs, allowing others to lead. Its prevailing strategy was to be seen as a responder rather than an initiator. Others could take the credit as long as the project was developed.

On the whole Livingstone was interested in the ideas that the A+UU generated but would intervene where necessary to ensure that they were in accordance with his political agenda. His agenda moved from the global to the local. He knew London intimately and could read plans and drawings. From his pivotal position at the centre of London government, he knew how to exercise control and if necessary play parts of the organisation off against each other. Inevitably within this environment the A+UU, while strategic, had to operate tactically. It did the drawings and coined the phrases that framed an important set of new initiatives that it carefully inserted into parts of the organisation that were open to its approach. Ultimately, these had a significant impact on the way London developed under the new mayor.

First projects

City East

Initially, the A+UU decided to concentrate on engaging with a small number of locations that were experiencing major change and where it could have a significant impact. The first places that were selected included Bishopsgate Goods Yard and the Thames Gateway. Bishopsgate Goods Yard had a long and complex planning and development history and was a highly contentious site. It soon became apparent that existing stakeholders would not welcome a new (and largely untried) organisation to the party. Such places were not suited to a 'light touch' approach and the experiment was not repeated.

The London Thames Gateway offered better opportunities for involvement. Despite the obvious potential in the area, little was actually happening and Deputy Prime Minister John Prescott wanted action. A key issue was the property market's perception of the area. The 'Thames Gateway' was perceived as too vague a concept, too big and frankly too difficult. The infrastructure was poor, many of the sites were contaminated and low market values deterred risk-taking. There was also no single project to catch the imagination. In the early days of the A+UU, Tim Williams, Director of the Thames Gateway Partnership and a ministerial advisor to the Blair government, counselled the unit to 'focus on the east and work in Barking and Havering'. The two boroughs were rather 'off the radar' for those thinking about London, but they were acutely aware of the problems that they were facing and were open to assistance.

City East was effectively a simple exercise in branding the area that was both vague and precise. The proposition started with a set of bold statements that City East might only constitute 3 per cent of the area of London but it was set to accommodate 25 per cent of London's growth (Figure 1.5). This conceptual work was based on survey work and a detailed knowledge of the area. Each area was considered through a set of questions around 'the consequence of change in each area'. This allowed a set of propositions to be discussed with the boroughs through a process of 'negotiated urbanism'. Because the options highlighted the consequences of different scenarios, the A+UU were able to assess the degree of change that was acceptable to boroughs and agree where plans and proposals might be developed further. This form of non-statutory plan-making set many of the parameters for the subsequent regeneration of east London. It took place before London was awarded the 2012

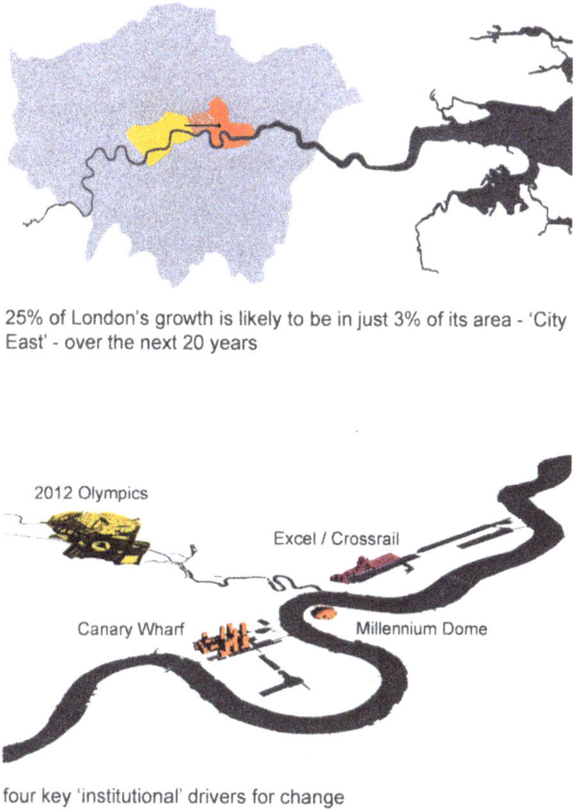

Figure 1.5 City East: the centre for London's growth. Source: A+UU/ Mark Brearley/GLA.

Olympics and considered alternative scenarios for the area that could respond to whether London won the Games or not. It also left behind strong working relationships that made the A+UU the natural point of coordination for cross-borough projects. The A+UU presented the concept in a diagrammatic and non-threatening way that demonstrated the potential of east London and was designed to build enthusiasm and support (Figure 1.6).

While this was an entirely conceptual piece of work, it did refocus discussion on London's eastward growth and underline the area's potential. The LDA responded by redirecting funds into land decontamination and infrastructure improvements. City East also articulated an important characteristic of the regeneration of east London. Despite being a priority for both national and local government for over a decade,

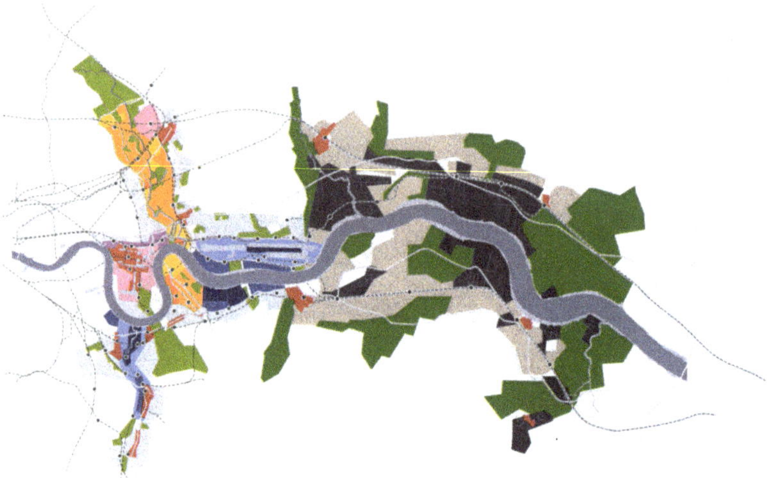

Figure 1.6 City East: analysis of the morphology of the London Thames Gateway. Source: A+UU/Mark Brearley/GLA.

progress had never been smooth or easy. Change had occurred, but in a series of 'eastward lurches' – Canary Wharf, City Airport, the London Exhibition Centre (ExCeL London) and the Millennium Dome/Greenwich Peninsula. Between each of these 'lurches' there had been no continuity. Infrastructure had often been put in retrospectively and, while each 'move' was important in its own right, none had provided sufficient momentum to trigger the next move. Where there had been development, it had been driven by the public rather than private sector. Although not attributable to the A+UU and the City East concept, the next big 'lurch' eastward would be the 2012 London Olympics. Arguably, this has finally produced the momentum to achieve the long-term regeneration of east London.

The City East concept spawned a series of smaller initiatives that latched onto mayoral budgets that were allocated within the Thames Gateway. These funds were channelled into projects in specific places and coherent strategies were written to aid the consolidation of existing town centres and growth areas. One such initiative was Barking town centre, where a sympathetic borough (Barking and Dagenham) was keen to improve one of the poorest places in London. The A+UU set up a methodology for town-centre and high-street interventions that were later developed by DfL (Figure 1.7). This programme is covered in more detail in Chapter 3.

Figure 1.7 Barking town centre: analysis of form and connections. Source: A+UU/GLA/Mark Brearley.

The Mayor's 100 Public Spaces programme

A second initiative, influenced by both Barcelona and Copenhagen, drew on the theme of public space improvements and became the Mayor's 100 Public Spaces programme (Figure 1.8). The title of the programme reflected the philosophy of 'Big Ideas'. In fact, there were never 100 public spaces in the programme, just a desire to create as many as possible. The programme would be design-driven and was specifically structured to address the fact that there was no budget and that implementation would require partnership. The effects of this initiative and its evolution into the Mayor's Great Spaces programme are covered in more

Figure 1.8 The Mayor's 100 Public Spaces programme. Source: A+UU/ Mark Brearley.

Figure 1.9 London Green Grid. Source: *East London Green Grid Primer*, GLA, 2006.

detail in Chapter 3. The first 10 spaces were identified in 2004, design teams were selected and work commenced.[23]

The East London Green Grid

The East London Green Grid (ELGG) developed the ideas of public space at the metropolitan scale and reimagined London as a regional park (Figure 1.9). It was significantly influenced by Florian Beigel's masterplans in Berlin and Leipzig. In Richard Rogers' words, it aimed to create 'peopled landscapes'.[24] The project mapped and recorded east London's neglected and often degraded urban spaces, its *terrains vagues* – landscapes of electricity pylons and wastelands, of commons, heaths, marshes and forgotten watercourses. These were neglected urban leftovers, but they were rich in potential. The ELGG devised multiple interventions to upgrade them, manage them and link them strategically into a connected green network. This network would eventually join the countryside outside London. The project is covered in more detail in Chapter 5.

Housing and the Compact City

Housing and the Compact City[25] developed ideas from the Urban Task Force and applied them to London. London's population was growing but the city was constrained from expanding outwards by the green belt.

The book spelt out a vision for a compact city on a European model, that recycled brownfield land and provided new public spaces within well-designed but high-rise, dense developments. The book explained the mayor's policies on housing density and illustrated them with different typologies at different densities. It was part design manual, part policy document and part manifesto and it fed into the new London Plan. It was the basis for a later involvement in housing policy that led to the 2010 London Housing Design Guide, covered in more detail in Chapter 4.

Streetscape Design Manual

The final major initiative was the Streetscape Design Manual. This stemmed from an early concern with the fundamental importance of the street. It reflected a reaction to the orthodoxy of the 1970s and 1980s where the segregation of cars and pedestrians had so damaged the richness of civic life.

The work of thinkers and practitioners such as Jan Gehl had already permeated approaches to street design in the UK. From the 1990s, the supremacy of the car was being challenged in the UK in favour of an improved public realm and the notion that streets could be people-oriented social spaces. An early practical illustration of these ideas may be seen in the series of interventions that improved pedestrian routes to the new Tate Modern as part of the extension of London's South Bank, on which Brearley had worked for several years before joining the A+UU.[26] With the establishment of the GLA and the new office of mayor, the Architecture Foundation launched an ideas competition that featured the theme of 'Car Free London',[27] ideas that chimed with the findings of the Urban Task Force.

The work on street design was the beginning of an important new interface between the A+UU and TfL. TfL was now under the direction of the mayor who was transforming it from a highway agency into a transport agency. A new commissioner, Bob Kiley, brought in from New York, was charged with developing an integrated agency under the political control of the mayor. His appointment opened up London to new ideas, influences and business practices from America. He also knew Richard Rogers, and this gave the A+UU useful access into TfL.

The Streetscape Design Manual was initially a reaction to the poor quality of London's streets. The 1980s and 1990s had been difficult times for many of the inner London Labour-controlled boroughs. They had resisted the spending cuts of the Thatcher government and had borrowed heavily in the expectation of a change of government. When this did not happen a number of boroughs faced serious financial difficulties. Added to this was a degree of internal mismanagement. In many cases money had been diverted away from highways maintenance to fund other programmes such as housing, leisure and community buildings. In certain areas London's streets were literally falling apart. Even where this was not happening the boroughs generally lacked long-term plans for street maintenance and the result was a hotchpotch of different styles and materials. These problems were compounded by the split of responsibilities for maintenance between TfL and the boroughs. Although TfL had leverage in the form of annual capital grants to the boroughs, these were based on traffic flow and safety criteria and there was no design control or project sign-off.

The catalyst for a comprehensive streetscape design guide was a walk that the A+UU team and Richard Rogers made around Bermondsey (actually en route to their Christmas lunch). A file of photos was put together documenting the appalling state of street surfaces and this was sent to TfL. Kiley responded with an invitation to undertake research into best practice and compile a design manual. The principles were simple enough:

- Streets were background, not foreground.
- Over-elaborate design was costly, was likely to be difficult to maintain and would soon look dated.
- A simple palette of materials, including granite kerbs and large block paving slabs, best reflected the existing character of London streets.
- Good design was about getting the basics right and this included care over construction and finishes (Figure 1.10).
- Excessive street furniture, including guard rails, should be removed wherever practical.
- Street lighting should be rationalised and attached to buildings wherever possible.

The *London Streetscape Design Manual* was published in 2006, and eventually its use became a condition of TfL funding for capital projects. It is still used extensively today. This was the A+UU's first major success in influencing design quality through policy rather than through project appraisal. It became a template for the future work of DfL.

1 Traditional paving extended to kerb

2 Traditional kerbs retained

3 Inspection cover replaced with insert cover

4 Concrete bollards replaced

5 Signal head on lighting column

6 Footway lighting added

7 Luminaire appropriate for urban centre location

8 Traffic bollards replaced by 'hoop' design

9 'Heritage' lighting retained

10 All street furniture finished in black (excluding central reserve barrier)

11 Bus lane surface pigmentation corrected to end at stop line

Figure 1.10 Images from the *London Streetscape Design Manual* showing principles and examples of detailing. Source: *London Streetscape Design Manual*, GLA/TfL, 2006.

An end and a new beginning

In the 2004 London mayoral election, Ken Livingstone was re-elected. With a second political term came the opportunity to prioritise different agendas, and Livingstone sought to develop London government's design capacity further by bringing together the different regeneration teams in the GLA family to form one team.

While the collaborative nature of the work that the unit initiated was widely supported, their style and working methods were being questioned by those unfamiliar with a design-led process and there was a managerial desire to bring it under closer operational control. In 2006 the regeneration and urban design teams from the GLA (the A+UU), the LDA and TfL joined to form one new design team, renamed Design for London (DfL). The professional backgrounds to this agglomeration of teams included architects, planners, road engineers, urban designers and general office support. The director of this new team, Peter Bishop, had previously been the Director of Planning and Environment at the London Borough of Camden. He was a planner by training but had worked closely with architects and urbanists throughout his career and at Camden had overseen the planning of the King's Cross scheme. He was also seen as a government insider who had delivered major projects in overtly political environments. This was a strategic move to 'enable design to be understood and communicated to all professions involved in city regeneration'.[28]

Conclusions

The A+UU was a small and innovative unit that survived for five years in the formative days of the GLA. It developed a set of powerful ideas for London and was successful in inserting these subversively into other agencies' agendas. It established both a design methodology and a modus operandi that were later taken up by DfL. This methodology signified a return to a debate about urban living and the importance of urban form. It was optimistic and at times idealistic, but its work was always rigorous and value-based. Such values are often overlooked in the day-to-day world of urban government. One of the A+UU's significant contributions was to explore the limits of design and to pilot new ideas, thus acting as a bridge between the proposals of the Urban Task Force (and the agenda of the Blair government) and the real world. London, with its new confidence and booming economy, was a fertile ground for experimentation. It is difficult to assess the A+UU's long-term success and impact. It certainly achieved a 'niche' position and a small but influential international following, particularly in Germany and the Netherlands. Some of its early programmes, such as the 100 Public Spaces and East London Green Grid, continue in different forms today. Others, like the town-centre work, have had lasting beneficial impacts.

The problems that the unit faced were as much organisational and political as anything else. The mayor was interested in architecture and design, but it was not central to his agenda. He could see how it fitted into his broader political objectives and, all other things being equal, he recognised that design had a role to play in his strategies for promoting London on the global stage. Richard Rogers, though respected, did not have the same degree of influence over the mayor as other, full-time advisors. The model of a mayor driving urban change through design, as had been the case with Barcelona, was not on the agenda for London. In addition, the structure of political advisors based around the mayor in City Hall meant that the A+UU was always seen as slightly suspect and was kept on the periphery. Its work would be appreciated where it coincided with another agenda, but where it did not it was viewed as lightweight and at times an irritant. In this context there was no automatic mechanism for follow-through on many good ideas, which ultimately limited the influence of the team.

The A+UU was made up of young architects, few of whom had had any senior experience in the public sector. It was on a steep learning curve in an environment dominated by experienced, and at times cynical, operators. In embarking on some projects it failed to understand the complexity of the problems, particularly on public space programmes that entailed working within labyrinthine internal procedures and where there were legitimate technical objections to their ideas. That said, the A+UU pioneered public realm programmes in a period when the emphasis was still biased in favour of vehicles and when public space was seen by many in government as a somewhat frivolous luxury.

The impact of the unit also needs to be viewed in the context of the re-establishment of the GLA. The boroughs had enjoyed a degree of freedom since the abolition of the GLC, and a new metropolitan body, although largely welcomed, was not necessarily trusted. This lack of trust extended to the new mayor, who was seen by some as trying to carve out a role at their expense.[29]

There was a gradual change in the management of the unit. The initial freedom that it enjoyed was slowly curtailed as it became embedded in the bureaucracy of London government. It is possible that its freedom and patronage were resented, but it is certain that a free-thinking and occasionally maverick team was treated with suspicion within a management hierarchy which sensed the potential danger of initiatives that could not be tightly controlled.

The A+UU operated in a difficult political environment. Much of the thinking that it developed in the early years of the GLA around public space, streets and landscape is now mainstream, but was not then. It benefited from the fluid nature of the newly constituted GLA but lacked experience in working in a government bureaucracy that was dominated by politically savvy operators. That said, the A+UU did have a significant impact on London and many of its initiatives are still apparent today. The real strength of the A+UU and possibly its most important legacy was its deeply held belief that the condition of the city could be improved, and that design was essentially a *political* activity that could do this. It set a foundation of thinking and work without which DfL would have struggled to make a mark.

Notes

1 Initiated by the Thatcher government as a response to political opposition from the left-wing Greater London Council. See Department of the Environment 1983 and *Local Government Act 1985*.
2 The population declined from 8.6 million in 1939 to 6.7 million in 1986. Source: Greater London Authority 2017.
3 Kleihues and Klotz 1986.
4 Originally coined in 1967 by the Bonzo Dog Doo Dah Band, this 'brand' generally embraced the emerging club, art, fashion and music scene of the 1990s.
5 Urban Task Force 1999.
6 Urban Task Force 1999.
7 Office of the Deputy Prime Minister 2000.
8 Urban Task Force 2005.
9 Livingstone's nomination as the Labour candidate was opposed by Tony Blair and the Party. He stood as an independent candidate against the Labour candidate Frank Dobson. He was later readmitted to the Party.
10 Conversation with Peter Bishop in March 2001.
11 Richard Brown, interviewed by Lara Kinneir, 9 March 2017.
12 Brown 2002.
13 Chase, Crawford and Kaliski 1999.
14 Chase, Crawford and Kaliski 1999.
15 Bishop and Williams 2012.
16 Ungers and Koolhaas 2013.
17 Ward 2011.
18 Interview with Mark Brearley, February 2020.
19 Interview with Mark Brearley, March 2019.
20 https://www.architecturefoundation.org.uk/programme/1996/future-southwark
21 Brearley 1997.

22 Alexander 1965.
23 The first 10 spaces were Windrush Square (Brixton), Exhibition Road and Sloane Square (Kensington & Chelsea), Euston underpass (Camden), Gillett Square (Hackney), Lewisham town centre, Lower Marsh (Lambeth), Coulsdon High Street (Croydon), Rainham village centre (Havering), Victoria Embankment gardens (Westminster).
24 Scalbert 2013.
25 Greater London Authority 2003.
26 East 1998.
27 Architecture Foundation, September 1998 to February 1999, competition for a car-free London.
28 Richard Brown, interviewed by Lara Kinneir, 9 March 2017.
29 For further detail, see Bishop and Williams 2016.

Bibliography

Alexander, Christopher, 'A City is Not a Tree', *Architectural Forum*, Vol. 122, No. 1, April 1965, pp. 58–62 (Part I), Vol. 122, No. 2, May 1965, pp. 58–62 (Part II). https://www.patternlanguage.com/archive/cityisnotatree.html (accessed 15 March 2020).

Bishop, Peter, and Williams, Lesley, *The Temporary City*, London: Routledge, 2012.

Bishop, Peter, and Williams, Lesley, *Planning, Politics and City Making: A Case Study of King's Cross*, London: RIBA Publishing, 2016.

Brearley, Mark, 'Determining Places', *Cambridge Architecture Journal*, No. 9, 1997, pp. 4–5.

Brearley, Mark, 'A Conversation with Mark Brearley', *Scroope*: *Cambridge Architecture Journal*, No. 14, 2002, pp. 28–9.

Brown, Richard, *GLA Business Report No. 8: Architecture and Urbanism Unit Staff*, Greater London Authority, 2 December 2002.

Chase, John, Crawford, Margaret, and Kaliski, John (eds), *Everyday Urbanism*, New York: Monacelli Press, 1999.

Department of the Environment, *Streamlining the Cities: White Paper*, London: HMSO, 1983.

East (Brearley, Mark), 'Adjusting a Street', *Scroope: Cambridge Architecture Journal*, No. 10, 1998, pp. 74–7.

Greater London Authority, *Housing and the Compact City*, Greater London Authority, 2003.

Greater London Authority, *East London Green Grid Primer*, Greater London Authority, 2006.

Greater London Authority, *London Plan 2016*, January 2017. https://www.london.gov.uk/what-we-do/planning/london-plan/current-london-plan/london-plan-2016-pdf (accessed 24 February 2020).

Greater London Authority/Transport for London, *London Streetscape Design Manual*, Greater London Authority/Transport for London, 2006.

Kleihues, Josef Paul, and Klotz, Heinrich, *International Building Exhibition Berlin 1987: Examples of New Architecture*, New York: Rizzoli, 1986.

Lichtenstein, Claude, and Schregenberger, Thomas (eds), *As Found: The Discovery of the Ordinary*, Zurich, Switzerland: Lars Müller Publishers, 1993.

Lluís Mateo, Josep (ed.), *Quaderns*, No. 177. Barcelona, Spain: Association of Catalan Architects, 1988.

Local Government Act 1985, London: HMSO, 1985.

McCreery, Sandy, 'East: Practice Profile', *Architectural Design*, Vol. 70, No. 4, 2000, pp. 106–9.

Office of the Deputy Prime Minister (ODPM), *Our Towns and Cities – the Future: The Urban White Paper,* ODPM, 2000.

Scalbert, Irénée, 'London After the Green Belt', *AA Files*, No. 66, 2013. https://www.thomasdanegallery.com/usr/documents/press/download_url/510/ml-aa-files-2013.pdf (accessed 24 February 2020).

Smithson, Alison, and Smithson, Peter, *Ordinariness and Light: Urban Theories 1952–1960 and Their Application in a Building Project 1963–1970*, Cambridge, MA: MIT Press, 1970.

Ungers, Oswald Mathias, and Koolhaas, Rem, *The City in The City – Berlin: A Green Archipelago: A Manifesto (1977) by Oswald Mathias Ungers and Rem Koolhaas [with others]*, edited by

Florian Hertweck and Sébastien Marot, UAA Ungers Archives for Architectural Research, Zurich, Switzerland: Lars Müller Publishers, 2013.
Urban Task Force, *Towards an Urban Renaissance*, London: HMSO, 1999.
Urban Task Force, *Towards a Strong Urban Renaissance*, London: HMSO, 2005. http://image.guardian.co.uk/sys-files/Society/documents/2005/11/22/UTF_final_report.pdf (accessed 24 February 2020).
Ward, Colin, *Autonomy, Solidarity, Possibility: The Colin Ward Reader*, edited by Damian F. White and Chris Wilbert, Edinburgh: AK Press, 2011.

2

Design for London: an interesting but short life

Peter Bishop, Lara Kinneir and Mark Brearley

The preceding chapter examined the background to the setting up of London government under Mayor Ken Livingstone, the structure of its various agencies and the establishment of the Architecture and Urbanism Unit (A+UU) under Richard Rogers. It also looked at the early work and approach of the A+UU as well as its successes and weaknesses. This chapter examines the reasons for the formation of Design for London (DfL), which replaced the A+UU, and considers its methodology and operational approach.

The first decade of the twenty-first century was a heady time for the UK and London. The Labour government under Tony Blair was in its second term, the economy was growing rapidly and London was emerging as one of the most powerful cities in the global economy. There was every sign that this would continue well into the future. Any clouds on the horizon were those arising from London's rapid growth, with shortages in affordable housing and the market distortions caused by property speculation for short-term returns.

Perhaps the high point was in July 2005 when London was awarded the 2012 Olympic Games. Mayor Livingstone was now back in the Labour Party and the London bid had been fully supported by the national government. The bid centred on the regeneration of Stratford, one of the poorer areas of London, and presented the opportunity to realise the strategy to push development eastwards into the Thames Gateway at a scale that would create long-term momentum for change. The way was open for London to emerge as the pre-eminent city in the world.

The institutions of London government

Ken Livingstone had been re-elected in 2004 without any serious challenge and the mechanisms of London government were maturing. The creative chaos of the early days of the Greater London Authority (GLA) was being replaced with more formalised structures. Critically, the two main agencies outside the GLA, Transport for London (TfL) and the London Development Agency (LDA), were now under a degree of political direction from the mayor's office. TfL in particular was under a new transport commissioner, Peter Hendy, and was continuing to transform into a transport agency. Capital funds were shifting from highways to buses and the underground. Walking and cycling were considered as legitimate transport modes in their own right and, despite still being low in the pecking order, were now receiving resources. These new programmes were largely uncommitted and offered opportunities for new public space projects.

The LDA was still finding its feet. Created as part of a national network of regional development agencies, its remit was to intervene in areas of market failure in order to stimulate regional economic growth. However, in London the market failures did not stem from industrial decline but were due to rapid growth and an overheating economy that had left behind areas of social and geographical deprivation. In these circumstances the measures in the traditional armoury of a regional development agency – land acquisition and decontamination, training and support for enterprise and incentives for inward investment – were not easily applicable.

The LDA's land portfolio, inherited from English Partnerships, was a ragbag of difficult sites and the agency soon became bogged down in a series of cumbersome development initiatives that were both costly and ineffective. In an overheated economy, the LDA was just getting in the way. Other programmes such as training and support for enterprise were also yielding mixed results and the agency was constantly firefighting to rescue poorly conceived initiatives that had been pursued for overtly political objectives. In the absence of well-developed management and performance structures, the LDA was operating well below its potential. It did, however, play one particular role with alacrity. It picked up specific projects that the mayor wanted to pursue but for which no other budgets were available. While TfL had a strong internal management structure that could act as a counterweight to the mayor, the LDA was malleable and compliant.

Background to the creation of Design for London

Ken Livingstone's re-election provided the opportunity for more ambitious long-term strategies and a chance to consolidate inter-agency working. Public interest in architecture and urban design had been stimulated by a series of lottery-funded projects, in particular the new Tate Modern, housed in the former Bankside power station originally designed by Sir Giles Gilbert Scott and converted into a gallery by the architects Herzog & de Meuron. Design was suddenly newsworthy, and architects were media stars. Following in the footsteps of the Pompidou Centre in Paris and the Guggenheim in Bilbao, the creation of Tate Modern brought about a significant transformation of London's South Bank. Exhibitions in the newly refurbished Turbine Hall created an important visitor attraction, and the building also completed the link along the South Bank between the Royal Festival Hall, Southwark Cathedral, Borough Market and Tower Bridge.

The development of Tate Modern had been accompanied by wider design thinking driven by Fred Manson, who had been Director of Regeneration and Environment at the London Borough of Southwark in the 1990s. Following its subsequent comprehensive upgrade, the Southbank Centre (Allies and Morrison, 2005–7) was connected to the Embankment and Covent Garden by the new Hungerford Bridge foot crossings (Lifschutz Davidson, 2002), while Norman Foster's Millennium Bridge provided a new link to St Paul's Cathedral. The partial pedestrianisation of Trafalgar Square (Norman Foster, 2003) under the Mayor's World Spaces for All programme had also proved instantly popular.[1] These projects had not been part of a grand design by a centralised authority – they were a triumph for pragmatic incremental urbanism driven by individual architects and agencies. There was widespread public recognition that such interventions, particularly around public spaces, represented a significant improvement. London was at last catching up with other cities.

Another force promoting good design was the Commission for Architecture and the Built Environment (CABE). Founded in 1999 as a response to recommendations in the Urban Task Force, it replaced the Royal Fine Arts Commission's role in design review. It also commissioned numerous best practice papers. It was a highly influential, if sometimes controversial, voice in support of contemporary architecture and design. CABE's role in raising the profile of the design debate in England (there were separate bodies for Wales, Scotland and Northern Ireland) was significant. It had responded to the government's agenda and had captured the public mood, acting as an important counterweight to the more conservative approach of English Heritage.

Purpose and structure of Design for London

Some in the GLA viewed the A+UU as maverick and difficult to control – more of a problem than an asset. Its fraught relationship with the GLA planning team was causing problems and its direct channel to the mayor through Richard Rogers represented another cause for mistrust. The idea of a new and more powerful design agency for London was first mooted in early 2005 by Deputy Mayor Nicky Gavron, Richard Rogers and senior managers in the GLA. The rationale was to strengthen the role of design within London government and at the same time to exercise greater control over projects in TfL and the LDA. The intention was also to regularise the position and managerial structure of the A+UU.

The A+UU had established good working relationships with project officers in the LDA and TfL, and the GLA hoped that an integrated design team would be able to extend inter-agency working and access to capital budgets for mayoral projects. Architecture and design were still part of the mayor's agenda and the creation of a single team represented an opportunity to establish a degree of common purpose between the GLA, the LDA and TfL, especially in the context of the rapid growth of the London economy and the forthcoming Olympics. The consolidation of design resources into a single unit would also increase the mayor's design capacity without the need to find additional funding.

With the agreement of Ken Livingstone and Richard Rogers, David Lunts, Director of Regeneration at the GLA, brokered an agreement with TfL and the LDA to pool their resources into a new pan-London design unit. The jealousy with which the agencies defended their independence meant that this new unit could not be located in the GLA, but the GLA did not want to lose control of it to either of the other agencies. The compromise was that it would be outside the existing structure of London government and would have a degree of managerial and operational independence. While the LDA would provide 'pay and rations', it would have no managerial control over the new organisation. Instead, it would report to a board chaired by Lunts that would include a senior representative from TfL and from the LDA. Richard Rogers would also be on the board. The new agency would have access to the mayor through the board. Whether this was a deliberate attempt to reduce

Richard Rogers' influence is unclear, but on paper at least the new agency would be managerially accountable for its activities. The new organisation was to be called Design for London (DfL), Richard Rogers would take a more strategic role in directing its work and a new director would be appointed to lead the integrated team. The arrangements were signed off by the mayor in the summer of 2006.

There was considerable media interest in the new agency, due partly to Richard Rogers' involvement and the high profile of design in London. Media interest had already been sparked by controversy around CABE, which was facing accusations of conflicts of interest. These were possibly due to perceptions that it had become overly powerful. There was also friction between CABE and English Heritage, and criticism from some within the architectural profession that CABE was promoting a 'modernist' as opposed to a 'traditionalist' agenda. Either way, design agencies were fruitful news stories for the architectural press. Another reason for the press interest was the name: Design for London represented a powerful brand image. It *implied* the power to shape and change London, as well as the independence to carry through projects. This was in keeping with the zeitgeist of the period. It also implied the prospect of conflict with CABE and English Heritage, and a potentially endless series of news stories. It brought in a period of intense speculation over who would be appointed as the new Director of Design for London.

The job was advertised in summer 2006 and a number of well-known architects were rumoured to be applying. The advertisement also caught the eye of Peter Bishop, then working as Planning Director at Camden Council. Bishop had worked as a planning director in central London for 25 years, at Tower Hamlets, Haringey, and Hammersmith and Fulham, and recognised that 'this looked like the best job in the world'.[2] An informal 'interview' – a lunch with Richard Rogers, Renzo Piano and others at the Venice Architecture Biennale – was followed by a formal interview with Rogers and senior officials from the LDA, TfL and the GLA. 'I didn't think I'd get the job,' says Bishop, 'but it became clear to me they were actually looking for a manager with experience in operating at the political interface. I knew London, I had been involved in urban design, but critically I also understood and could work within the systems of London government.'[3] Bishop was appointed, and Design for London was launched to some fanfare from the design press, in October 2006.[4] Peter Murray, director of New London Architecture, commented:

> We are very glad Peter Bishop has won this very important appointment. He has always been a great supporter of quality

architecture as shown by the work he did while at Hammersmith and at Camden. He is someone who can provide the link between the GLA and the Boroughs which will be so important for the successful implementation of the London Plan. We look forward to working with Peter Bishop in the future to encourage the best of design for the capital.[5]

The appointment of a director who was not from an architectural background surprised many people, as did the fact that the new director was from local government. Possibly there was no room for two big-name architects in London government. The appointment made a clear statement that DfL was to be an agency of government and was expected to move the propositional work of the A+UU onwards to achieve more delivered projects on the ground. The director was also expected to manage the A+UU and evolve the design team by amalgamating design staff from TfL and the LDA. To do this the director needed to understand the processes of government and be able to work within the politics of City Hall.

Approach and methodology of Design for London

DfL inherited the staff and work programmes of the A+UU together with the design teams at the LDA and TfL. The staff came with their existing work programmes, time commitments and approaches, but only the A+UU had a clear working methodology based on sound theoretical frameworks. Few staff from the LDA and TfL had design skills, but they did bring project implementation skills and a knowledge of organisational procedures – both of which had been areas of weakness of the A+UU. The A+UU's tight-knit, energetic and talented team formed the core of the new organisation and its previous work provided a firm basis from which to build new momentum. Richard Rogers retained his close working relationship with the team and usually spent one day a week working in their offices, critiquing projects and discussing new policy ideas.[6]

Bishop shared the A+UU's recognition that London was never going to be shaped by *grands projets*. The limited power of the mayor and the shortage of capital budgets for London in any case precluded major intervention. Bishop brought to the team his experience of working on major development projects, a knowledge of the development industry, the skills needed to access public funding and a pragmatic approach to steering urban change through tortuous political processes. He was also more comfortable working in a political environment than the A+UU had been and understood the power of intercorporate working and networks.

As a planner Bishop had always been interested in the social and economic impacts of urban change and viewed urban design as an essential tool of the planning profession. He had been involved in major development projects and saw planning as a means to drive social improvement in the form of affordable housing, public space and the creation of economic opportunities for local communities.[7] For Bishop, planning was a flexible and creative discipline that could be *used* to achieve urban change – planning process was of interest only inasmuch as it achieved tangible (and desirable) results. That said, Bishop understood process and understood politics and this combination had enabled him to drive through transformative change in the parts of London that he had worked in. He had been trained in urban design and was scathing of planning's inability to be involved in the wider design debate. From the outset, he viewed DfL as a planning agency, but one that was able to use architectural approaches to shape the city.[8]

Bishop had been particularly influenced by the methodology of everyday or incremental urbanism, as developed by Margaret Crawford and Stephen Marshall, a theory of the city based on a degree of tolerated disorder.[9] This approach is critical of '[b]anal suburbs, shiny but empty downtowns, formal office parks and abandoned districts [that] result from policies that neither recognise the everyday nor allow it to assert and reassert itself'.[10] The everyday urbanism proposed by Crawford favours interventions that reinforce the heterogeneous qualities of small, temporary, not-intended, undistinguished though well-used spaces. It takes ordinary places, 'the nooks and crannies of existing urban environments', thinks about them in new ways and makes small changes that may accumulate to have a transformative effect on the wider locality.[11] It aims to reconnect urban design with ordinary human and social meanings and thus strengthen 'the connective tissue that binds daily lives together'.[12] Inherent in this approach is an appreciation of the fine grain of the city.

Bishop's thinking was very close to that of Mark Brearley and the A+UU team, whose way of working he easily embraced. This approach sat comfortably with the pragmatism required to orchestrate urban change from the position of organisational weakness that DfL had inherited. To be effective, DfL had to be able to play a weak hand well. It had no power or money, but these could be considerable assets. In the absence of power there was no requirement to comply with the stifling conformity of government. If it could deploy the soft power of its access to the mayor, then other agencies would willingly work with it and could be influenced by its approach. If other agencies carried out the project work then DfL would be free of all of the responsibilities of dealing with public money and could be a strategic design agency. The ambiguity of its position in the structure of London government was to be its greatest asset.

From the outset DfL adopted much of the A+UU's methodology, projects and programmes and fully embraced the approach of urban narratives rather than urban plans. Its more powerful position in London government, high public profile and ability to work more adeptly in a political environment allowed it to extend its influence further in the following ways:

– *Partnership with stakeholders who controlled budgets*. DfL set out to be collaborative and not didactic. The A+UU had been effective at finding allies within the boroughs, the LDA and TfL, and DfL was able to build on these networks. In particular it could now access a greater number of senior decision-makers. At the same time, it continued to 'infiltrate' key agencies of London government to persuade them to take a wider design perspective. This 'soft power' approach allowed DfL to build wider and deeper networks. To back up these networks, DfL worked hard to identify available resources within government budgets and programmes. By knowing where the money was and working with those who controlled resources, the team could assemble complex funding packages to implement its own project priorities. This ability to harness the power of funding set the new agency apart from the A+UU and enabled it to make an early impact.
– *Influencing procurement and supporting the client role.* The mantra 'good architects *can* design good buildings, bad architects never will' is explored in more detail in Chapter 7. Influencing the procurement of architects was seen as one of the most effective ways of improving project design. Support from the mayor (real or perceived) gave the team access to stronger influence over the procurement of architects and designers. Over time DfL advised clients on development briefs and took on a pivotal role in

setting up new framework agreements. DfL deliberately used procurement to promote a new generation of practices – smaller, younger and more experimental – that had often been excluded by traditional procurement processes. It recognised the potential of such practices to move the design agenda forward with new ideas and approaches.

- *Campaigning and publicity.* DfL made the decision to exploit the high profile generated by its formation. This was a departure from the A+UU's policy of keeping a low profile. There was a major press launch for the new agency, frequent contact with the architectural press, events and exhibitions. All were aimed at creating continuous media (and public) interest. In its publications, DfL deliberately eschewed any recognised public-sector house style. The graphics, covers, photos and plans were a deliberate departure from public-sector norms. They were part of the branding of the team. This is covered in more detail in Chapter 7.
- *International profile.* European influences were evident in the methodology and early projects of the A+UU and it had built a good network with other cities and practitioners. Under DfL connections with German and Dutch practices were refreshed. Dutch masterplanning in particular was considered to be ahead of current thinking in the UK, as were German ideas around landscape. Consequently, links were strengthened with a range of practices such as KCAP, Maxwan, Vogt, and Latz+Partner. DfL became a significant conduit for new ideas for London. It also became an advocate for emerging UK and international practices to gain commissions in London.

At the heart of DfL's approach was a detailed knowledge of London and an understanding of its uniqueness. London's urban morphology is not as formal as that of other European cities and has an ingrained flexibility of form. Outside the areas of historical importance, the city has a wide range of diverse places that offered opportunities for experimentation. The team did consider whether there might indeed be a specific London 'style' but concluded that it was the *approach* to urban thinking that defined the city (Figure 2.1). *Grands projets*, certainly before the Olympics, were to be left to private-sector developers with the land and money to execute them. The strategic design team aimed to develop ideas and projects that could sit within the everyday fabric of the city. These could then be implemented by other agencies as the opportunities permitted.

Figure 2.1 Open city: London, a cosmopolitan city of many nationalities. Source: KCAP.

Design in a benign environment: 2007–2008

DfL's first priority was to bring all the staff together while there was still momentum. This was achieved in less than two months. The second priority was an early and high-profile launch where major figures in London architecture and the press would be present. This took place in March 2007. Presentations by Richard Rogers and Ken Livingstone reinforced the impression that the new organisation had high-level support and would be a force to be reckoned with. Its inherited body of work gave DfL a head start and the first projects in the 100 Public Spaces programme were nearing completion. Although Gillett Square in Hackney (Figure 2.2) was officially opened in November 2006, two months before the new agency actually came into existence, it was badged as a DfL scheme and an instant sense of momentum was established. Similarly, the *East London Green Grid Primer* was published in 2006 and DfL was credited with the project. Richard Rogers' association with DfL provided both national and international kudos, and he dedicated much time to boosting the team's public influence.

Figure 2.2 Proposals for Gillett Square in Hackney as part of the 100 Public Spaces programme. Source: A+UU/GLA.

Soon after DfL's establishment, a new advisory panel was set up. This was recruited through open competition and provided more positive press coverage. DfL's profile allowed it to attract some of the best practitioners from the UK and abroad (see Chapter 7). The panel deliberately included names that were unexpected, as well as representatives from development, landscape, engineering and environmental disciplines. It met quarterly and its role was flexible. It rarely advised on the design of specific projects. Its main purpose was to connect DfL to the world of practice (and to be seen to do so). Outside the formal meetings, a number of the panel members put in time to advise and mentor on projects. The panel was also an important conduit of new ideas and provided a powerful set of friends and advocates for the new team (Figure 2.3).

The creation of a new agency provided a good opportunity to reappraise projects that had been inherited from the A+UU, the LDA and TfL. The core programmes of town centre renewal, public spaces and the East London Green Grid were continued (Figure 2.4) and are covered in more detail in Chapters 3 and 5. Other initiatives, such as an ambitious idea for a cross-river park in east London, were dropped (when Mayor Johnson abandoned the Beckton river crossing in 2008). City East was not pursued as a project (it had achieved its purpose), but it did provide a strong foundation for later plans for the regeneration of east London and the Royal Docks.

The most significant change was one of traction. DfL had the profile and power to gain momentum for its projects. Complex funding

Figure 2.3 Richard Rogers (centre, in a characteristic coloured shirt) at the Design for London Advisory Panel. Source: Design for London Archive, DfL/GLA.

Figure 2.4 Influencing through policy documents. Source: Design for London Archive, DfL/GLA.

arrangements were knitted together from various agencies to progress projects, in particular for the 100 Public Spaces programme. Direct involvement in procurement allowed the team to influence some LDA and TfL projects and the team expanded its involvement in writing briefs, setting up competitions and selecting design teams on behalf of London government and boroughs. The development and architectural sectors began to respond with better designs. Town centre projects were brought forward, most notably in Dalston and Barking, and the growing maturity of the team was apparent in its ability to extend its networks and work with local politicians. The style was cooperative, gentle, persuasive. Mayoral agencies had expected DfL to throw its weight about. The very name 'Design for London' suggested a body that would direct and impose its views and there was understandable suspicion, especially as the organisation reported directly to the mayor. From the start DfL recognised the danger of taking a high-handed position and sought to collaborate with agencies within London government. They were surprised and became more comfortable in cooperating with the team. In practice there was little friction in working relationships.

Perhaps DfL's most influential work was in the field of policy. The GLA had responsibility for producing the London Plan – a task that they executed effectively. However, there are limitations to what can be achieved through planning policy and DfL was able to move into these openings. The London Housing Design Guide project (covered in Chapter 4) is an example of how a policy debate that was considered too controversial and politically sensitive for a statutory planning team to engage with could be moved forward. Ken Livingstone had concerns about any policy framework that would impose higher design requirements that might stifle private-sector development and increase already high land values. Initially it was agreed that the *Design Guide* could be produced as long as it only applied to a small handful of LDA-owned sites. However, eventually it was incorporated in the London Plan and became the basis for national housing policy. In a similar way, the team was able to float big conceptual ideas and spatial strategies without any requirement to justify them within the restrictions of the UK planning system. Thus, City East was developed into the Green Enterprise Zone and a strategy for the Royal Docks that led to the London cable car, the Siemens Crystal and the new business district at Albert Dock (commenced in 2017 by the Chinese company ABP). These are all covered in more detail in Chapter 6.

DfL's other area of work was the London Olympics (see Chapter 6). The award of the Olympic Games to London in 2005 had completely transformed the regeneration agenda for east London. The A+UU had been ahead of the game with City East and planning work in the Lower Lea Valley, but had not had the political strength to be involved more directly in the Games bid. Once the Games had been awarded, the Olympics project went into implementation mode and questions about architecture and design were sidelined. In fairness, there were significant concerns about the UK's ability to deliver the Games on time and within budget, and agencies promoting design strategies were not welcome at the table. The Olympic Development Authority (ODA) was tasked with delivering the Games while the LDA took on the role of land acquisition and the relocation of existing businesses. Delivery of the Games' legacy was also allocated to the LDA but, for the time being, was politely put to one side. There followed a long period of working behind the scenes to influence the ODA, first through the (eventual) establishment of design review panels and then through commenting on and altering the most inflexible parts of the Games plans. When the Games' legacy was finally brought forward, DfL was fully involved in the appointment of a masterplanning team, the Dutch practice KCAP.[13] DfL also produced various Olympic Fringe masterplans that aimed to spread the benefits of the Games into the wider community. Several DfL team members eventually joined the London Legacy Development Corporation (LLDC).

DfL's relationship with CABE was generally good, even if the two agencies had very different philosophical approaches. CABE saw itself as an influencer (very much top-down) and employed design review, design policy and best practice as its principal workstreams. DfL viewed this approach as one of detachment rather than involvement. DfL was not overly interested in questions of aesthetics and saw design agency more as a matter for proactive involvement and the political empowerment of local communities. The difference was illustrated when CABE offered to pass design review in London over to DfL, an offer that was turned down. DfL considered that design review was a distraction that failed to address the central issues of why parts of London were deprived and of poor quality. The design review process would also have been administratively onerous, a distraction from the team's core business and likely to create more enemies in the profession than friends.

Although the two organisations were largely promoting the same values, DfL was critical of CABE where it was seen to be 'improving' poor projects rather than intervening to change them. English Heritage, on the other hand, was often perceived as being at loggerheads with CABE. Some members of the architectural press and the profession made the rather artificial distinction that CABE was a supporter of 'modernism' and English Heritage of more traditional approaches to design. DfL attempted to distance itself from this debate and saw such definitions as irrelevant to its work. There was certainly a perception from some in the industry that CABE was a creation of the Blair government and this association may have contributed to its ultimate demise under the Conservative administration of David Cameron in 2011. Political changes were to impact on DfL as well.

First challenge: the transition to a new mayor, 2008

Within 18 months DfL was maturing as an organisation. Its work programme was delivering results and it was strengthening its influence on the agencies that made up London government. It had chosen to concentrate on working with amenable boroughs and not to bother with those that were not. Its unique governance model provided independence. It might report to a board, but this only met quarterly. Richard Rogers continued to put in one day a week with the team and was their figurehead and champion. DfL relished its ambiguous relationship within London government and enjoyed access to support from the mayor. It was skilled at deploying its soft power and was viewed as an organisation to work with rather than against. Its Achilles heel was that its power rested on its political patronage and this was about to change.

The 2008 London mayoral election initially seemed one-sided. Ken Livingstone was generally popular and initially the Conservative challenger, Boris Johnson, was not taken seriously. Two factors changed that. The first was a campaign in the *London Evening Standard* that was critical of Livingstone. The second, and more important, was the mobilisation by the Tories of the outer London vote. In a campaign that was to have shades of the later Brexit referendum, Livingstone was portrayed as elitist and out of touch with 'ordinary Londoners'. His achievements were painted as having benefited inner (and Labour-controlled) boroughs. What had he achieved for the suburbs?

Johnson's election in May 2008 caught many by surprise, including DfL. London government had not experienced a change in political leadership and had no way of ensuring a smooth transition. Mayoral advisors were cleared out overnight and replaced by a new team. Some key appointments had apparently been made directly by Conservative Central Office. Simon Milton, who had been Leader of Conservative-run Westminster City Council, was appointed as Johnson's special advisor on planning. Peter Hendy retained his position as TfL Transport Commissioner, but the chief executive and board of the LDA were replaced.

DfL mistakenly assumed that it was too small to be caught up in this shake-up and was in any case so obviously a force for good that it would retain its special relationship with the mayor. It was only a matter of keeping its head down and waiting for the right moment to impress. What was not clear at the time was that Milton had no love for DfL and that tensions within the GLA, dating back to the days of the A+UU, would resurface. DfL's public profile – one of its strengths – suddenly became a weakness. It was too visible a target to escape notice. DfL's re-emergence had been planned to coincide with the new mayor opening a major exhibition as part of the London Festival of Architecture at Somerset House. Curated by Isabel Allen and Morag Myerscough together with the team, it was intentionally quirky and thought-provoking. However, it soon became abundantly clear that DfL was peripheral to the mayor's interests (see Chapter 7). Richard Rogers stepped down from his role as advisor, and DfL was left exposed and without support.

As members of its board focused on their own survival, there was a real possibility that DfL would be wound up. Peter Rogers was appointed as the new Chief Executive of the LDA with a remit to reform the agency. Rogers' motives for retaining the team are unclear, but it is possible that he could see a role for it within an agency where new ideas were needed. Although it was notionally within the LDA, DfL had scrupulously avoided association with it. It was fortunate that Peter Rogers had known Peter Bishop when he worked in Camden (and had tried to recruit him to Westminster). Bishop was offered the role of Deputy Chief Executive of the LDA, a position he accepted reluctantly and on condition that DfL came with him and remained intact.

DfL survived the transfer of power but no longer had the independent position that it had enjoyed under Livingstone. It was now part of the LDA and had to report through line management structures to a board. However, DfL did have some advantages. First, it was a new organisation that had not been part of the traditional institutions of government. Second, it had a portfolio of projects that were ready to be implemented if the funding was available, and the decimation of LDA projects from the previous mayor meant that it was. Third, it was sufficiently agile to read and respond to the political changes. In return for its loss of independence, DfL gained direct access to LDA funding and took control of its land portfolio and environmental programmes. It had to undergo a rapid and painful process of growing up but could now deliver its programmes. It had traded soft power for tangible power. Now, with Mark Brearley pushed forward as Head of Design for London and the close collaboration with Bishop sustained, the team changed its mode of operation in a number of ways:

- With the fresh closeness to those who controlled the LDA's land portfolio, it developed new ways of using land as leverage to implement big spatial strategies and town centre regeneration.
- It shed design staff back to TfL since it could no longer exert significant influence over transport programmes.
- It developed expertise in the LDA's Byzantine processes of internal project management.
- It rebadged core programmes. The Mayor's 100 Public Spaces programme was replaced with London's Great Outdoors. It covered the same set of schemes but was more flexible and included Better Streets and London's Water Spaces. The East London Green Grid was reworked as the All London Green Grid, and the town centre projects evolved in response to the new understanding gained from the team's research work on high streets, and after the 2011 riots, DfL was able to re-present these as 'oven-ready' projects that could become a core element of the Outer London Fund.
- It moved staff out into other agencies. Peter Rogers had given away the LDA's lead role in delivering the Olympic legacy and a new development corporation had been set up – the Olympic Legacy Development Corporation (LLDC). The new chief executive of the agency, Andy Altman, was an American architect and a friend of Richard Rogers and Peter Bishop. He was a natural ally and took two staff from DfL, thus allowing a degree of direct influence over the Olympics that had previously been absent.
- It found new friends. The Advisory Board was now effectively defunct, so a new London Design Advisory Board was recruited. Its role was less clearly defined under Johnson, but it demonstrated to the press and professions that the mayor was maintaining continuity in design policy and that DfL was still alive. Johnson appointed Daniel Moylan, a councillor from Kensington and Chelsea, as his advisor on public realm. Moylan was also the chair of the TfL board and had pioneered a series of public realm projects in Kensington. He was also a friend of Richard Rogers and a supporter of public space programmes. This gave an important degree of continuity and Moylan was to prove an important supporter of, and collaborator with, the team.

Design in a hostile environment: 2008–2011

If working for Ken Livingstone was like being in the court of the Medicis (cf. Chapter 1), the period under Boris Johnson was more like the Sublime Porte of the Ottomans: the courtiers were replaced with a group of powerful advisors whose role was to ensure that no one was allowed access to the 'sultan'. Contact with the new mayor was closely controlled by his chief of staff, Simon Milton. Meetings were formal and agendas were agreed in advance. Simon Milton, who also controlled planning, viewed DfL with deep mistrust.

In such an environment DfL was forced to rethink its mode of operation and develop new strategies. It focused on the art of the possible and dropped some of the more ambitious schemes that would have required political commitment from the mayor. The highest-profile of these was the second of the World Squares for All projects, the partial closure to traffic and re-landscaping of Parliament Square (Chapter 5). It was clear that under the new mayor the project, designed by the Swiss landscape architect Günther Vogt, would never be realised. English Heritage and Westminster Council opposed it and the mayor could see no reason to change the existing layout. Other schemes, however, could be rebadged more easily.

On the positive side, the Johnson administration was far more conciliatory to the boroughs than Livingstone's had been and there was a view, probably stemming from Milton's own background in Westminster Council, that the boroughs should largely be left alone. Money was reallocated to the outer London boroughs to honour election pledges and this opened up opportunities for new partnerships.[14] Otherwise, DfL's work with boroughs was largely unaffected and indeed some new opportunities for collaboration opened up. A degree of refocusing took place and greater emphasis was placed on suburban town centres and high streets across London. This suited the design philosophy of the team. Projects such as Making Space in Dalston, typical of this period, are covered in Chapter 3. In addition, the London's Great Outdoors programme identified new opportunities and, with access to LDA budgets and the political support of Daniel Moylan, the programme gained real traction. As a result, a flurry of new projects were completed, for example in Brixton (Windrush Square), Kensington (Exhibition Road) and Tower Hamlets (Aldgate Roundabout).

The team also dropped its campaigning profile and worked more deeply within the machinery of government. While it had been forced to become part of the institution of government, this did not prevent it from subverting that machine. As Deputy CEO of the LDA, Bishop saw his role as shielding the team and allowing it to function without being drawn into the LDA's difficult working environment. Brearley and his by now highly experienced team were familiar, from their A+UU days, with a subsurface way of working, so they readily adjusted, exercising influence while pushing credit to the mayor and others.

Bishop could also access new sources of funding through an investment subcommittee that was largely made up of business and financial consultants. The secret to working with this group was to use drawings and plans, which were an entirely new concept to many on the committee. They might challenge the business cases presented by other sections of the LDA, but found plans and drawings intoxicating. Public space improvements were also real and material. Although the projects might lack any output indicators or metrics, they were the subject of well-worked-through inter-agency funding packages where LDA money was leveraged to good effect. The committee members were also open to a good narrative. The idea of storytelling and narratives had been developed by the A+UU and perfected by DfL, and Bishop had employed the concept extensively in his work with politicians in his previous positions in London boroughs.

Access to the mayor was restricted. Through his role as Deputy CEO of the LDA, Bishop (and therefore DfL) had weekly meetings with the mayor, but these were carefully controlled and monitored by his advisors. Individual meetings were discouraged. The formal meetings covered the range of business of the LDA and the mayor rarely showed any interest in design. The trick was to find a way of engaging and holding his attention. Obscure historical references (especially classical ones) usually worked, as did unusual turns of phrase.

Nevertheless, this was the working environment and DfL did adapt. In some ways the mayor's working style was conducive to the team's approach of 'big ideas – small moves'. Livingstone was interested in detail; fail on this and he would dismiss the initiative. Johnson was capable of engaging with a big idea and was largely content to allow the team to get on with it as long as his advisors ensured there was no adverse political fallout.

DfL was sufficiently agile to work in this way and could package ideas and narratives quickly to suit the prevailing climate. A specific example was the creation of the Green Enterprise Zone (Figure 2.5). At the end of 2008, Bishop had a rare meeting with Johnson on his own. The conversation ranged from the economic slump and the risk of London being too heavily reliant on the financial industries sector to the lack of a

Figure 2.5 The Green Enterprise Zone: a conceptual plan for the regeneration of east London. Source: DfL/GLA.

credible Olympic legacy strategy and the pressure that the mayor was under to find a convincing environmental strategy. The response to 'Can you do something?' was the Green Enterprise Zone. The idea was simple: brand a large area of east London that included the Lower Lea Valley, the Royal Docks, Beckton and Barking as a zone for the emerging green economy. The zone would include district energy grids, research and development establishments, and state-of-the-art 'green' manufacturing. The strategy was written up in a morning and a plan was produced. It was presented to the mayor a week later and he liked it. It had not been anticipated that two weeks later he would show it to the prime minister, Gordon Brown, who liked it too. There followed a frantic post hoc justification of the project. Management consultants Ernst & Young were brought in to verify the concept and put numbers behind it, but the concept stood. It was then taken to the Shanghai Expo as part of the London pavilion curated by DfL (see Chapter 7). Later that year Siemens invested in the Green Enterprise District,[15] a move that triggered a new DfL workstream around regeneration of the Royal Docks (Chapter 6).

Johnson was always affable and enjoyable to work with and was undoubtedly popular with his staff and many Londoners. The key was to find a time when he was not being chaperoned by his advisors. The mayor cycled in and out of City Hall and it was often possible for Bishop, also a cyclist, to intercept him on his way home to Islington. A number of projects were discussed and ideas planted in this way. The London cable car (Emirates Air Line), for example, was mooted one evening at the traffic lights on Pentonville Road.

The period from 2008 to 2010 was a productive one for DfL. The LDA was used as a funding vehicle for projects, and the integration of design work with Bishop's control of property assets and environmental programmes opened up new possibilities for area-based design strategies. Town centre regeneration projects were being developed in new locations. The Royal Docks were beginning to attract investment interest and the doors were opening for greater involvement with the Olympic legacy work.

The Olympic Fringe masterplans (Chapter 6) were a response to agitation from the five 'host boroughs' for tangible investment in their communities. Central government and the mayor did not have answers, but DfL did. Indeed, many of its new projects were a response to problems that existed at the interface of the GLA, TfL, the boroughs and central government. Such power interfaces represent real problems for formal institutions of government but are fertile areas for creative design thinking. Consequently, DfL developed new strategies around the wider integration of land development, housing and environmental programmes. These were launched at the annual property conference at MIPIM in March 2010 as the New Urban Agenda. Other initiatives were developed around town centre regeneration on the back of the impact of Crossrail.[16] LDA land had dropped so sharply in value after the 2009 crash that it could no longer be considered as a significant asset. This triggered a period of intense policy development around how it could be used to support area-based regeneration programmes. This moved the policy emphasis away from financial returns towards design-based interventions which could achieve social and economic benefits.

But once again there were problems on the horizon. In May 2010, the newly elected Conservative government was determined to reduce public spending and slim down the agencies of government, especially the quangos (quasi non-governmental organisations). CABE's funding was removed and the regional development agencies were abolished. This included the LDA and once again DfL was both homeless and under threat.

An unwanted child: 2011–2013

Following the spending cuts in the 2010 autumn budget, the LDA began the process of winding down its organisation in preparation for its abolition. All programmes and projects that were not party to a binding contract (and some that were) were immediately suspended. Staff redundancies commenced, with a view to terminating the LDA by early 2012. DfL was caught up in this storm and initially no one in the mayor's administration showed interest in preventing its abolition. With disaster looming, Brearley worked behind the scenes, helped by Richard Rogers and several members of the London Design Advisory Board, to get a survival campaign going. In response the team received a huge amount of support from the professions and press. Ellis Woodman described it as 'an agency to be cherished'[17] and Merlin Fulcher wrote a piece in the *Architects' Journal* entitled 'Save Design for London'.[18] Letters were written to the mayor from the presidents of the Royal Institute of British Architects, the Landscape Institute and the Architecture Foundation. *Building Design* published an open letter from international architects including Renzo Piano, Zara Hadid, Rafael Viñoly and Frank Gehry urging the mayor to retain the team.[19] DfL had moved from the fringe to the mainstream! After an intense period of internal lobbying, a small core of staff of five architects from DfL were moved to the GLA, with other staff going to TfL and the Olympic Legacy Development Corporation.

In March 2011 Peter Bishop left the LDA to join the architects Allies and Morrison. Mark Brearley moved back to the GLA with a greatly reduced team to face an uncertain future. One of the conditions of survival for the design team was that it would be absorbed within the planning and regeneration group at City Hall and the name Design for London would be dropped. Brearley's team was almost back down to the size of the A+UU in 2006, but this time it had no obvious champion at either political or managerial level. The team took the decision to ignore abandonment of the name, judging that perhaps no one would challenge continuity. No one did, so the DfL name continued, and the team flourished for another two years, regrouping and adapting its strategy once again. The team focused on progressing its existing workload rather than becoming too distracted by events, but as it happens a number of external events presented unexpected new opportunities.

First, the unexpected death of Johnson's principal advisor, Simon Milton, led to Daniel Moylan taking over the mayor's responsibilities on the built environment and separating these from planning. This gave DfL both a committed champion and a clearer niche in London government. While he was a councillor at Kensington and Chelsea, Moylan had been responsible for streetscape improvements in Kensington High Street. These had set new benchmarks for design quality and Moylan was both interested in and knowledgeable about architectural design. He supported a number of DfL projects that might have otherwise been abandoned. In addition, he agreed to continue with the London Design Advisory Group, changing its membership to include Terry Farrell, Nick Serota (Director of the Tate), developer Roger Madelin and experienced civil servant Joyce Bridges. The mayor's occasional attendance, encouraged by Moylan, provided an opportunity to engage him in a design debate and float ideas that would otherwise never reach him. It was through these sessions that, for example, interest in high streets was nurtured and enthusiasm for the Great Outdoors programme was strengthened.

Many small projects that had been developed with the boroughs could still proceed, often with the explicit support of the mayor. With Moylan now keen to make use of DfL's skills, it became possible to dovetail with TfL projects and with borough projects funded by them. Moylan established a design review process for TfL-supported projects and he pushed the team's nimblest critics to the fore. The Green Grid work was promoted by the mayor after a pitch to him that it offered a big impact for a low cost and his advisors noticed that these projects also afforded several photo opportunities. The team's approach was low-key and opportunistic. Although in theory DfL had been wound up, the team's continuity and distinct status was validated by Daniel Moylan and he coached Brearley in the art of politics and survival. It was a matter of staying in the game and waiting for an opportunity to rebuild.

The second relevant external factor was the need to provide a tangible response to outer London, a political payback that was required in response to Johnson's 2008 election victory. Elections were coming up again in 2012, and the mayor's Outer London Commission[20] was struggling to find meaningful responses to the suburbs. The riots in August 2011 (a year before the Olympics were due to open) concentrated minds. The DfL team had a series of projects on town centres and high streets that had been prepared earlier in response to the economic downturn and demise of the high street. These were ready to be implemented (see Chapter 3). They had the advantage of being tangible and local, and were not funded from borough budgets. The resulting projects, initiated by DfL working with boroughs, were rolled forward through what became the Outer London Fund. This bold programme was acknowledged by Johnson as an important contribution to his re-election in 2012 (indeed, in May 2012 he spotted Brearley in the City Hall cafe and marched over to ask that he thank the team).

The third factor was the mayor's relationship with the boroughs. This was less confrontational than under Livingstone since the political assumption of the administration was that decisions, wherever possible, should be taken at local level. This was very much in keeping with the Cameron government's policy of localism. This gave the DfL team access to new political clients. As long as its work was well grounded and in boroughs that actively sought its involvement, it was seen in a relatively positive light within the GLA. In the weeks before his departure from the LDA, Peter Rogers had arranged for Brearley to present to the mayor a proposal to focus regeneration efforts on a scatter of smaller projects across London, in places identified as 'Good to grow and ready to go'. This approach was recognised as able to deliver much with small budgets, while enthusing boroughs and being welcomed by the public. Before long new initiatives and a flurry of projects had been tailored to respond to opportunities as they arose. The team thrived again, making rapid and substantial achievements. But this was to be short-lived.

Following Johnson's re-election in 2012, there was another reshuffle in City Hall and the design team was again left without any political or managerial support. Daniel Moylan was moved to another job outside City Hall and lost his key role at TfL. New advisors were appointed and the planning lead passed to Edward Lister, formerly leader of Wandsworth. The emphasis of policy moved to raising the density of new housing. With a new round of budget cuts on the horizon, time had run out for DfL and the team was abruptly disbanded. No reasons were given nor announcements made. This time there was to be no survival campaign as it was clear that it would be futile. Mark Brearley departed with several of his colleagues, and the remaining team members were incorporated within the GLA regeneration team as project managers, to see out existing commitments. This effectively marked the end of the design experiment that had started 12 years earlier with the A+UU.

Designing for London: the legacy

While the Design for London brand name came to an end, it was not the end of the work of the team. The final element to this story is the diaspora of the team. Some members (Peter Bishop, Lara Kinneir and Richa Mukhia) have gone into academia; others (Tobi Goevert and Adam Towle) moved to city government, while some (Eleanor Fawcett, Esther Everett and Steve Tomlinson) worked for Mayoral Development Corporations. Mark Brearley is a professor of urbanism and has taken over a manufacturing enterprise in south-east London. Eva Herr, Charlotte Kokken and Fenna Wagenaar are all senior planners and designers, in Germany, Belgium and the Netherlands respectively. Some have advisory roles to other cities (Mark Brearley: Brussels; Peter Bishop: Zhuhai, Goyang and Riyadh). Through this diaspora the promotion of good design within city government continues.

It was always envisaged that the team would operate through the networks that it built in London government and it has been successful in advocating the importance of good design within London government. There are today many individuals within the GLA and TfL who understand the importance of good design and who make efforts to promote it in their everyday work.

Ten staff remained in the GLA as part of a Regeneration Team within a larger department. The loss of the brand name proved to be liberating. It removed the profile that had made DfL such a target and allowed the team to be assimilated into the structure of government. There they were seen to be under management supervision and had 'proper jobs'. The team continued a number of projects with mayoral support on high streets, public space, town centre regeneration and the Green Grid.

When Sadiq Khan (Labour) was elected as mayor in 2016, there was no debate about re-establishing a design agency to replace DfL, but the process of transition was easier and there were no major upheavals. The remnants of the DfL team were by then well embedded in the GLA and had matured into a design-led regeneration team with sound relationships across London government. Khan's agenda is broad and ambitious in certain areas but does not place design and urbanism at its centre. The main threads of the team's design work – open space, landscape, town centres and high streets – all continue, as does work on housing standards and London Plan policy. The team continues to work in a refreshingly collaborative manner and has developed further strategies to support other parts of the GLA and TfL and the boroughs. There is political support for the team and its work. The team has learnt to play by the rules and is now an established voice for the promotion of good design in London.

Good Growth by Design, a programme of London's current mayor, Sadiq Khan, aims to promote quality and inclusion in the built environment.[21] It recognises the role of design in improving development and delivering quality of life in an ever-denser city. It has six pillars of activity:

– *Setting standards.* This involves design-related research to provide evidence and information to inform policy, investments and decision-making, including a refresh of the Housing Design Supplementary Planning Guidance, guidance to promote the reuse and recycling of materials across a building's life cycle, and guidance on making London child-friendly.

- *Applying standards.* This involves mechanisms to provide scrutiny of London's development, such as the London Review Panel (City Hall's design review panel), which has undertaken more than a hundred reviews since its launch.
- *Building capacity.* This concerns building and supporting local authority place-shaping capacity.
- *Supporting diversity*. The *Supporting Diversity Handbook*, launched in July 2019, addresses the barriers at each stage of career progression, from school age through to leadership.
- *Commissioning quality.* The programme recognises the role of good procurement and accessing the best design practitioners. Work includes the Design Quality Management Protocol – a framework for ensuring design quality, including design review and procurement. The Architecture Design and Urbanism Panel (ADUP) is a pre-approved panel of built environment consultants that can be used by public-sector bodies.
- *Championing good growth.* Advocacy work continues to be undertaken by Mayor's Design Advocates and Advocate Organisations engaging on behalf of the mayor across London, nationally and internationally. This includes events, conferences and design awards.

Conclusions: an agency to be cherished?

The Introduction to this book compared forms of city government in the UK and other countries. It would be a generalisation to say that UK politicians are more sceptical about professional advice than their European counterparts, but the generalisation is borne out by how few examples there are of architectural advice reaching the heart of city government in the UK. The period in which the A+UU and DfL operated was both exceptional and volatile. The team and its work survived a change of mayor, but ultimately could not survive both that and a change of national government. It was not alone here, since CABE and other agencies were also axed. It was particularly unfortunate to have been incorporated into the LDA, where it ultimately suffered from the agency's own demise.

There is always the need for champions at the political and operational level. When these existed in Ken Livingstone, Richard Rogers and Daniel Moylan, the team flourished; when they were absent, the team struggled. A design team will always be a fragile entity within city government. To be effective, DfL had to deploy a high public profile with an operational ability to influence and subvert. This worked when it was located close to the centre of political power, but it can make for an interesting but short operational life. Operating effectively within the heart of government inevitably makes enemies. Urbanism and design are approaches to shaping government programmes rather than core statutory requirements and therefore are always potentially expendable.

DfL was politically savvy and able to adapt and constantly reinvent itself. The approach of 'big ideas – small moves' (incremental urbanism) was robust enough even when architectural design was no longer at the centre of mayoral priorities. Programmes that deal with public space, climate change, town centre regeneration and streets are universal and should be able to cut across political boundaries. Some of DfL's most effective work was in the field of policy development. DfL did not take a detached and technocratic approach to this work. Policy was abstracted from an understanding of its likely design impacts and this in turn was derived from extensive and careful research. The team understood where power and money were located in government and was adept at accessing these to support its projects. It learnt to build allies in different government agencies and to find new clients, budgets and workstreams. During this volatile period, it repackaged its programmes and 'sold' the ideas to different politicians and organisations. In the final analysis DfL was tenacious, resilient and agile and did not become institutionalised. Some of its work around the Olympics, high streets, public space, street design and urban landscapes has achieved a lasting impact. Perhaps its greatest achievement was the way it changed the culture of design thinking in government and the organisations within it. It supported those who were working to improve design quality and helped to build common methodologies as well as an evidence base that demonstrated the benefits of well-crafted and thoughtful design-led interventions.

DfL sought to plan London strategically as a whole by transcending boundaries and making relationships beyond sites and masterplans and between boroughs. It recognised that a city is a live and changing entity and worked to bring convergence between the disciplines of planning, architecture and landscape through its multidisciplinary, multi-scaled approach. Its approach was simple: to collaborate with others as part of the design process; to value and present the existing city with clarity; to support its work with fresh research; to help improve the quality of design through influence; and, most crucially, to bring the designs of others together in one place, thus enabling a coordinated dialogue.

DfL was the kind of creative influence that London needed at the time (and still does). Its approach was loose. It could not shape the city through formal powers or the control of capital budgets. Instead it relied on its ability to influence and used the support of the mayor for this purpose. The approach to urbanism was to develop big ideas and implement them in small steps. DfL's effectiveness lay in its ability to forge alliances, to influence public agencies and private developers, and to improve design quality through better design procurement and constructive design critique. Its ad hoc and opportunistic approach can be seen to have lent itself successfully to the naturally piecemeal patterns and behaviours of city regeneration, particularly in the London context. Its form of practice was in response to this very London condition.

This brings us to the underlying questions of how cities can be shaped by design strategies, what methodologies are the most effective and how these can be implemented within the structures of government. Possible answers to these questions include the following:

- Political leadership is essential. City politicians need to recognise that architecture and design are not abstract concepts. Well-thought-through and carefully applied design strategies can transform a city for the better (and benefit all of its inhabitants).
- A tactical approach, utilising big ideas and then bringing them to realisation through small projects, is an effective methodology.
- Long-term commitment and design continuity are essential. Many of DfL's ideas and projects are still coming to fruition.
- A small design team that is unrestricted by city bureaucracy can act as a conscience, as a catalyst and as a conduit for new ideas. A design team needs to be given political licence to 'think about the city'.
- Partnership and cross-agency working are very effective ways of channelling resources for change.
- Strengthening client roles in procuring and managing design work is essential.
- Public engagement – winning hearts and minds both at the city scale and through public involvement in local schemes – is vital.
- Drawings, phrases and narratives are important mechanisms for framing ideas and engaging partners.

- Research and intelligence gathering are essential to make the case for design interventions.
- Finally, achieving better design outcomes is difficult. It requires tenacity and stubbornness.

Kees Christiaanse described the methodology of DfL as 'a negotiated approach, an urbanism of brokerage', and Kieran Long commented, 'Design for London is using guerrilla tactics to become the most influential city architect's office in the country'.[22] This legacy can be seen in many of the projects that have been delivered and in the continuing work of those who still work in London government. DfL and the A+UU might not have changed London, but they certainly shaped it, and in most cases for the better. At its height, from 2006 to 2011, DfL employed 25 people – the most concentrated group of city designers in the history of London government. The impacts of its projects and programmes are considered in more detail in later chapters.

Notes

1 The programme originally planned the partial pedestrianisation of Trafalgar Square, Leicester Square and Parliament Square. Plans for Leicester Square were implemented by Westminster City Council and the GLA in 2012. Those for Parliament Square were abandoned in 2008 when Boris Johnson became mayor (Chapter 5).
2 Interview with Richard Brown, writer and Senior Policy Officer at the Centre for London, May 2019.
3 Interview with Richard Brown, writer and Senior Policy Officer at the Centre for London, May 2019.
4 Building 2006.
5 New London Architecture 2006.
6 Richard's contribution and generosity deserves wider recognition. Not only did he give one day a week of his time without any payment; he was also available at any time to offer advice as well as to use his personal reputation and contacts to support the work of the team. He asked for no public recognition for this work.
7 Bishop and Williams 2016.
8 Interview with Richard Brown, May 2019.
9 Chase, Crawford and Kaliski 2008.
10 Kaliski 2008, p. 108.
11 Crawford 2008a, p.14.
12 Crawford 2008b, p. 25.
13 The mayor's team intervened to insist that KCAP were partnered with Allies and Morrison.
14 An Outer London Commission was set up to look at ways to do this, chaired by William McKee and advised by Terry Farrell. In reality little significant funding was diverted from existing programmes but recommendations did feed into the London Plan.
15 Siemens built the Crystal at Victoria Dock, opened in 2011.
16 The east-to-west cross-London railway, recently renamed as the Elizabeth line.
17 Woodman 2010.
18 Fulcher 2010.
19 Warmann 2011.
20 Set up to devise ways to move investment, the Outer London Commission (OLC) was established in 2008 by the Mayor of London. Chaired by William McKee CBE, it included

representatives of business, the boroughs, the development industry and the voluntary sector. The OLC published its Third Report in July 2014.

21 Summary of the Good Growth by Design programme provided by Jamie Dean and Sarah Considine, GLA (March 2020).

22 Long 2008. Editor of the *Architects' Journal* 2007–9.

Bibliography

Bishop, Peter, 'The Work of Design for London', in Harald Bodenschatz, Christina Gräwe, Harald Kegler, Hans-Dieter Nägelke and Wolfgang Sonne (eds), *Stadtvisionen 1910/2010*, Berlin, Germany: Technische Universität Berlin Architekturmuseum and DOM Publishers, 2010, pp. 406–11.

Bishop, Peter, and Williams, Lesley, *Planning, Politics and City Making: A Case Study of King's Cross*, London: RIBA Publishing, 2016.

Building, 'Peter Bishop Chosen for London's Top Design Job', *Building*, 29 September 2006. https://www.bdonline.co.uk/peter-bishop-chosen-for-londons-top-design-job/3074467.article (accessed 29 July 2020).

Chase, John, Crawford, Margaret, and Kaliski, John (eds), *Everyday Urbanism*, 2nd edn, New York: Monacelli Press, 2008.

Crawford, Margaret, 'The Current State of Everyday Urbanism', in John Chase, Margaret Crawford and John Kaliski (eds), *Everyday Urbanism*, 2nd edn, New York: Monacelli Press, 2008a.

Crawford, Margaret, 'Blurring the Boundaries: Public Space and Private Life', in John Chase, Margaret Crawford and John Kaliski (eds), *Everyday Urbanism*, 2nd edn, New York: Monacelli Press, 2008b.

Dowdy, Clare, A profile of Mark Brearley in his role as leader of Design for London, *Design Week*, Vol. 24, No. 27, 9 July 2009, p. 13.

Fulcher, Merlin, 'Save Design for London: Growing Group of Supporters Call for Survival of Development Enabling Body Design for London after Government Pulls Plug on London Development Agency', *Architects' Journal,* 25 November 2010, pp. 8–9.

Fulcher, Merlin, '"Saved" Design for London Heads to GLA', *Architects' Journal*, 17 February 2011, p. 6.

Kaliski, John, 'The Present City and the Practice of City Design', in John Chase, Margaret Crawford and John Kaliski (eds), *Everyday Urbanism*, 2nd edn, New York: Monacelli Press, 2008.

Krasny, Elke, 'Designing Dialogue', in Francesca Ferguson and Urban Drift Projects (eds), *Make-Shift City*, Berlin, Germany: Jovis, 2014, pp. 154–5.

Lefebvre, Henri, *The Urban Revolution*, Minneapolis, MN: University of Minnesota Press, 1970.

Long, Kieran, *Architects' Journal*, April 2008.

Long, Kieran, 'Say Goodbye to All This', *Evening Standard*, 3 November 2010, pp. 36–7.

New London Architecture, 'New London Architecture (NLA) Welcomes the Appointment of Peter Bishop as Head of Design for London', *New London Architecture*, 28 September 2006. http://legacy.newlondonarchitecture.org/news/2006/september/nla-welcomes-peter-bishop-as-head-of-design-for-london (accessed 17 March 2020).

Schultz, Brigitte, 'We Seed Enthusiasm: It is About Enabling It Rather Than Designing It', an interview with Mark Brearley and Peter Carl, in *Stadt Bauwelt 194*, Vol. 103, 26 October 2012, pp. 18–19.

Warmann, Catherine, 'Star Architects Appeal to Boris to Save Design for London', *Building Design,* 22 February 2011.

Wingham, Mark/Mayor of London, *London's Architecture Sector: Update 2018*, GLA Economics Working Paper 93, March 2018. https://www.london.gov.uk/sites/default/files/wp93-architecture_paper_2018.pdf (accessed 18 March 2020).

Woodman, Ellis, 'An Agency to be Cherished', *Building Design*, 29 October 2010. https://www.bdonline.co.uk/opinion/an-agency-to-be-cherished/5008074.article (accessed 17 March 2020).

3

High street places: doing a lot with a little

Tobias Goevert and Adam Towle

London might be one of the wealthiest cities in the world, but it also contains areas of intense deprivation. These are predominantly centred in east London around the docks and areas that had previously been centres of manufacturing. Unlike many other cities, London also has pockets of deprivation set in otherwise relatively wealthy districts. The planning system has recognised this problem and has formulated numerous plans to tackle it. These plans, however, are largely policy documents that have no real means of implementation.

When the Architecture and Urbanism Unit (A+UU) and Design for London (DfL) formulated their mission to nurture a compact, mixed-use, well-connected and well-designed London, the general consensus was that improvement strategies for London still required radical surgery. Vast swathes of development, usually on brownfield land, required considerable site preparation, infrastructure provision, financing and marketing. To date, the transformation of such sites had been slow through projects such as Canary Wharf, the Greenwich Peninsula and the London Olympics. For projects such as Barking Riverside, the scale of investment required has been a barrier to delivery for decades. Such large-scale regeneration can yield major change, but momentum and continuity can be hard to maintain and there is no certainty that the benefits will be spread across society. Furthermore, the resources available for regeneration were limited from the 1980s onwards and within the public sector they were almost non-existent. As a consequence, a number of districts, particularly in inner London, had been left behind. Where development was planned, it was largely piecemeal, rarely part of a wider strategy and often of very poor quality.

When Clive Dutton[1] joined Newham Council as Regeneration Director in 2009, he considered possibilities for redeveloping the Royal Docks. Having reviewed the tortuous planning history of the area and counted 74 development proposals, plans and strategies, he concluded that the area did not need a 75th masterplan, but a totally new planning approach. His solution, as described by Peter Bishop, was to 'throw away all the previous plans, write a short strategy, sign up the politicians and then broadcast it'.[2]

Looking back, it feels as if Clive drew the curtain on a 'Big Plan-making era' for London. He recognised that London needed a different form of strategy – one that was incremental, nimble and nurturing. London, of course, had seen major regeneration projects such as King's Cross, Bishopsgate and Paddington. These had to varying degrees been successful, but they were all driven by the private sector and were in areas traditionally considered commercially viable. There were no public-sector programmes to address the poorer neighbourhoods – interventions where success would be measured in social as well as financial returns. Previous attempts to regenerate these localities had been limited to superficial measures that had been inadequately funded. The *structural* reasons for an area's demise had not been tackled.

The centre of a locality is often its high street. Many in inner London were in a state of decline but they remained the psychological centre of the community and represented a unique opportunity for intervention. Get these places right and wider regeneration could occur that might benefit everyone.

Chapters 1 and 2 looked at the emergence of DfL's approach to promoting change through 'incremental urbanism'. Incremental urbanism focuses on small-scale interventions that are allied with compelling and overarching strategies. These strategies set the broad direction of the mayor's funding programmes and gave them clarity and coherence. Individual projects could then be devised and implemented as and when there were opportunities to do so (Figure 3.1). No single project would fundamentally change an area, but cumulatively and over time they could. This pragmatic form of urbanism proved to be especially effective for a team 'without power or money'[3] working within the complex institutional networks of London's government. In this chapter we look at how incremental urbanism was applied to regenerate town centres in some of London's poorest localities. In Mark Brearley's words, 'This was about how a sparky group of proposition-minded public planners was shaping ideas and initiatives, acting as entrepreneurial urban curators, making the case for care and flair, working in partnerships across London, all with the support of the mayor.'[4]

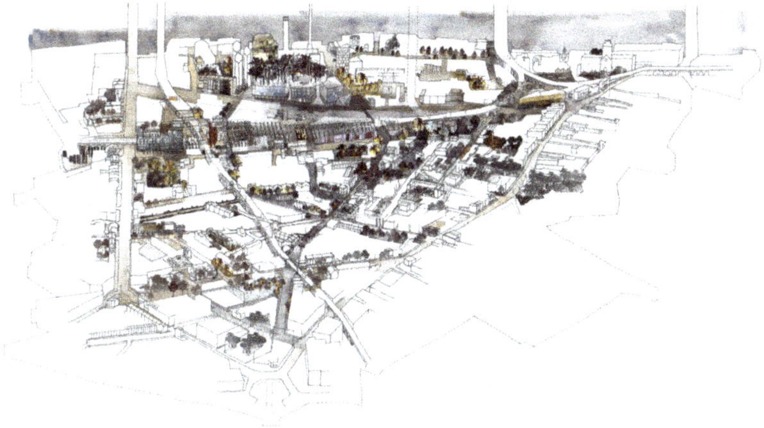

Figure 3.1 Incremental urbanism as a collection of interlinked small-scale interventions: Bankside Urban Forest. Source: Witherford Watson Mann/DfL/GLA.

London: a city of high streets

Matthew Carmona, who has written extensively about London's high streets, argues that London is distinct from cities such as Paris or Barcelona in that, while it has planned neighbourhoods (e.g. Bloomsbury), it is not a city of grand boulevards and civic set pieces. Instead, it is characterised by its continuous network of 'everyday streets', principal of which are its high streets.[5] London's high streets have been at the centre of its economic, social and civic life since they were first established along Roman roads such as Watling Street, Ermine Street and Portway Street. By the sixteenth century, as London grew beyond its medieval walls, these roads formed the backbone of the urban region (Figure 3.2). They attracted commerce and public services and joined existing villages together. In time they became a part of the morphology of London – its connections and nodes.

These lively and varied streets came under pressure during the twentieth century, when planning started to respond to mass car ownership. Since many high streets formed major transport arteries, many were damaged by road building. Some town centres, such as Paddington, were more or less destroyed before schemes like the 1960s Motorway Box proposals were shelved in the 1970s. The damage was lasting and was compounded by the popularity of out-of-town shopping centres and retail sheds in the 1970s and 1980s and by the subsequent

Figure 3.2 Map of London (1832) showing Roman roads (in crimson). Source: Fiona Scott/DfL/GLA.

withdrawal of major players like department stores. At the same time car-based policies saw the development of ring roads to bypass town centres and of large car parks to serve superstores that severed them from adjacent high streets. At the end of the 1980s it was clear that high streets across the UK were in decline and this had become a *political* problem. National planning policy responded by placing restrictions on the growth of out-of-town shopping. When considering superstores in urban areas, local councils were required to use a sequential test that put existing town centres first. Developers had to demonstrate that there were no available opportunities within existing town centres before they could create new out-of-town or edge-of-town complexes.

The turn of the century brought in new shopping trends. Apart from online shopping, inner urban shopping malls were developed, such as the Westfield developments in White City and Stratford. These catered for a younger clientele that had high disposable income and low car dependency. While arguably less damaging than out-of-town centres, these large retail

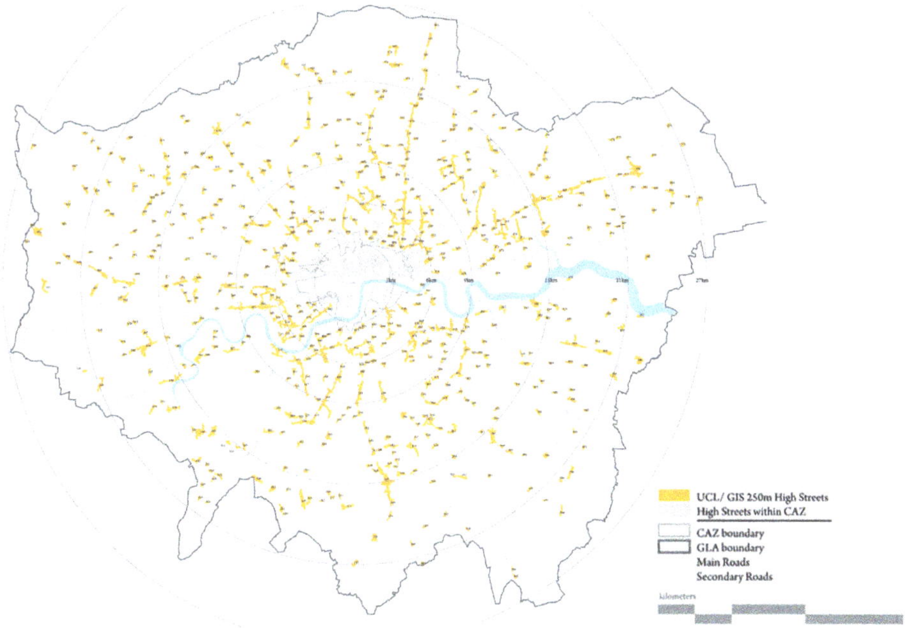

Figure 3.3 London's 600 high streets (outside the Central Activities Zone). Source: Greater London Authority, *Learning from London's High Streets*, 2014 (originally *High Street London*), Fiona Scott/DfL/GLA.

malls still pulled yet more of the 'high street brands' off the high street. By 2005, many of London's high streets were experiencing significant decline, with well-known chain stores like Woolworths or HMV going into administration. The aftershocks of the 2008 financial crash and the rise of internet shopping created a perfect storm.

In early 2020, London still has over 600 high streets and has fared well in comparison to the rest of the UK, with the vacancy rate on its high streets two thirds of the national average.[6] High streets might be busy roads and they might be suffering from structural changes in shopping habits, but they are still diverse places and provide community hubs where activity of all types can prosper and grow. They still take advantage of flows of people and goods, opportunities for trade, and have easy access to the economy of the metropolis. The future of these areas, as with their past, cannot be defined by shopping alone. High streets provide pubs, restaurants, schools and colleges, town halls, stations, markets, libraries, doctors, dentists, banks, workshops and yards, cinemas, offices, parks, museums and of course shops (which typically account for only half of the activity along high streets). They are the places where the city's community and its economy are at their most vibrant and obvious.

High streets define certain localities and their communities and they therefore define the spatial and social geography of London (Figure 3.3). They typify Alexander's semilattice[7] and Jacobs' view that cities are complex systems of enormous heterogeneity, which maximise economic and social opportunities[8] (Figure 3.4). Consequently, they provide an excellent framework for the incremental growth of the city.

While most of London's high streets survive, they are struggling to recover from the planning mistakes of the late twentieth century. Changes in consumer shopping habits facilitated by online shopping have made the future of many of them precarious, and structural changes in the local retail economy have led to the loss of small local independent stores, especially in the food sector. Bread, meat and grocery shops are being squeezed out by the supermarkets and many of the UK's high

Figure 3.4 Whitechapel Road and Market. Source: GLA/DfL.

streets have lost their local character, diversity and distinctiveness. Across London, many high streets are indistinguishable from one another and are dominated by clone retailers and chain stores.[9] Many of the chain store owners have little interest in the future of the places in which they are located.

To compound matters, many high streets have lost their pride, spark and quality. The public realm often lacks investment in maintenance and many pavements are in a poor condition. Some boroughs reached crisis point in the 1990s when street maintenance budgets had been slashed to the point where a cycle of continuous decline was occurring.[10] The *Streetscape Design Manual* (Chapter 1) was an early response by the A+UU to the problems of poor street maintenance. Lack of investment in high streets can set off a spiral of decline as busy street life ebbs away, people start to avoid them for fear of crime, and they become abandoned. This is more than the loss of local shopping; it is a cancer that eats away at community identity.

London's high level of housing need (along with rising land values) has meant that surplus retail and office space is being converted into housing, often of poor quality. This has been supported by planning policy that sought to shrink core town centre retail areas. While shopping 'core areas' were generally protected, 'fringe areas' that extended out along the city's arteries were released for other development. This was compounded by the relaxation of 'permitted development' rules (introduced in 2014), which relieved developers of the need to seek local planning consent for conversions from commercial to residential use. Paradoxically, planning policies to protect high streets often seek to restrict non-retail in the protected core areas – uses such as cafes and local businesses – and thus hinder their diversification.

The decline of high streets had become a popular concern. In 2011, Prime Minister David Cameron commissioned the TV presenter and entrepreneur Mary Portas to investigate and be the national face of the struggle of small towns to revitalise their high streets. Portas's final report recognises the irreversible nature of the structural changes that have impacted on the British high street:

> New benchmarks have been forged against which our high streets are now being judged. New expectations have been created in terms of value, service, entertainment and experience against which the average high street has in many cases simply failed to deliver. These reasons alone conspire to create a new shopper mind-set which cannot and should not be reversed.[11]

She advocated a range of measures to revitalise high streets that were taken forward by the government. These included the setting up of 27 Portas Pilots across the country where Town Teams would take control of the operation and management of high streets. These were supported by a Future High Streets Fund that allocated up to £100,000 per high street. Such paltry funding could not have a lasting impact on struggling localities. It was a populist response to a deep-seated structural problem. The reasons for decline were far more complex.

A methodology for town centre and high street regeneration

The re-establishment of London government created a political and organisational opportunity to address the problem. Under Mayor Livingstone, Transport for London (TfL) funding was redirected from road building to public transport and then to schemes to promote a modal shift to walking and cycling. This presented the A+UU and DfL with an opportunity to generate new renewal strategies. If powerful narratives for high streets could be developed, then political influence could be used to access significant budgets within the transport authority. DfL set about refocusing its research and drew attention to both the plight of, and opportunities on, high streets. By doing this it was able to devise a wide range of new programmes and projects for the mayor.

High streets have always been at the centre of many Londoners' everyday lives and vital to the spatial, economic and social structure of the city. A strategy that sought to nurture them back into healthy centres of community life was both strategic *and* local. It would also provide a relatively easy and popular set of projects that could be branded and communicated to a wider audience. A focus on town centres and high streets had other advantages for the design team. First, the programmes could focus on some of the most deprived communities and this was in line with Mayor Livingstone's social objectives. Second, it addressed an issue of universal concern. Third, it allowed the A+UU, and later DfL, to build working relationships with a number of boroughs which were welcomed when the team could bring funding from the various mayoral agencies that the boroughs could not access alone. Fourth, the methodology of incremental urbanism coupled with intense community engagement provided an effective modus operandi. As Rowan Moore commented in *The Observer* in 2012: 'The idea, therefore, is to do a lot with a little'.[12] The little money available for regeneration needed to be spent in those localities most ready and able to show tangible benefits quickly and efficiently to give the greatest 'pops per pound'.[13] High streets and town centres offered the opportunity to use all the talent within local communities to create multiple and overlapping benefits.

In a comprehensive study on high streets (commissioned by DfL), Jones, Roberts and Morris[14] describe what makes high streets so critical to the growth of the city:

- They are key components in the strategic transport network.
- As transport interchanges they accommodate movement between different modes of transport in London, including tube and rail, as well as buses and walking.
- As pseudo-estuaries they channel movement from the surrounding catchment of, typically, residential streets.
- They contain a rich mix of uses – retail, services and residential and office uses above the ground floor.
- They are locations for a wide range of on-street facilities and services, from the infrastructure under the street to that on top, such as kiosks, cash points, telephone boxes, public art, parking, benches, bins, signage, CCTV, street lighting and so forth.
- They are identifiable public spaces (positively defined by continuous street walls and active frontages) for social encounter and exchange.
- They are centres of local identity, often peppered with landmark features that give them a distinctive/historic appearance.

Carmona[15] also draws attention to the fact that high streets are a key driver of entrepreneurship. They are places where business space is generally more affordable and they offer local employment, space for innovation and sophisticated business networks. Businesses within high streets are generally small, lean and able to adapt (up to a point) to changing local circumstances.[16]

One-size-fits-all solutions to the decline of London's high streets were unlikely to be appropriate. Neither would purely physical (cosmetic) interventions work. Regeneration programmes had tried cosmetic 'improvements' in the 1980s and 1990s and it was clear that painted lamp posts and hanging baskets would not impact on the structural problems that these places were facing. A far more considered methodology was required, one that understood the reasons for decline and would find new carefully crafted responses. Incremental urbanism is such a methodology. It requires a detailed understanding of the politics of the city – its governance, its organisation and its institutions. It is based on deep research and community dialogue and works within the system to positively distort its outcomes. It is patient and subtle, and in many cases the design outcome is a product of the process – the art of the possible. At heart it is subversive. Barcelona first inspired DfL's incremental approach: 'the scale of action does not need to be immense; rather, a cumulative effect should be sought'.[17] This, of course, is also echoed in North American urban thinking, going back to the work of Jane Jacobs, the 'tactical urbanism' of Stephen Marshall[18] and the 'deliberative planning' of John Forester.[19]

DfL coordinated delivery agencies within deliberately loose but long-term urban strategies, each tailored to the needs of the particular locality. It commissioned design teams and acted as the 'intelligent client'. It identified the gaps and invented small-scale projects to work on the ground in these often very deprived communities. Peter Bishop described the work of DfL as 'urban curation' and provocatively referred to the architects in the team as planners, but ones who understood how cities worked, could visualise and draw better future scenarios and work the system to get physical things built. This is a far cry from how the planning system sees its role today.

In July 2014 the Greater London Authority regeneration team, the successor body to DfL, produced the internal report *Learning from London's High Streets*, which identified a number of different ways to stimulate and facilitate a growing and prosperous high street.[20] These measures start on a micro-level with improvements to pedestrian and cyclist priorities. They also include the redesign of shop fronts with new colour, materials, imagery, improved signage and enhanced architectural features. Empty shops, disused buildings and vacant land can be revived through temporary 'pop-up' uses and exemplar projects. These present essential opportunities to experiment, test and celebrate the variety of uses along high streets. Public events – regular, seasonal or one-off – can bring liveliness, public interest, consumer confidence and media attention. In the long term, such small interventions help to strengthen community cohesion and the unique identity of a place, be it through food, arts or local history. The sustained organisation of local stakeholders and authorities into town teams or trader associations, or in Business Improvement Districts (BIDs), can strengthen local networks and facilitate long-term improvement. Such groups can help to engage local businesses, especially start-ups, through providing access to business advice or low-cost workspace. The physical activation of high streets can be achieved through simple, qualitative and durable pavement improvements, good lighting and places to sit and rest. Works to buildings, traffic-calming measures and adjustments to parking layouts can all create a better experience for the pedestrian. These are all straightforward measures but they do need to be combined into a coherent strategy, and having the appropriate design quality governance in place is essential.

First projects

The first project, focusing on 'opportunity centres', was developed in 2002. The A+UU introduced area-focused working with team members looking after particular places and borough relationships on a long-term basis. The aim was to bring together all the opportunities – spatial planning, physical regeneration, and skill and employment initiatives – into a single conversation. Part of the Mayor's 100 Public Spaces programme (Chapter 5) sought to tackle the problems of major thoroughfares through town centres. It chose Coulsdon High Street, Lewisham town centre and Brixton as early schemes that would demonstrate both the value of public space and ways to carve it out from existing highways. The A+UU was also involved in two comprehensive town centre studies. The report *TEN: Town Centre Enhancement in North London* in 2006[21] was followed in 2009 by *SEVEN: Housing Intensification in Seven South London Town Centres.*[22] These two reports proposed strategies for suburban town centre improvements under themes that were tailored to the particular conditions in each locality. They were well researched and grounded in the particularities of each place. They included strategies for landscaping, pedestrianisation, connectivity, diversity and growth. These documents did not seek to address the problems on the ground through the creation of another raft of planning policy. Instead, they were design-led studies that included practical projects that could be implemented quickly.

The association of many of these projects with transport gave them a common theme but also opened up the process of implementation. TfL controlled the largest available source of funding in London and the mayor had radically shifted its priorities towards pedestrians, cycling and the public realm. Follow the money, develop an idea that could capture the public imagination, find a sympathetic champion in TfL and a project could be realised. Better still, DfL did not need to manage the tedious public procurement processes but could remain strategic, agile and inventive.

This work started a set of experiments in design-led planning in Barking town centre and Dalston, described by Long as 'a feedback loop of thinking and doing that resulted in a range of carefully crafted public realm projects that were diverse in their nature but rooted in a deep understanding of the area'.[23] This was incremental urbanism by retrofit and by constant refinement. By engaging the communities in the design process, this work was overtly democratic and well founded.

Barking town centre: an east London phoenix

Since the early 2000s Barking town centre had been the focus of public-sector-led regeneration. The trigger was the council's commitment to counter social and economic decline caused by loss of traditional industries, including the scaling down of the Ford Motor plant at Dagenham. The resulting deprivation had encouraged the emergence of the far-right British National Party. There was a particular need to respond with regeneration programmes that would achieve visible change on the ground. The London Borough of Barking and Dagenham (LBB&D) was eager to experiment with new ideas and saw DfL as an ally and agent for change. Through this emerging partnership, an opportunity came up to rethink the town centre.

Barking town centre was blighted by disjointed public spaces, poor-quality social housing blocks and the decline of local business. It lacked any sense of urban coherence and was not an obviously attractive area, but it had a rich historic and cultural heritage that could be used as a basis for regeneration. Overall it had real potential to be so much better. In early 2006 the LBB&D initially commissioned DfL to help prepare and implement a town centre strategy to support a major housing development that was being sponsored by the London Development Agency (LDA). From this a series of projects ensued and DfL commissioned the architectural practices muf architecture/art, AHMM and Witherford Watson Mann. These projects included a new town square, estate improvements, and housing and cultural developments.

The projects started with a series of street theatre events that were designed to engage the population in a debate. One of these involved a group of polar explorers on an expedition to 'search for Barking town centre'. A design-led masterplan was then developed in consultation with the local community to provide the context to turn around the fortunes of this once vibrant hub of civic life in east London. Barking had always suffered from poor-quality public realm so DfL's approach deliberately incorporated crisp well-finished contemporary design and sought to use striking and innovative design to raise local aspirations.

This made it an exemplary case study of design-led regeneration. Design-led regeneration continues in Barking 14 years later and is still based on close collaboration between the local council and the Greater London Authority (GLA). The reworking of the Town Hall car park was part-funded through a mixed-use high-density development. New public realm was laid out in line with a coherent design palette that included locally made street furniture – the 'Barking bench'. Multi-award-winning interventions led by muf architecture/art included a folly (Figure 3.5),[24] an urban arcade lit by 13 chandeliers designed in collaboration with Tom Dixon, and an arboretum (Figures 3.6 and 3.7).[25] Thoughtful masterplanning along the River Roding and elsewhere is beginning to deliver high-quality new housing (including council social rented housing) and is continuing the spirit of proactive planning, now driven by the council-owned regeneration company BeFirst.

Figure 3.5 Barking town centre folly. The folly wall was designed as a ruin to recapture Barking's sense of its past. The wall references Barking Abbey and nearby Eastbury Manor House. Source: muf/DfL/GLA.

Figure 3.6 Barking town centre arcade beneath affordable housing by AHMM. Source: muf/DfL/GLA.

Figure 3.7 Barking town centre arboretum. Source: DfL Archive.

Making Space in Dalston

The project that best illustrates incremental urbanism as applied to town centre regeneration is the multiple-award-winning Making Space in Dalston programme that was carried out between 2007 and 2012.[26] It established the mantra: 'Value what's there, nurture the possible, define what's missing' (Figure 3.8).

The project started in Gillett Square, one of the first of the Mayor's 100 Spaces (see Chapter 5 and Figure 2.2). This was opened in 2006 and included new public space, affordable workspace and a new home for the Vortex Jazz Club. As with many DfL projects, it acted as a 'foot in the door'. Once local contacts had been established and networks formed, other projects invariably followed. Incremental urbanism was as much about the incremental development of client relationships as about projects on the ground.

The impetus to return to Dalston was provided by the revamp of the East London line (as part of London Overground), which involved a

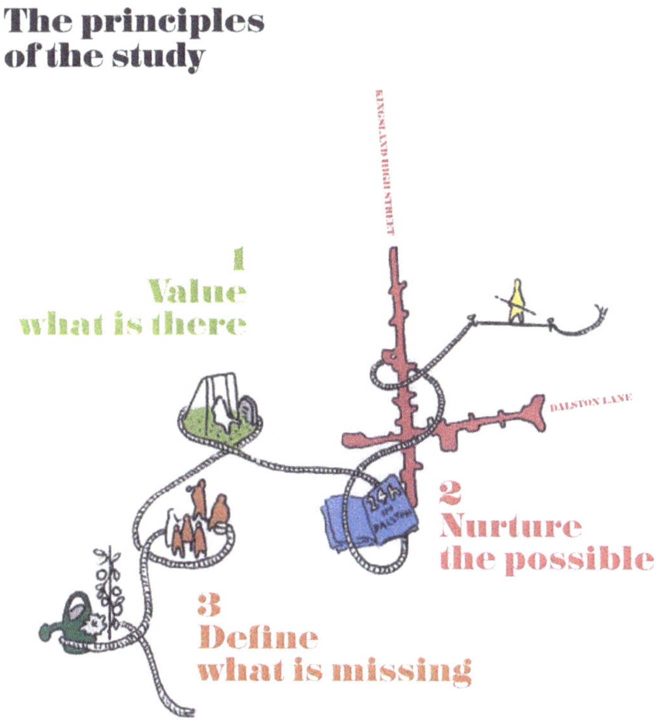

Figure 3.8 Value, nurture, define, deliver: a methodology for incremental urbanism. Source: J & L Gibbons and muf/DfL/GLA, Making Space in Dalston.

new station at Dalston Junction.[27] The station was built on a deck that also provided housing, public space and a library. Development of the transport hub was driven by public bodies – TfL, the LDA, and Hackney Council – with the publicly procured development partner Barratt London. The development provided the catalyst for local regeneration. A case for £1.5 million funding for new public realm had to be made to a sceptical LDA. The argument was that if £250 million had been spent on transport infrastructure, not to complete the public realm would be the equivalent of buying an expensive house and then economising by not fitting any carpets.[28] The money was agreed without dissent.

The project addressed local concerns within a broad strategic framework and an evolving process of communication and action research (Figure 3.9) that helped develop a shared vision with the residents, businesses and organisations. The project focused on achieving a higher-quality and more extensive public realm without losing the place's

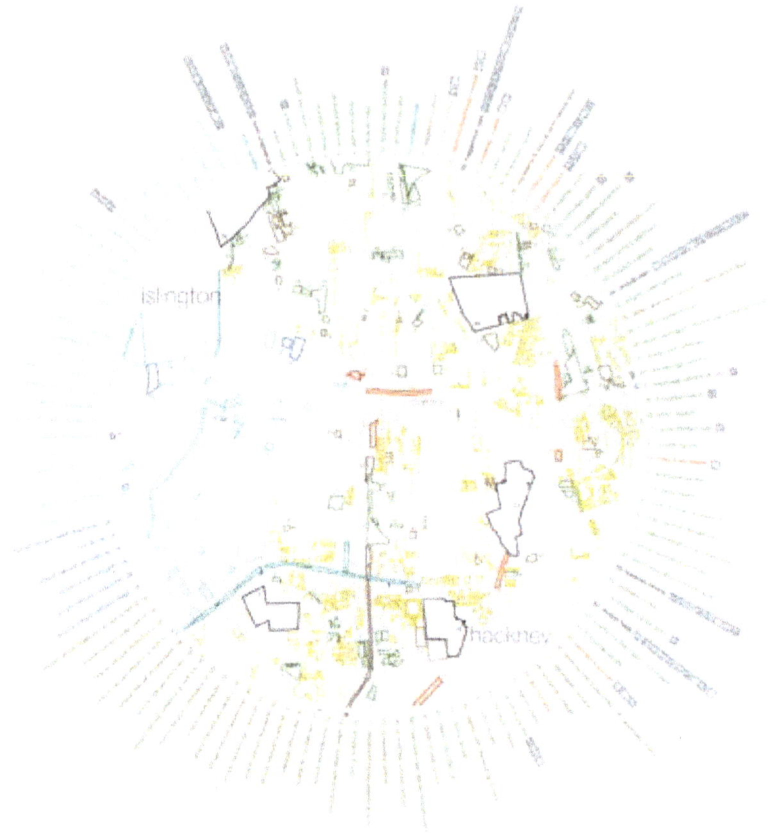

Figure 3.9 Mapping community assets in Dalston. Source: J & L Gibbons and muf/DfL/GLA, Making Space in Dalston.

existing assets. The active public involvement helped a once struggling locality to turn the corner and find new momentum and civic pride. The public space network, framed by the new development, was at the centre of proposals. Muf architecture/art and J & L Gibbons – teams that DfL had worked with on previous community collaborations – were appointed as designers. The initial brief sought to identify 10 costed projects and an action plan for cultural programming and management. In fact, over 70 projects were identified in 10 themes, based on discussions with almost 200 individuals and groups. Frequent steering group and stakeholder meetings were held in local venues, and numerous presentations were made to the community and other stakeholders. The initial mapping work[29] secured funding for 10 demonstration projects that ranged from small-scale interventions in collaboration with local artists to larger phased engineering projects. Bird-boxes, a green wall, new lights for the local cinema and the Eastern Curve Community Garden[30] were all completed. Improvements to Ridley Road Market and public realm along the High Street attracted further resources in later funding rounds.

Making Space in Dalston is an example of design-led, incremental masterplanning.[31] This is a process based on constant feedback between thinking and doing. Partners need to 'get their hands dirty' in collaboration with local people, rather than spending money on reports or following the conventional top-down approaches typical of traditional masterplanning processes. The grassroots-based methodology of 'valuing what's there, nurturing the possible and defining what's missing' allows for a shift in the balance of power to local residents. Involving local people in decision-making meant that local partners were able to take ownership of the projects (Figures 3.10 and 3.11) and from this evolved the mechanisms for future partnership working.

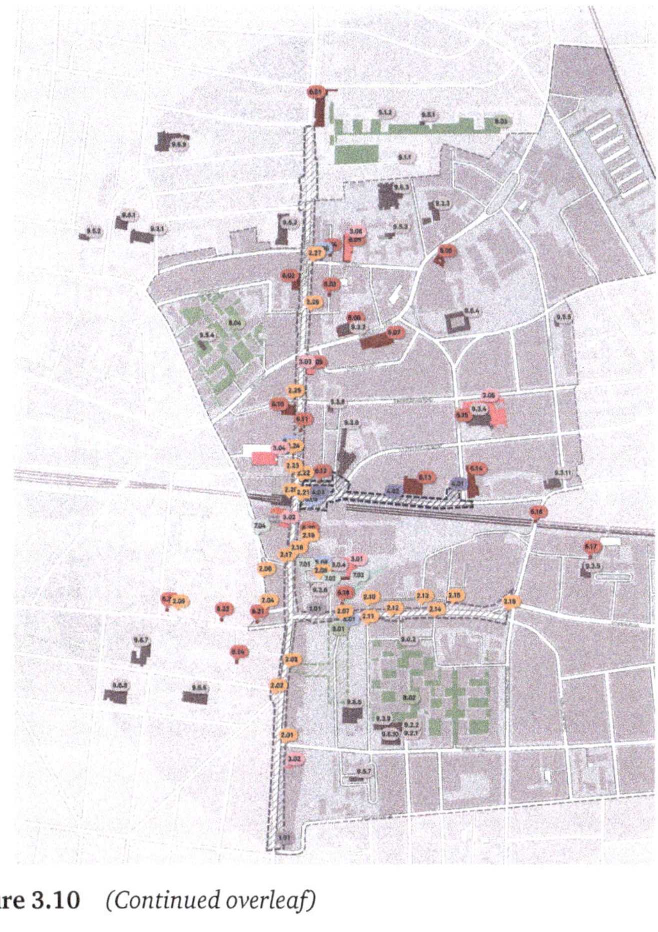

Figure 3.10 *(Continued overleaf)*

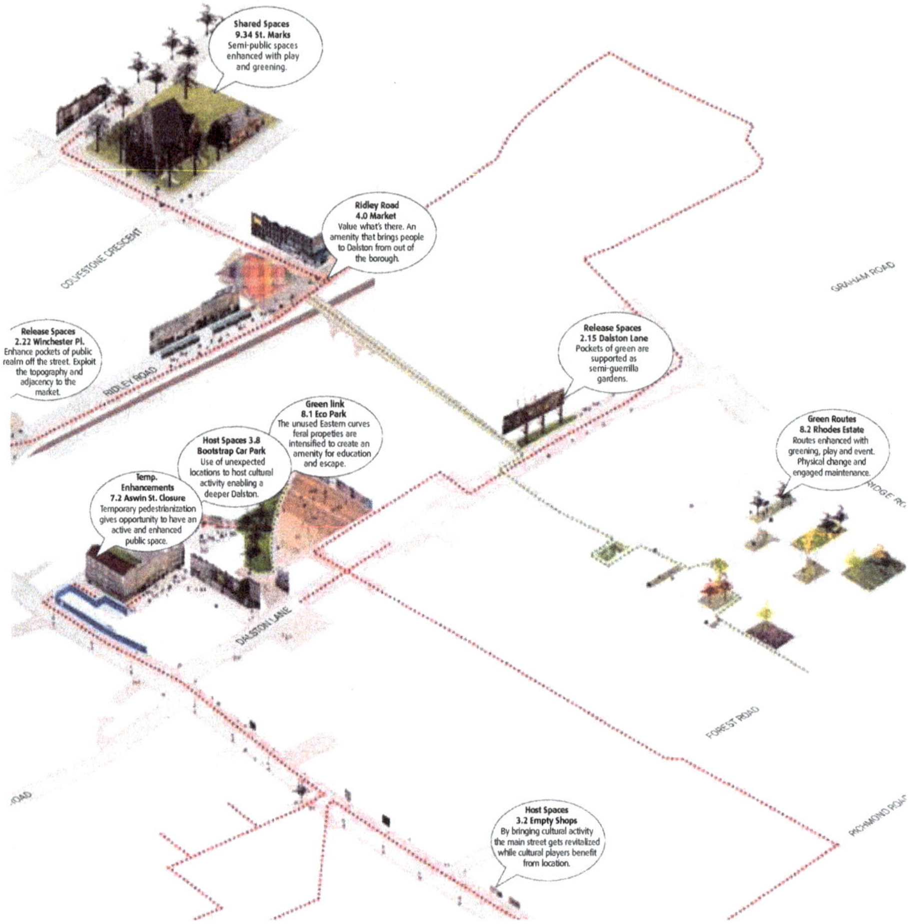

Figure 3.10 'Lots of projects everywhere': incremental urbanism in Dalston. Source: J & L Gibbons and muf/DfL/GLA, Making Space in Dalston. *(Continued from p. 89)*

Kieran Long[32] provides a good summary of the outcomes. He argues that the projects are a 'test case for how the idea of the Big Society will play out at the point of delivery of new urban plans'.[33] The brief for the projects was cowritten by the local community and developed gradually in response to conversations. Long says: '[i]t demonstrates that the results of engaging meaningfully […] are not predictable, and the outcomes are sometimes born out of conflict as much as consensus.' Interestingly, the foreword by Mayor Boris Johnson celebrated the success of the project by quoting Horace's phrase *concordia discors* ('harmony in discord').

Figure 3.11 The Eastern Curve Community Garden summer project as wheatfield and flour mill. Source: J & L Gibbons and muf/DfL/GLA, Making Space in Dalston.

High street places

Early in 2009, in response to the election of a new Mayor of London, DfL started to focus on high streets as a core part of its programme. The argument was that London was fortunate in having 600 or more high streets that could provide an excellent basis for future growth. They were vital, if neglected, elements in the city's structure. Such high streets were ideal locations for new regeneration programmes that would spread investment outside central London. This had been part of the mayor's electoral pledge, and programmes that centred on high streets and town centres would strike a chord with the new mayor and his team. Nearly 70 per cent of London's high streets did not fall within a designated town centre boundary and this meant that the majority of high streets lacked policy designation and consequently were potentially vulnerable to development pressures.[34] At the same time, high streets were also some of the most congested, polluted, complex but neglected spaces in the city. For this reason, they often languished on the 'too difficult to handle' register.[35]

The High Street 2012 project (beginning in 2008 with London's Great Outdoors; see Chapter 5) aimed to inject new life into one of London's most famous arterial high streets: the A13, or Whitechapel Road.[36] By examining the condition of the road from Aldgate to Stratford, and the places that it connected (Figures 3.12 and 3.13), the aim was to demonstrate that incremental rather than comprehensive change was the most effective way to realise the potential of such vital urban arteries. This approach was in stark contrast to that which prevailed for most transport projects at the time. These saw such roads as corridors where single funded programmes would implement *linear* improvements along the length of the carriageway. Consequently, the places that these roads ran through and connected were either ignored or were considered to be expedient. The choice of name was a piece of DfL opportunism – using the '2012' from the Olympics logo to create a 'project brand' and applying this to lever out the funding.[37]

Whitechapel Road was the archetypal DfL project. The area had a rich history and cultural diversity. It was damaged and poor, yet the road had historic buildings, institutions and street markets. It was a series of town centres, each with its local identity. Although it was a busy and congested transport corridor, it still had sufficient space to accommodate

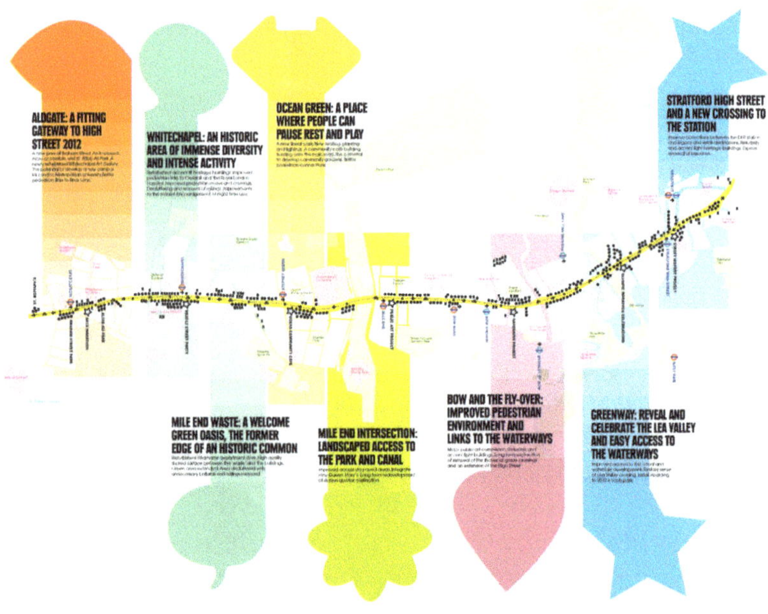

Figure 3.12 High Street 2012: conceptual design strategy. Source: DfL.

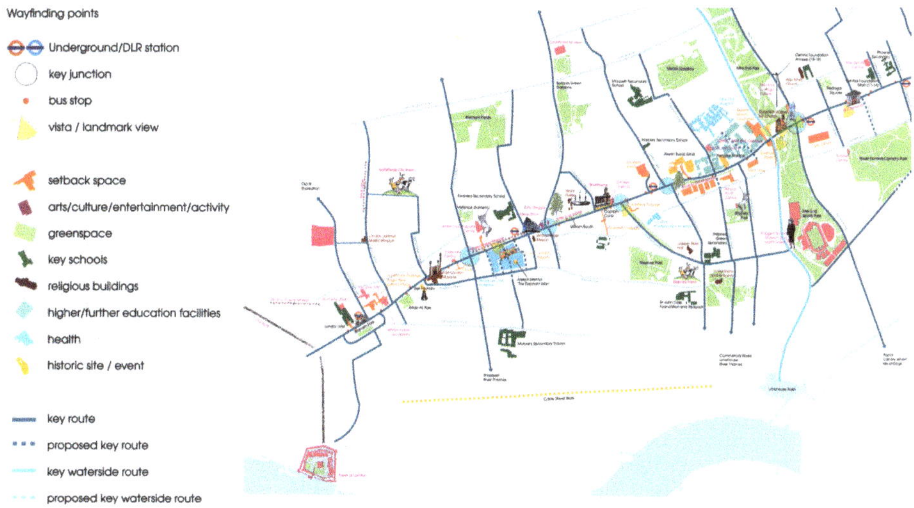

Figure 3.13 High Street 2012: projects and interventions. Source: DfL/GLA.

interventions to widen pavements and to improve the public realm. The remarkable historic buildings along its length provided a framework to create distinctive places (Figure 3.14).

High Street 2012 followed the approach of incremental urbanism. It celebrated the everyday, built on local identity and creativity, and brought about effective, durable and lasting change. The project was divided into eight sections, each of which had a punchy theme:

- Aldgate: A fitting gateway to High Street 2012
- Whitechapel: A historic area of immense diversity and intense activity
- Mile End Waste: A welcome green oasis
- Ocean Green: A place where people can pause, rest and play
- Mile End Intersection: Landscaped access to the park and canal
- Bow Flyover: Improved pedestrian environment and links to the waterways
- Greenway: Reveal and celebrate the Lea Valley
- Stratford High Street: New crossings to connect to the station.

Alongside these area-based design-led projects were themed interventions to improve lighting, landscape and pavements, to remove street clutter and to reinforce wayfinding. The entire initiative was built around an intense community involvement programme.

Figure 3.14 High Street 2012: refurbished terrace on Whitechapel Road, illustrating heritage as a key design anchor. Source: Peter Bishop.

In Aldgate, a new park – Braham Street Park – was created through unravelling a one-way traffic system (Figure 3.15). This project was funded by a private developer who recognised that offices next to a park would be much more attractive than offices next to an urban gyratory. Since the park's construction a new food and drink outlet has occupied part of the ground floor of a building fronting the space. This has helped to activate one edge and draw people into and through the park. The park

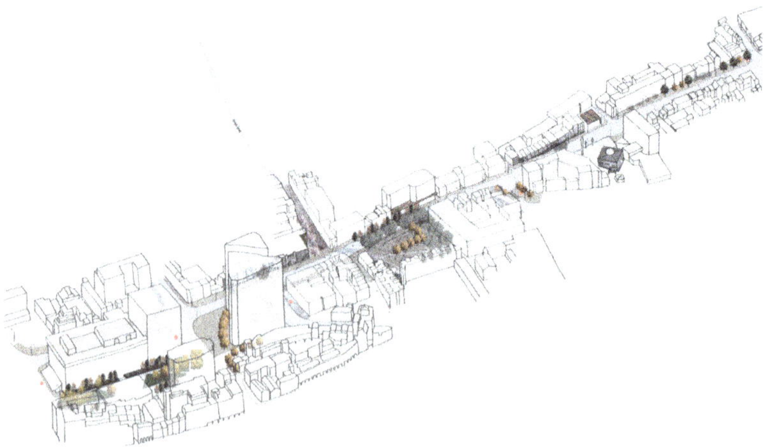

Figure 3.15 High Street 2012: Aldgate to Whitechapel Road. Source: High Street 2012, Vision document (2009), DfL/GLA.

itself was designed to be a flexible and programmable space. The design (EDCO Design with WilkinsonEyre, 2010) was a simple creation of 'space out of nothing' and provides a moment of reprieve in a busy and congested area. One of the greatest challenges was to find a public body to maintain the park.[38] The decision was taken that without a long-term management regime, the project would fail and it was consequently put on hold, but after lengthy negotiations the space was adopted by the City of London.[39]

At Altab Ali Park, the team worked with the local community to map its historical and cultural significance (Figure 3.16). A community-based archaeological dig excavated the site (the White Chapel) while an Alpana street painting event revealed the rich culture of the local Bangladeshi community (Figure 3.17).[40] These events opened up a meaningful dialogue between those using the park and those living, working and studying nearby. This helped the design team to produce a sophisticated and layered design that provided space for sitting, chatting, playing, and for social and political gatherings, as well as being a space to learn about the local history. A similar process of engagement helped to produce a new multilayered landscape at Mile End Waste. Whitechapel Market was the most complex project and the most difficult to deliver. The improvements led by East Architects were subtle and designed to make the market work better. They incorporated improved lighting, drainage and servicing (anticipating the arrival of the new Crossrail services nearby). English Heritage was involved as a significant partner and provided funding to restore historic buildings along the route.

Figure 3.16 High Street 2012: Altab Ali Park provides room to breathe just off Whitechapel Road. Source: Peter Bishop.

Figure 3.17 High Street 2012: Altab Ali Park community programme, using traditional Bangladeshi chalk paints. Source: muf/DfL/GLA.

At Ocean Green (Figure 3.18), plans were already well advanced and were incorporated into the High Street 2012 project. The resulting design uses landscape at the edge of the estate to reconnect it to the high street while maintaining privacy and protection for residents. Access to Mile End Park was also improved and the Green Bridge was replanted. A new floating towpath was constructed on the canal and the cycle superhighway now snakes down part of the street. At the end of the route, paving, lighting and carriageway changes have started to make Stratford High Street a little more like a street than an urban motorway.

Getting good designers on board was crucial to the success of this project, as was coordinating an expanded client team for them to work with. This team included highway authorities, local authorities, heritage organisations, private developers, parks departments, artists, market traders, schools, museums, women's groups, religious organisations and many more. The scope of this partnership allowed the project to tap into shared visions of the future and plan the appropriate physical changes to improve everyday life.

A key lesson from this and other projects was that the design process is not limited to the architect and the drawing board. Perhaps the most creative aspect of DfL's work was in brokering common interests and managing creative inputs. High Street 2012 was a lesson in collaboration and partnership building. Not only were there many funding partners, but some of the improvements were done in partnership with private

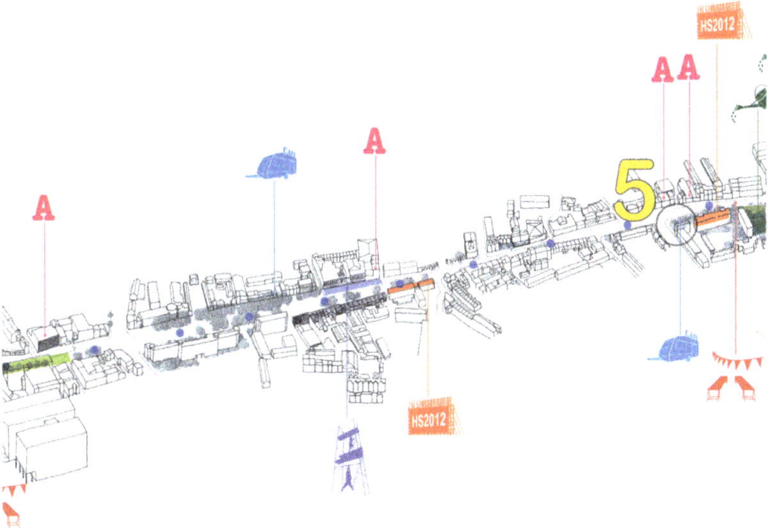

Figure 3.18 High Street 2012: proposals for Ocean Green and Mile End Waste. Source: High Street 2012, Vision document (2009), DfL/GLA.

landowners and developers. This involved harnessing disparate funding pots, levering in further investment and ensuring that the execution of works was of a consistently high quality across the statutory authorities. All of this required time and negotiation. Finally, more mundane issues such as management and maintenance (and securing the long-term funding for this) had to be addressed.

High Street London: understanding the problem and developing responses

Over the past 30 years, the capacity of public bodies to undertake research has been cut significantly. At its peak, DfL had 23 staff, but it never employed dedicated researchers.[41] The team had to rely on other institutions of London government for facts and data to support its work and recognised this as a weakness. An attempt to address this was the Urban Design Scholarships programme.[42] This was sponsored by the planning consultancy RPS and launched in 2008. It created funded secondments for talented practitioners to work with the team on applied research. One of these was Fiona Scott.[43]

There was very little systematic spatial analysis or quantitative data on London's high streets and in order to make a case for investment in London's high streets, DfL needed statistical, economic, planning and

Figure 3.19 London, a city of high streets. Source: Fiona Scott/GLA.

cultural research. Working as a sponsored 'scholar' in the DfL team, Fiona Scott set about creating a new interpretation of London's polycentric urbanism – one that focused not on the point (the town centre), but on the line (the high street; Figure 3.19). This is not to deny the importance of the town centre, which has both historical and cultural precedents, but it takes into account another history – that of the city which grows along linear space (in this case its Roman roads). The urban artery has its own significance and value; it is both 'place' and 'connector' at the same time. Initially, the study focused on a stretch of road between Ilford and Chadwell Heath – part of the old Roman road running from the City of London to Colchester in Essex. Its scope soon expanded to investigate the full 51-kilometre length of the 'high street' connecting Uxbridge to Romford through central London, with Oxford Street at its centre (Figure 3.20).

The research, and its meticulous drawings (Figure 3.21), revealed a wealth of new facts about the hidden economy of this stretch of road, such as it being home to 80,000 jobs and 6,500 businesses – more than Canary Wharf. The initial research was followed by a commission for research into London's entire high street network, identifying the role of high streets in supporting London's sustainable growth and development.[44] This became the High Street London project.

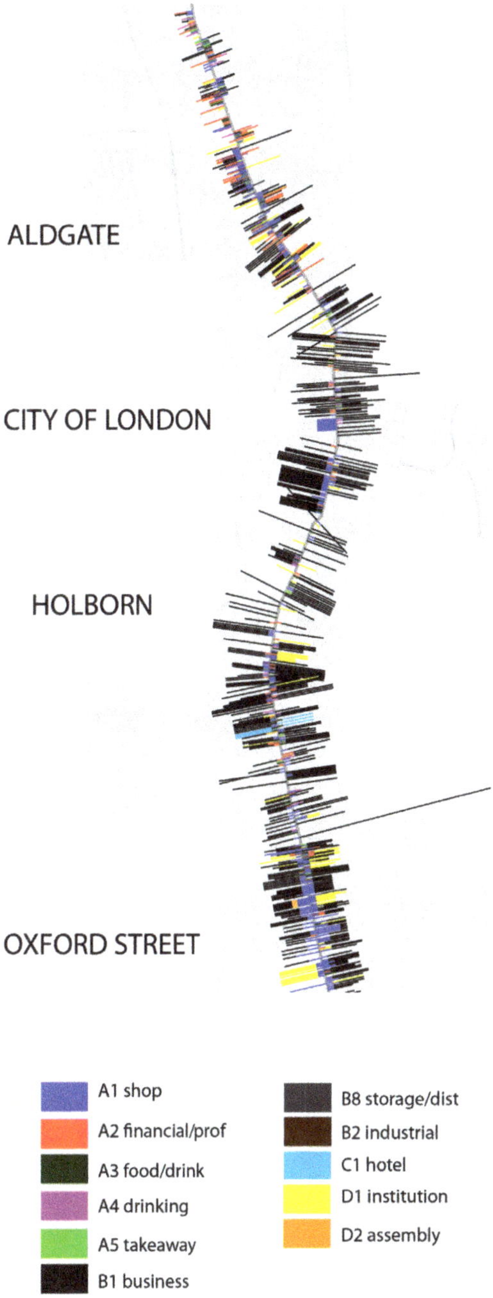

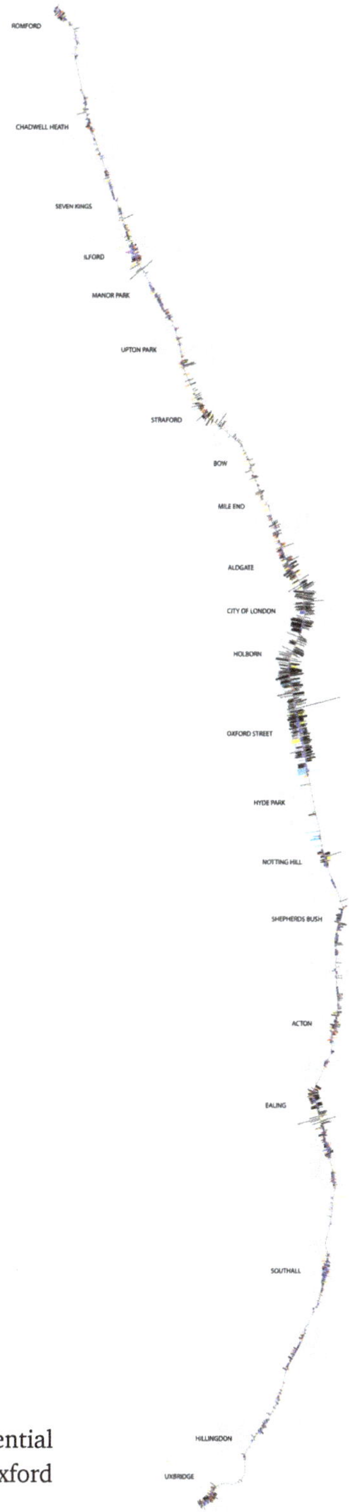

Figure 3.20 Uxbridge to Romford: non-residential land uses. Enlarged section shows Aldgate to Oxford Street. Source: Fiona Scott/GLA.

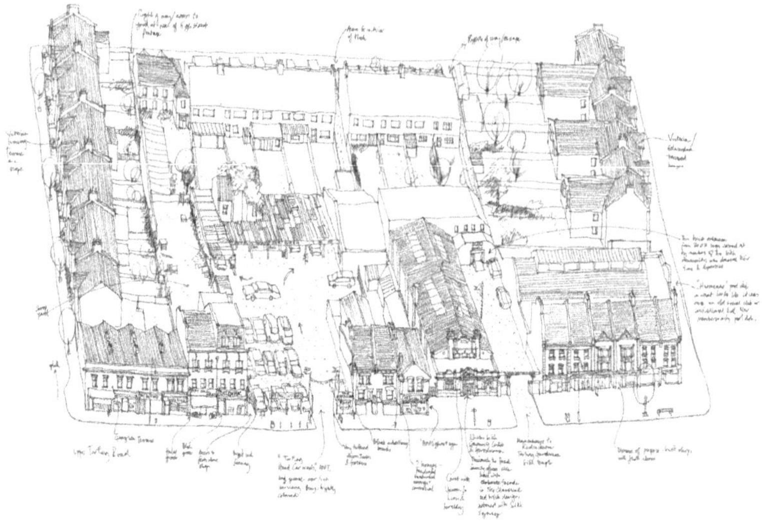

Figure 3.21 Diverse economic and cultural activity on Tooting High Street. Source: Fiona Scott/GLA.

Much of the previous discussion about failing high streets had focused on their very obvious problems rather than their potential. Underpinning the city-wide study was the proposition that London's high streets represented an important element in the city's urban fabric and could play a vital strategic and local role across the capital. High streets had great potential to accommodate much of London's predicted future growth, through the provision of new jobs and housing.

High Street London found that London's high streets are an economic system made up of some 175,000 businesses, employing almost 1.5 million people (or 35 per cent of London's total jobs), and home to a significant portion of London's micro and small businesses. The analysis also showed that half of London's brownfield land is on or within 200 metres of a high street. The Strategic Housing Land Availability Assessment at the time identified over 3,369 large sites (within a 300-metre buffer around the newly defined high street) with a capacity to deliver 155,137 dwellings over a 10-year period.[45] This was 54 per cent of the overall capacity of large sites in London for this period. Furthermore, two thirds of Londoners (5 million people) lived within a five-minute walk of a local high street and many did not venture beyond it in their day-to-day lives.

Two publications stemming from this research, *High Street London*[46] and the mayor's *Action for High Streets*,[47] focused hearts and minds on these social, economic and structural assets and formed the foundation of work over the years to come. They built the business case to support and strengthen the resilience of high streets strategically and pointed out the huge potential in them.

Crossrail: a new impetus for town centre regeneration

High Street London set the basis for a serious rethink by policy-makers at a time when almost all investment was being focused on big regeneration projects in the Thames Gateway and east London, particularly around the Olympic area. Outer London suburbia, where a large proportion of London's population lives, had been largely ignored (a point emphasised by Boris Johnson's campaign team during the 2008 mayoral elections). The fact that suburbia is rather 'ordinary' should not make it uninteresting to policy-makers. Indeed, designing in lower-density locations presents unique challenges. The interest in suburbia culminated in the 2016 London Plan's suggestion for increased intensification targets for suburban areas.

Once again transport investment, this time for Crossrail, presented the opportunity for the team to become involved at the local level.[48] The *Crossrail Atlas*, commissioned from the architects' practice 5th Studio, explored the opportunities for change that might be opened up by the new railway line, particularly in some of the outer London town centres.[49] The business case for the Crossrail infrastructure project had been based on economic growth, and, while the railway line was undoubtedly encouraging speculation in places like Ilford, a key growth centre along the new line, there were no specific local studies to ascertain where growth might occur or the form that it might take. There was a real risk that the scale and quality of regeneration activity would actually be damaging to the local area.

The case for local growth linked to Crossrail was examined by 5th Studio, Regeneris and Cyril Sweett. Their study aimed to establish the points where regeneration activity might be focused to create opportunities for local benefits, and a series of maps visualising the opportunities were brought together in the *Crossrail Atlas*.[50] This provided a comprehensive description of the regeneration potential and possible geography of urban change that might be triggered by the Crossrail project. Each station was first ranked by indicators of deprivation and economic performance. Second, each station locality was ranked according to its development opportunity. This took into account deprivation indicators, market opportunities and those areas where investment could have the greatest proportionate impact. Six stations where GLA/LDA investment could bring the furthest-reaching benefits were shortlisted for further study. These were then split into two priority groups: one where the current opportunity related to existing town centres and would be driven by residential development, the other where the opportunity was for commercial or mixed-use development. The project built a strong case for town centre renewal by gathering detailed data that identified where modest investment would have the biggest impact.

A change of political priorities: the Outer London Commission

Following his election in 2008, Mayor Boris Johnson set up the Outer London Commission to investigate actions which could help areas that had not seen much regeneration investment. These were also areas where many Conservative voters lived.

Chapter 5 considers the tactics that DfL used to rebrand existing programmes to adapt to a change in political leadership. In the case of town centres, the team successfully pitched a new idea that was really a rebranding of existing work: programmes of comprehensive change focused on high streets *across all of London*. High-street-based regeneration was well suited to suburban London and an initial £50 million was pledged over three years, with local authorities and organisations bidding for funds. The 'new' programme targeted high streets in London's outer areas. The political programme continued after the election in 2010 of a Conservative-led coalition central government that severely reduced public spending. In order to survive, DfL had to change its focus from town centres like Barking, with brownfield sites and high levels of deprivation, to a more opportunistic approach that was geared towards economic growth opportunities.

Town centre programmes repackaged: 'good to grow and ready to go'

In 2012, central government abolished the LDA and brought together, under one roof at the GLA, what was left of DfL, the London region of the Homes and Communities Agency and the London Thames Gateway Development Corporation. The GLA now had a broad remit for public space projects, town centre and high street schemes, housing renewal and development, public transportation, place-shaping, and growth corridor and Opportunity Area planning. Although it was significantly reduced in size, DfL saw this as an opportunity to create a new methodology for investing in localities that were 'good to grow and ready to go'. This term best described decisions made in a time of declining public funding and based on both need and opportunity.

The repackaged town centre programme reflected how political decisions on funding allocation had changed and where there might be support for new interventions – in particular, where there might be a measurable opportunity for growth arising from small-scale public subsidies. Inspired by the diagram 'London: Social and Functional Analysis',[51] which elegantly described London as a series of places with distinct identities, the team (with the property firm GVA) collated pan-London data to identify and evaluate all of London's 600-plus high street localities. This provided an evidence base for better-informed regeneration and investment strategies. Analysis of the data identified places that were 'good to grow' (had the capability to support housing and job growth, and were 'good' as in virtuous or right) and 'ready to go' (had all the ingredients in place to grow: willing and proactive people, space in the right ownership and supportive planning policy). Adding these layers of analysis to the localities map enabled a detailed and complex picture of the city to be drawn up. From this, multiple approaches to investment and regeneration could be derived. The study corroborated the places in which the GLA Regeneration Team (and previously DfL) had been investing over the last few years. It also strengthened the case for investment in overlooked (at the time) places like Southall, Sidcup, Erith and Blackhorse Lane.

The 2011 riots provided an unexpected catalyst for this new work. Civil unrest erupted first in Tottenham and later spread to other centres, including Croydon and Clapham Junction. Urban riots form a subline through English history from the twelfth century (religious riots and gang warfare between guild apprentices) to the eighteenth century (the 1780 Gordon riots, against Catholics) and the nineteenth century (a series of riots over electoral reform). More recently London had seen civil unrest in the Brixton riots of 1981 and the poll tax riots of 1990. As always, the riots caught the authorities by surprise, and with the Olympics scheduled to open in less than a year, an instant response was demanded. The riots had of course focused on high streets as these are the natural places for community congregation, and these seemed to be the places to start rebuilding community confidence. Additional funding was made available as part of the £70 million Mayor's Regeneration Fund, with a focus on Tottenham and Croydon, which had been the worst-affected areas.

Figure 3.22 Good to grow. Source: Adam Towle, DfL/GLA.

The 'good to grow and ready to go' high street strategy (Figure 3.22) was able to secure a significant proportion of the £221 million total[52] that had been allocated since 2011 by the mayor and others to help boost high streets, strengthen local trade, create new jobs and shape better-quality places. These schemes had been carefully researched and well designed – sadly, an unusual occurrence for short-term politically driven initiatives. More important projects were based on a clear rationale and could be implemented quickly.

The ensuing regeneration programmes acknowledged the importance of combining analysis and place-based mapping to identify the opportunities for each locality. Practical action was accompanied with strategic research on a London-wide level to understand the implications of change in the economy, including impacts on retailing, commerce, civic activities and housing demand. Projects were both practical and at a stage where implementation could occur as soon as the funding was made available and the green light given. The partnerships were already in place with partners ready to provide support.

The impact of the high street and town centre work

One question is whether the high street is uniquely British and whether the work of DfL was a response to a unique London problem. High streets may have different names in Paris, Milan, Amsterdam or Hamburg but in essence their structure, use and socio-economic importance are very similar. Some of DfL's ideas have proved transferable to other cities and the team has worked with a group of German academic researchers called Think Berl!n, led by Dr Cordelia Polinna, to apply London's tried and tested approaches. This work has ranged from articles to political workshops on Design for Berlin.[53] It was recently commissioned to prepare a proposal for an International Building Exhibition (IBA) based on Berlin's high streets (the Radialen) and called Radikal Radial (Figure 3.23).

On the dissolution of DfL, many of its team members secured new jobs in different cities and took with them their networks, methodologies and approaches to urban regeneration. A number of the programmes have been adapted to new circumstances. The London Borough of Harrow, for example, took on Tobias Goevert, Adam Towle and other ex-members of DfL who shaped the Building a Better Harrow regeneration programme, which owed much to the Barking and Dalston town centre projects. Fenna Haakma Wagenaar is now Design Lead (Hoofdontwerper) in Amsterdam, where a variation of the high street strategy, *Stadtstraten*, 'is the most used (and abused) strategy for combining improved pedestrian links and public space with the general demand for densification'.[54] Another team member, Eva Herr, works in the planning department in Hamburg on improving and

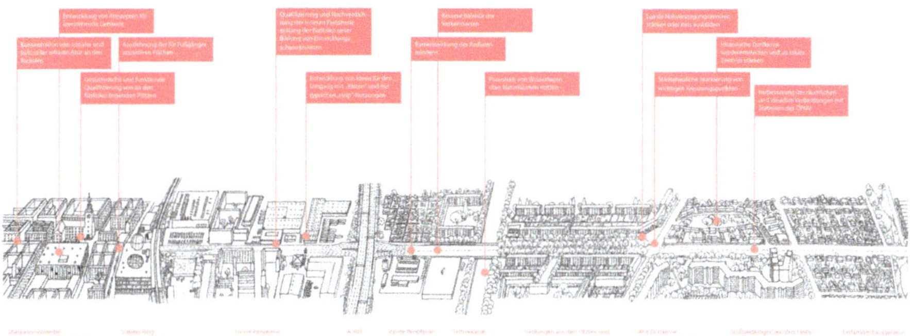

Figure 3.23 Schematic representation of a Berlin radial road that runs from the city centre to the outer city through various types of neighbourhoods (2011). Source: Thomas Hauck.

densifying the city's arteries in outer areas, called the *Magistralen*. The city commissioned a major design workshop, Bauforum, in 2019, using 200 experts and audiences of 8,000 to inform a programme of high street demonstration projects.[55] Peter Bishop has just completed new masterplans for Barking town centre.

The UK government has launched a national Future High Streets grant programme, with the first round of bids in 2019. This has picked up on the approach applied in DfL's original high street funds and is looking at opportunities beyond high street improvements, including major housing-led town centre restructuring.[56]

Conclusions

DfL's high street work is not without parallels, but it is hard to find a comparable initiative that rode successive political changes and funding fluctuations and delivered such a range of projects. Opportunism is important in times of uncertainty. This is not to say that a number of the town centres would not anyway have seen changes or indeed improvement. But that change would have been piecemeal without the team's active involvement.

The work on town centres and high streets was a response to economic and social forces that were manifest in radical shifts in consumer behaviour. It was also a response to the volatile and turbulent politics of the period. Simple programmes for town centre and high street regeneration had to be constantly repackaged and adapted to new sources of funding and new political priorities. Agility, invention and opportunism are central elements of survival, and incremental urbanism is possibly the only approach that is able to withstand the stresses and uncertainties of local government.

High street and town centre regeneration projects show the importance of carefully designed small-scale interventions that emphasise sensitive urban design. London is under constant development pressure and this growth is taking place through infill and brownfield site development as well as through the reuse and reactivation of empty buildings. Strengthening retail functions is an important first step, but the future of the high street lies in the diversification of use through developing the whole ecosystem – small firms on upper floors and production in backyards. Structural changes in the UK and London economies are heralding the return of small businesses and customised manufacturing. This 'creative milieu' is essential to the future development of cities. These jobs are more resilient in the face of financial crisis, create a local economy and are able to react flexibly to new circumstances and changes in demand. The high street is a perfect seedbed for such activities.

The projects illustrated in this chapter show that robust relationships with (and within) local authorities, business and resident groups are the key to developing, implementing and maintaining good urban change. Local charrettes (workshops carried out over a number of weeks involving the architects and the local community) and design reviews with all stakeholders are a key element in this process. They helped to create a climate supportive of design quality which was hard for private investors, local planning departments and engineers to disregard. Targeted public-sector investment is just the starting point of a regeneration process, but it does set the agenda for longer-term programmes and further investment from local authorities, developers and businesses. Coordination between the various bodies involved in high-street-related activities is essential. The projects with the most impact were those that involved communities from the outset, took local needs into account, fostered uniqueness and diversity, nurtured individual assets and developed strong partnerships between all stakeholders.

However, not all lessons from the last decade of high street interventions are positive. Shopfront improvements, popular as 'quick fix' local programmes, are often ephemeral due to short retail leases and lack of understanding by shopkeepers of their 'design value'. The problems of high streets are deeper than the quality of shopfronts. Physical improvements that fail to address the root causes of decline lose any regenerative impact quickly. Long-term improvements in the quality of high streets cannot be achieved by politically driven quick fixes. High streets and town centres are complex places that are built on a web of social and economic relationships. Long-lasting improvements are driven by meticulous research, skilful design-led interventions and programmes that build capacity and resilience. Most of all they require long-term commitment and agency. The projects that DfL brokered in Dalston and Barking demonstrate a methodology for renewal that has an enduring legacy.

If the high street is to have a future, there must be more innovation to diversify and grow the high street ecosystem. It is probably true that the high street is no longer the centre for a neighbourhood's shopping needs. Some, especially where they have the benefit of an attractive historical environment and a wealthy residential hinterland, will continue to thrive. Many other high streets will have to reinvent themselves. In a time when local shopping is declining in importance, high streets are still centres of their communities and can diversify to become local economic, service, leisure and transport hubs. They still need to have a welcoming and well-maintained public realm and a distinctive local identity. The London high street of the twenty-first century will need to become more resilient and capable of ongoing reinvention. This might include the use of buildings and space for local markets, digital manufacturing and fabrication, community enterprises, leisure and recreation, or food production. High streets must also improve their capacity for walking and cycling in order to reduce vehicular flows on London's already congested medieval street pattern.

London's future development challenges can only be addressed through sensitive place-based strategies and plans. In some places that may mean incremental change and adjustment; in others it might mean more comprehensive redevelopment. Town centres and high streets will continue to play a key role in supporting urban change, but this requires a recognition of their important physical, social and economic attributes and continued support.

Notes

1 Clive Dutton, OBE, 1953–2015. Clive Dutton was an unconventional and inspiring figure in a world that is too often viewed as dull and regimented. His career spanned Birmingham, Newham and Belfast. His affable nature hid a polished operator who had the panache to generate ideas. Critically, he had the energy and political acumen to navigate the political mazes to make them happen. DfL welcomed his arrival in London as a chance to work with an ally and sympathiser.
2 Bishop 2015, and see Chapter 6.
3 Interview with Mark Brearley (DfL), January 2020.
4 Interview with Mark Brearley (DfL), January 2020.
5 Carmona 2015. Carmona contributed a huge amount to the High Street London report.
6 Local Data Company 2020.
7 Alexander 1965.
8 Jacobs 2002 (first published 1961).
9 Simms, Kjell and Potts 2005.
10 Indeed, in some inner London boroughs the compensation payments made to pedestrians injured through tripping over uneven pavements exceeded the pavement maintenance budget.
11 Portas 2011.
12 Moore 2012.
13 A phrase used by Mark Brearley in an attempt to anglicise the American idiom 'bang for your buck'. A regular slide in Mark's presentations read, 'telling stories and minting phrases, from "catch and steer" to "good to grow, ready to go"'. Minting phrases was a common and important feature of DfL's communication.
14 Jones, Roberts and Morris 2007.
15 Carmona 2015.
16 This was part of the reasoning for the GLA's expansion of the high street agenda to include street and covered markets and 'places of work' in 2014/15.
17 Latham 1990, p. 31, cited in van der Heijden 2015, p. 9.
18 Marshall 2008.

19 Forester 2006.
20 Greater London Authority 2014b.
21 Urhahn Urban Design 2006.
22 Urhahn Urban Design 2009.
23 Long 2010.
24 The folly was designed by muf and finished in 2010. It has already acquired its own folklore, with local schoolchildren relating that it is a haunted ruined castle. In a current scheme by Bishop & Williams and DaeWha Kang design, the leader of the council has insisted that the folly be retained or moved to another nearby location.
25 Barking Town Square, http://morethanonefragile.co.uk/barking-town-square/
26 Winner, Hackney Design Award 2010: Eastern Curve (Making Space in Dalston); Winner, Communications and Presentation Category, Landscape Institute Awards 2010; Finalist, Urban Intervention Award Berlin 2010; Winner, President's Award, Landscape Institute Awards 2011; Winner, Urban Design and Masterplanning Category, Landscape Institute Awards 2011; Commended, Place Making Category, NLA Awards 2011; Finalist, Rosa Barba World Landscape Prize 2014.
27 London Overground was a highly successful amalgamation of various rail lines, mainly in north London. The lines were transferred to TfL and train frequencies were increased to make services similar to those of the underground. It was opened in 2007.
28 Interview with Peter Bishop.
29 muf architecture/art, 2009.
30 This is now in its 10th year and has become an exemplar of best practice of community-managed public space.
31 Long 2010.
32 Long 2010.
33 The Big Society was an initiative by the Conservative government under David Cameron; see https://en.wikipedia.org/wiki/Big_Society
34 A focus on town centres as they are commonly considered, namely as foci of high-end retail and office space, is retrograde. The DfL view was that a broader conception of a town centre was needed: one that encompassed a wider area of relatively inter-accessible streets that enable the co-location of the full gamut of non-residential activity, including primary schools, workshops and so on. This creates extensive and varied activity which seeds daily, weekly and periodic movement as well as engagement of individuals with their locality.
35 Carmona 2015.
36 Like many of London's major roads, Whitechapel Road was part of the Roman link between London and Colchester.
37 Originally, the project was called Olympic High Street, but this was blocked by the London Olympic Organising Committee as misuse of their brand (which corporates like McDonald's and Coca-Cola had paid to use). Originally it was planned that the marathon would go along Whitechapel Road, and DfL argued successfully for funding to improve the route. The fact that the Olympic Committee decided to reroute the marathon on the grounds that Whitechapel Road did not present a picturesque enough route illustrates the shortsightedness of some institutions of London government. The project went ahead regardless. A number of other key routes were eventually tidied up, in particular those that would take participants and press between the different venues.
38 An offer by the Royal Bank of Scotland to adopt it was rejected as inappropriate for a new piece of public space.
39 The park is actually in the London Borough of Tower Hamlets.
40 By muf architects.
41 The extensive research that was used to support its work was carried out by the team members themselves as part of its design methodology.
42 The Urban Design Scholarships programme was sponsored by the planning consultancy RPS with a launch at London Met and publicised by the *Architects' Journal*. The programme ran for two years. Based on a public call for submissions, it placed talented practitioners in the DfL team to develop a specific research programme under close mentoring from DfL leads (see Chapter 7).
43 Fiona Scott now runs the London-based architecture practice Gort Scott with Jay Gort.
44 The commission was awarded to the young practice Gort Scott, assisted by The Bartlett Faculty of the Built Environment at UCL.

45 https://www.london.gov.uk/what-we-do/planning/london-plan/new-london-plan/strategic-housing-land-availability-assessment
46 Gort Scott Architects, 2010.
47 Greater London Authority 2014a.
48 Now renamed the Elizabeth line, this new high-speed railway line under central London will connect Heathrow Airport to the east of London, radically altering transport accessibility and land values.
49 The *Crossrail Atlas* attempts to provide a comprehensive description of the regeneration potential of the Crossrail project. The atlas was prepared by 5th Studio on behalf of DfL/LDA, and was undertaken in parallel with an economic study by Regeneris Consulting and Cyril Sweett. See http://www.5thstudio.co.uk/projects/crossrail-atlas-london/
50 5th Studio, 2011.
51 Drawn by Arthur Ling and D. K. Johnson and first produced in the *County of London Plan 1943* by Patrick Abercrombie and others. Variously described as the 'Abercrombie Plan', 'Potato Plan' or 'blob map' (see Chapter 1).
52 This sum was made up of the Outer London Fund (£50 million), the Mayor's Regeneration Fund (£70 million), and other TfL and GLA funds and injections from Central London funds.
53 *Urban Design*, Winter 2013, Issue 125. and a book, Bodenschatz, Hofmann and Polinna 2014.
54 Interview, Fenna Haakma Wagenaar.
55 https://www.hamburg.de/bauforum/
56 The budget for the fund was increased significantly in August 2019 after Boris Johnson became prime minister; see https://www.gov.uk/government/news/1-billion-future-high-streets-fund-expanded-to-50-more-areas

Bibliography

5th Studio, Holbrook, T., et al., *Crossrail Atlas*. http://www.5thstudio.co.uk/projects/crossrail-atlas-london/ (accessed November 2019).

Alexander, Christopher, 'A City is Not a Tree', *Architectural Forum*, Vol. 122, No. 1, April 1965, pp. 58–62 (Part I), Vol. 122, No. 2, May 1965, pp. 58–62 (Part II). https://www.patternlanguage.com/archive/cityisnotatree.html (accessed 15 March 2020).

Bishop, Peter, 'Clive Dutton Obituary', *The Guardian*, 29 June 2015. https://www.theguardian.com/society/2015/jun/29/clive-dutton (accessed 29 August 2020).

Bishop, Peter, and Williams, Lesley, *The Temporary City*, London: Routledge, 2012.

Bishop, Peter, and Williams, Lesley, *Planning, Politics and City Making: A Case Study of King's Cross*, London: RIBA Publishing, 2016.

Bodenschatz, Harald, Hofmann, Aljoscha, and Polinna, Cordelia (eds), *Radialer Städtebau: Abschied von der auto-gerechten Stadtregion* ('Radial Urban Development: Farewell to the Car-Friendly City'), Berlin, Germany: DOM, 2014.

Boomen, Tijs van den, Frijters, Eric, Assen, Sandra van, and Broekman, Marco (eds), *High Streets – London (UK), Urban Challenges, Resilient Solutions*, Trancity x Valiz and Future Urban Regions, 2017, pp. 170–5.

Brearley, Mark, 'Determining Places', *Cambridge Architecture Journal*, No. 9, 1997, pp. 4–5.

Brearley, Mark, 'I'll Take the High Road', *Architectural Review*, March 2015, pp. 20–1.

Brown, Richard, *GLA Business Report No. 8: Architecture and Urbanism Unit Staff*, London: Greater London Authority, 2 December 2002.

Carmona, Matthew, 'London's Local High Streets: The Problems and Complexities of Mixed-Use Corridors', *Progress in Planning*, Vol. 100, August 2015, pp. 1–84.

Chase, John, Crawford, Margaret, and Kaliski, John (eds), *Everyday Urbanism*, New York: Monacelli Press, 1999.

Department of the Environment, *Streamlining the Cities: White Paper*, London: HMSO, 1983.

Forester, John, *The Deliberative Practitioner: Encouraging Participatory Planning Processes*, Cambridge, MA: MIT Press, 2006.

Greater London Authority, *Housing and the Compact City*, Greater London Authority, 2003.

Greater London Authority, *East London Green Grid Primer*, Greater London Authority, 2006.

Greater London Authority, *Action for High Streets,* London: GLA, July 2014a.

Greater London Authority, *Learning from London's High Streets,* London: GLA, July 2014b.
Greater London Authority, *London Plan 2016*, January 2017. https://www.london.gov.uk/what-we-do/planning/london-plan/current-london-plan/london-plan-2016-pdf (accessed 24 February 2020).
Greater London Authority/Transport for London, *London Streetscape Design Manual*, Greater London Authority/Transport for London, 2006.
J & L Gibbons LLP and muf architecture/art, *Making Space in Dalston*, London Borough of Hackney and Design for London/LDA, July 2009.
Jacobs, Jane, *The Death and Life of Great American Cities*, New York, NY: Random House, 2002 (first published 1961).
Jones, Peter, Roberts, Marion, and Morris, Linda, *Rediscovering Mixed-Use Streets: The Contribution of Local High Streets to Sustainable Communities,* Bristol, England: Policy Press, 2007.
Kleihues, Josef Paul, and Klotz, Heinrich, *International Building Exhibition Berlin 1987: Examples of New Architecture*, New York: Rizzoli, 1986.
Local Data Company, 'Trouble Ahead for Retail Vacancy Rates', 11 May 2020 [with data for Q1]. https://www.localdatacompany.com/blog/brc-vacancy-monitor (accessed 29 August 2020).
Local Government Act 1985, London: HMSO, 1985.
Long, Kieran, 'UDS: Designing for London', *Architects' Journal*, 14 May 2009, pp. 26–35.
Long, Kieran, 'The Big Society Begins in Dalston', *Evening Standard*, 30 June 2010, p. 31.
Long, Kieran, 'Regenerating Barking', *Architects' Journal*, 13 September 2013, pp. 24–35.
Marshall, Stephen, *Cities, Design and Evolution*, Oxford: Routledge, 2008.
Masey, Anthea, 'Barking up the Right Tree', *Evening Standard*, 5 August 2009, p. 7.
Moore, Rowan, 'How Barking is This?', *Evening Standard*, Life and Arts, 11 September 2007, p. 39.
Moore, Rowan, 'Borisopolis: London under Boris Johnson', *The Observer*, 29 April 2012. https://www.theguardian.com/artanddesign/2012/apr/29/london-architecture-boris-johnson-livingstone (accessed 29 August 2020).
Office of the Deputy Prime Minister (ODPM), *Our Towns and Cities – the Future: The Urban White Paper,* ODPM, 2000.
Portas, Mary, *The Portas Review: An Independent Review into the Future of Our High Streets*, December 2011. http://www.bis.gov.uk/Portas (accessed 7 November 2019).
Scalbert, Irénée, 'London After the Green Belt', *AA Files*, No. 66, 2013. https://www.thomasdanegallery.com/usr/documents/press/download_url/510/ml-aa-files-2013.pdf (accessed 24 February 2020).
Simms, Andrew, Kjell, Petra, and Potts, Ruth, *Clone Town Britain: The Survey Results on the Bland State of the Nation,* London: New Economics Foundation, 2005.
Ungers, Oswald Mathias, and Koolhaas, Rem, *The City in The City – Berlin: A Green Archipelago: A Manifesto (1977) by Oswald Mathias Ungers and Rem Koolhaas [with others]*, edited by Florian Hertweck and Sébastien Marot, UAA Ungers Archives for Architectural Research, Zurich: Lars Müller Publishers, 2013.
Urban Task Force, *Towards an Urban Renaissance*, London: HMSO, 1999.
Urban Task Force, *Towards a Strong Urban Renaissance*, London: HMSO, 2005. http://image.guardian.co.uk/sys-files/Society/documents/2005/11/22/UTF_final_report.pdf (accessed 24 February 2020).
Urhahn Urban Design, *TEN: Town Centre Enhancement in North London*, Amsterdam, The Netherlands: Urhahn Urban Design, June 2006. http://www.urhahn.com/wp-content/uploads/town-centre-enhancement-in-north-london-lowres.pdf (accessed 29 August 2020).
Urhahn Urban Design, *SEVEN: Housing Intensification in Seven South London Town Centres*, Amsterdam, The Netherlands: Urhahn Urban Design, 2009. http://www.urhahn.com/wp-content/uploads/housing-intensification-in-seven-south-london-town-centres-lowres.pdf (accessed 29 August 2020).
van der Heijden, Hans, 'Catch and Steer' (Version AF), 2015. https://hvdha.com/20/wp-content/uploads/2015/07/HvdH_Catch_and_Steer_Eng_Illustrated.pdf (accessed 13 October 2020).
Wainwright, Oliver, 'Review 2010', *Building Design*, 17 December 2010, p. 10.
Ward, Colin, *Autonomy, Solidarity, Possibility: The Colin Ward Reader*, edited by Damian F. White and Chris Wilbert, Edinburgh: AK Press, 2011.

4

Better housing for London: how on earth did we pull that off?

Richa Mukhia

> *It [the London Housing Design Guide] is quietly radical. It demonstrates that it is still possible for public authorities to direct city building for the better.*
>
> – Rowan Moore, *Slow Burn City*[1]

The London Housing Design Guide (LHDG) was arguably the boldest and most influential of all the projects of Design for London (DfL). It was a conviction-driven mission, fighting for a better standard of housing for the average Londoner.

This fragile project survived against the odds and steered a new course for housing in London. In essence, the LHDG proposed 90 standards that set out a confident vision for housing quality in the capital. Of the suite of standards, the most controversial were the minimum space standards. These have now been transplanted into national policy through the *National Technical Standards* published in March 2015. Now, for the first time in history, Britain has minimum space standards for all housing tenures. London really did lead the way, under the watch of a Conservative mayor and a Conservative government and during a turbulent era of financial crisis and public-sector cutbacks in Britain.

Writing this chapter has presented a valuable opportunity to revisit this story, speak to the protagonists involved and learn lessons from a most unlikely success story. The focus of this text is the process of delivering the LHDG and not the standards as published. These can be found in the guide itself.[2]

UK housing standards: historical background

Since the publication of the London Building Act of 1667, London has always had some form of regulations concerning housing design. These were often put in place with urgency after national disasters or wars and were invariably at the mercy of politics and economics.

In the late nineteenth century, the Disraeli government passed a raft of legislation to tackle poor and insanitary housing, including the Public Health Act 1875, which set out construction bylaws for terrace housing, and the Artisans' Dwellings Act 1875, which empowered councils to buy and demolish slum housing and construct new public housing. The Tudor Walters report (1918) arose from the Homes Fit for Heroes campaign after the First World War and sought to raise the standard of housing in the country. Crucially, it acknowledged the importance of housing quality in improving living conditions and made the link to space standards by proposing minimum floor areas for a range of dwelling types. The Dudley report (1944) and the *Housing Manual* (1949) built on this legacy. These standards applied to public housing and did much to bolster quality.

In the 1950s, as private house building accelerated and political priorities shifted to increasing the supply, there was a notable deterioration in housing quality. The amount of space in homes was falling just as living standards were rising and people were demanding more space. In response, Sir Parker Morris was appointed to chair a committee tasked to 'consider the standards of design and equipment applicable to family dwellings and other forms of residential accommodation, whether provided by public authorities or by private enterprise, and to make recommendations'.[3] The committee was open and outward-facing, and consulted with a wide array of stakeholders and interested parties. There was also a great deal of fieldwork, with visits to over 600 dwellings supported by a functional analysis of needs and requirements of 'new patterns of living'. The committee's hugely influential report *Homes for Today and Tomorrow* was published in 1961 (Figure 4.1) and made the case for space standards: 'Additional floor space takes first priority in the evidence, and this call cannot and must not be ignored, for a good house or flat can never be made out of premises which are too small.'[4]

The Parker Morris standards were derived by examining how residents used their homes, what equipment and furniture they needed, and the space required to perform household activities. The report concentrates on the usability of a home but also devotes an entire chapter

Figure 4.1 The Parker Morris report: (a) Cover; (b) Livable housing. Source: *Homes for Today and Tomorrow*, HMSO, 1961.

to 'The Home in Its Setting', focusing on the relationship of the dwelling to the street and surrounding context. Initially, the standards were applied through good practice guidance, but in 1967 they were made mandatory, first for the New Towns and subsequently (1969) for all new council housing.

While the standards had an influence on the private housing market, the ambition to apply the guidance across tenures failed to materialise, apart from in the New Towns. However, since local authorities remained the primary deliverers of housing in the 1960s and 1970s, this ensured a legacy of well-sized and functional housing stock from this period.

In 1980 a new Conservative government, led by Margaret Thatcher, rescinded the Parker Morris standards and introduced the Local Government, Planning and Land Act. The Act had further far-reaching consequences for the delivery of housing in the UK. New financial controls curbed local authority house building, and as a result housing associations became the main providers of social housing and private enterprise the main supplier of housing overall. This marked a structural shift in the way housing was delivered in the UK and sowed the seeds for the market-led approach to housing that defined the following decades.

A new millennium: housing in London

The year 2000 was significant for governance and planning in London. Ken Livingstone was elected as Mayor of London in May 2000. The same year, *Planning Policy Guidance 3* (*PPG3*) was launched, sanctioning higher densities and development on urban and brownfield sites. As David Birkbeck notes: 'Prior to *PPG3* no one built very high or very dense. After it launched everything changed very quickly. Developers who had been building four-storey blocks were suddenly building 12-storey schemes with very little thought given to design or the particular challenges of living at higher density.'[5]

The first mayoral *London Plan* was published in 2004. It promoted London as a high-density global city, giving developers another charter to densify. Critics voiced concerns that 'the quality debate had been blindsided'.[6] In the publication *Towards a Strong Urban Renaissance*, Lord Rogers and his fellow Urban Task Force members demanded that:

> the design of individual housing units must be improved, and the quality increased to reflect advances in new technologies, construction techniques and environmental efficiency. The Urban

> Task Force did not address the issue of the private residential sector in detail, but it is clear that new measures are needed to ensure that private housebuilders – despite their best intentions – do not build a new generation of mono-functional enclaves based on lowest common denominator design.[7]

At City Hall, the focus remained on housing output and the ever-growing pressure to 'get the numbers up'. Housing targets were in the low 20,000s in 2000, after which they rose steadily, reaching a target of 42,000 by 2015. In 2000 densities in London (56 dwellings per hectare or dph) were already higher than the national average (25 dph), as observed by Christine Whitehead, who further states: 'By 2005 national average densities had increased by almost two thirds to 41 dph. Densities in London had doubled to 112 dph – almost 175% above that average.'[8]

Community groups were increasingly concerned about the impact of this growth on their communities. They put pressure on members of the London Assembly, who in turn began to discuss the issue of housing 'quality'. In 2003 *Housing for a Compact City* was published by Richard Rogers, as the mayor's Chief Advisor on Architecture and Urbanism, and the Architecture and Urbanism Unit (A+UU; Figure 4.2). This promoted successful high-density housing projects from across Europe along with a clear message about quality: 'In seeking to meet our targets, we must not put quantity before quality. We must provide future generations of Londoners with the best of contemporary housing, creating places that will accommodate and sustain London's vibrant and diverse communities. High quality design and increased densities are critical to this equation.'[9]

The London property market showed no sign of slowing down. A rising population, ready access to credit and international investors fuelled the booming housing market. Despite the warnings about quality, little changed, and it was clear that self-regulation by the private housing market was not working.

The A+UU and, later, DfL were at the front line in reviewing housing proposals across the capital, and these were of increasingly poor quality. The prevalent typology was the double-loaded corridor serving two-bedroom, low-ceilinged, single-aspect flats. Homes seemed to be shrinking at a startling rate and there was real concern that a sustainable housing stock was not being created. Our instinct and awareness told us London was in danger of leaving an alarming legacy of poor housing for future generations to sort out. Of course, we were not alone in observing these

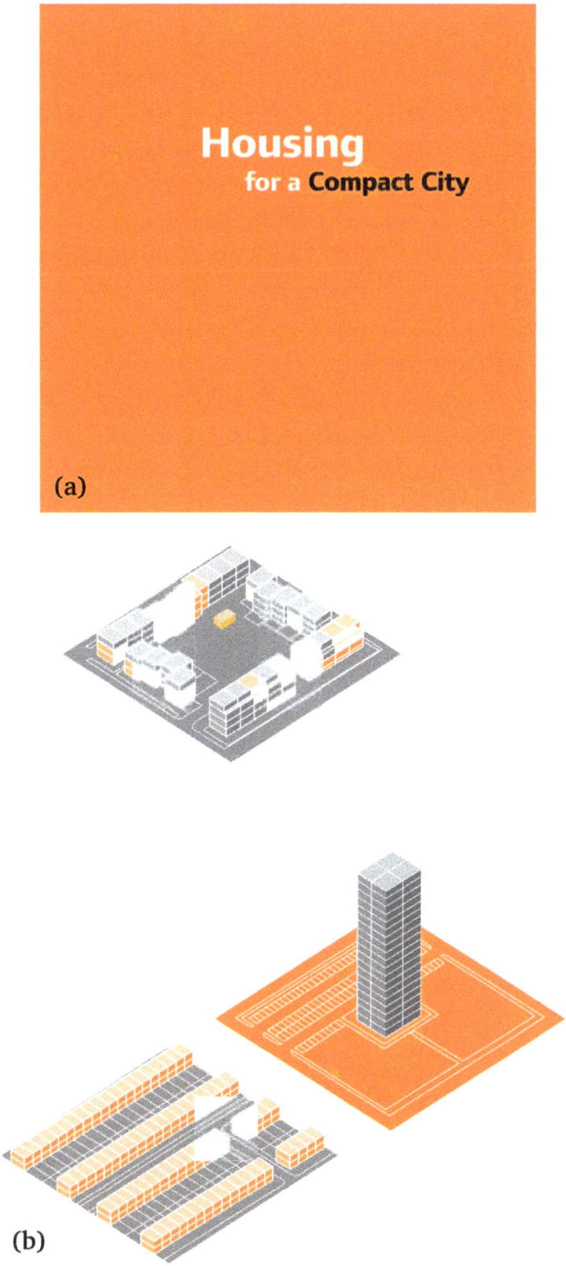

Figure 4.2 *Housing for a Compact City*: (a) Cover; (b) Three alternative approaches to designing at the same density. Source: Architecture and Urbanism Unit, *Housing for a Compact City*, Greater London Authority, 2003.

worrying trends, as shown by this anonymous post from the blog of the Commission for Architecture and the Built Environment (CABE):

> Where does one start? The shrinking new builds since 1980 and the Thatcher removal of mandatory space standards? The disappearance of the bath to be replaced by a shower only in new flats? The disappearance of the kitchen to be replaced by a corner unit stuck in the living room without a window over the sink or being in its own four walls? The loss of what was formerly loft space in a building by bedrooms with Velux and not dormer windows such that the occupant has no direct view out? The increase in double loaded corridor apartment blocks leading to vast numbers of poky single aspect flats in blocks that will stand for 30 years at least? Much has been built that even a lay person would find unacceptable as a flat dweller and I am one such, not an architect but you don't need to be an architect to see that rooms are too small, ceilings too low, that places lack storage space, and that there is an absurd number of toilets and showers in newly built flats. Since when did people refuse to share a toilet? I could show you the floor plan of a two bedroomed flat in Essex that has three toilets, one in each ensuite and one presumably for visitors. Are we now so precious about our backsides that sitting on a toilet somebody else has used is anathema? I don't think so.[10]

Research, articles and campaign documents published by CABE, the Royal Institute of British Architects, the Joseph Rowntree Foundation, HATC, Shelter, Design for Homes and others added to the groundswell of concern. The studies confirmed that London was producing some of the smallest homes in western Europe.[11,12] Not only were these homes small, but also only 18 per cent of schemes assessed by CABE were rated as 'good' or 'very good', 'revealing overall a disappointing picture of housing quality, and demonstrating that consumers are getting a raw deal when it comes to new homes and neighbourhoods'.[13]

In response to this growing pressure, the Greater London Authority (GLA) commissioned the housing consultants HATC to produce a report investigating 'the potential role of internal space standards for dwellings … to be considered within the forthcoming review of the London Plan …The purpose of this study is to attain an understanding of the evolution, role, operation, and impact that space standards have had and may have in the future within London and to propose policy for incorporation in the London Plan and related guidance'.[14]

As Andrew Drury of HATC explained, 'We were being asked to answer two fundamental questions: 1. Should the GLA establish minimum space standards? and 2. Could the GLA legally establish minimum space standards? Our answer was yes and yes.'[15] There was a clear case for space standards and associated guidance on design quality. Homes in London were shrinking and there was a case for the GLA to intervene.

Despite the mounting evidence, there was little change to the status quo. The house builders out-lobbied everyone else, insisting that the introduction of space standards would be catastrophic for delivery. The spectre of housing targets loomed over the politicians, quantity was prioritised over quality and the HATC report and recommendations regarding the introduction of standards were shelved.

Design for London

Design for London (DfL) was established in October 2006, two months after the publication of the HATC report. There was an awareness from the outset that the team was a political creation that was unlikely to last. In Mark Brearley's words,[16] 'Design for London was inherently vulnerable, not likely to survive for many years, as there was no legal or procedural requirement for us to exist. Hence we made a concerted effort to have as big an impact as possible, as soon as we could.' During their time at the A+UU, Mark Brearley and Richard Brown had realised that work on strategy and policy had a greater impact than location-specific projects. With the establishment of DfL, the involvement with policy work increased. The team was involved in a wide range of policy work on Opportunity Areas, the London Plan, industry, high streets, streetscape guidance, public space and housing. As Peter Bishop commented, 'We were given freedom to ask big questions, which civil servants embedded within the GLA could never do. Design for London was allowed to initiate policy debates. We had an open brief and the productive naivety of having direct access to the mayor. We had licence to generate ideas and licence to upset people.'[17]

In the early days we did not always have a seat at the table when housing policy decisions were being made, but the team continued to push the conversation on housing quality and worked to build momentum for the cause. Mark Brearley observed: 'We were conviction-driven people and we found others who supported the mission and were interested in positive action. It was an innocent mission – we wanted to make the city better.'[18]

Although at arm's length from City Hall, DfL were still consulted when policy drafts were circulated. We also had direct access to the London Development Agency (LDA), particularly their land development team. A last-minute review of the mayor's draft Housing Strategy by Deborah Mathieson[19] revealed that 'there was virtually no mention of design or quality. I sent some comments about design just before it got sent to the mayor, and Alan Benson (Head of Housing Strategy at the GLA) agreed that the document must include a narrative about quality.'[20] The GLA agreed that a supplementary guide focusing on housing design should be produced. This was to give very general design guidance, focusing solely on consolidating existing standards. No one wanted us to include anything new or propositional, as this would have been far too controversial politically. We agreed but, of course, did not abide by this. In stealth, we looked at the issues holistically, produced a one-page brief and sought out a sympathetic collaborator at the LDA, who funded the project.

In parallel, the DfL team continued 'making the argument for standards in different ways to different levels and layers of the bureaucracy. They were out there convincing people. A project like this needs leaders who have the ear of politicians.'[21] For example, when a group of prominent housing architects and Design for Homes informally presented the findings of a report on living at superdensity in 2007,[22] the team capitalised on the opportunity to build up sympathy for the cause within the LDA. As David Birkbeck commented, 'Peter Bishop stage-managed a presentation to David Lunts and the LDA.'[23] (Lunts was the executive director for regeneration at the GLA.)

Peter Bishop later recalled:

> There was no appetite from the mayor's office for any kind of housing standards, his senior aides fearing that they would discourage investment from house builders. The agreement (already brokered with the agencies concerned) was that the team would produce standards that would only apply to LDA land holdings and HCA-funded schemes – the argument being that if there were cost implications, then they would be reflected in lower land values (that the LDA was willing to accept) or higher subsidies (that the HCA were willing to accept). In other words, I explained as politely as possible that it was none of the GLA planners' business. Design for London then secured support (with strings attached) to test some of the emerging principles on an LDA-owned site in Bow (St Andrews).[24]

There were many mountains to climb. The project was deeply contentious; there were many cooks, many stakeholders; the evidence needed pulling together; there was a complex web of existing regulations to navigate that were often contradictory or onerous; there was a well-funded lobby from the house builders, and scepticism and reluctance from the delivery community generally. There were, however, many voices lobbying for change and they all contributed to the growing momentum to address the problem of housing quality. DfL was fortunate to take the lead on the project. Strict instructions from the GLA and the LDA ensured that our brief and public statements on the project would apply to publicly funded projects only. However, in truth the prize was always the application of standards to all tenures across London. In the early days this seemed like a fragile, distant ambition rather than an inevitability.

Doing the homework

The project started with an intensive research period. We looked at historical precedents (Parker Morris, *Housing as if People Mattered*,[25] the Smithsons' writings on housing[26]) and at best practice across Europe and beyond. We pooled our collective knowledge about what makes good housing. Richard Rogers was a strong advocate for balconies and private outdoor spaces; others brought experience from practice and design reviews. There was also considerable observation and reflection, drawing on the team's own experiences of living in London.

DfL was an atypical policy-making unit. It was a diverse group of individuals from different backgrounds. Many of us had trained as architects and brought with us experience of working in practice and delivery. Most of us had experience of living in other cities and countries, and very few fitted the stereotype of white-collar civil servants living in suburban homes in the commuter belt. We brought with us experiences of living in studios, in homes with no storage and with poor insulation and security, in single-aspect flats with no outdoor space. Such experiences were highly relevant but unusual given that decision-makers are often far removed from the realities of some issues. Personal experiences helped us to pitch action and policy with added persuasiveness.

We knew we needed support with the project as we were not in a position to devise standards or check for consequences. Unlike the Parker Morris committee with its 19 members, we had one officer, working with Mark Brearley, leading the project (Deborah Mathieson from 2006 to 2009 and Richa Mukhia from 2009 to 2011). As with all DfL projects, we started by pulling together the best team for the project. The tender for the draft LHDG was won by a team led by Urban Initiatives and supported by Proctor and Matthews Architects and Mae Architects.

The project team began by addressing the pressing need for consolidation and consistency. The guidance was to be primarily a consolidation of existing standards, bringing together existing policies and guidelines already embraced by the mayor (Lifetime Homes, Code for Sustainable Homes, Building for Life and Secured by Design). A survey of existing regulation revealed inconsistencies. Standards varied depending on whether schemes were funded privately or publicly and this added to the complexity of delivering mixed-tenure schemes. Additionally, it was clear that some of the guidance developed at a national level did not relate well to the high-density London context.

This started a long period of consultation and dialogue. We went back to the commissioners and authors of existing guidance. We worked out where there was scope for flexibility (particularly in standards developed by single-interest groups) and negotiated clarity and compromise where the standards produced by different groups seemed contradictory or overlapped.

As well as rationalising the plethora of existing guidance, it was clear that to really improve quality, the guidance would have to plug the missing gap in terms of space standards. Alex Ely of Mae Architects later recalled another issue:

> Developers were focused on promoting a certain type of residential block layout that was leading to other problems. The double-loaded corridor plan created a high proportion of single-aspect dwellings, many of which received no sunlight or alternatively suffered from overheating. Given that there was a growing trend towards apartments [80 per cent of dwellings produced were flats], we felt something should be done about access to outdoor space as well.[27]

Minimum space standards, private open space, ceiling heights, dual aspect and shared circulation were the key new additions that the research suggested would make the greatest difference. The spatial and ergonomic parameters that formed the basis of many of the new standards are universal. The amount of space required to live comfortably in a home does not vary from borough to borough, and therefore it was appropriate that the issue was addressed at a strategic level by City Hall. Alex Ely later commented:

> We did a huge amount of research into housing standards across the UK and internationally. The most widely used were the Housing Corporation's Housing Quality Indicators, English Partnerships' Quality Standards Delivering Quality Places and Habinteg's Lifetime Homes Standards. To some extent our commission was about synthesising these standards into one set of requirements. Nonetheless, I was interested in the whole history of standards from the Tudor Walters report of 1918, which promoted low-density solutions for housing that complemented the garden city movement of the time, through to the Parker Morris report of 1961, *Homes for Today and Tomorrow*, which, for the first time, linked space standards with occupancy. The report took a functional approach to determining space standards in the home by considering what furniture was needed in rooms, the space needed to use the furniture and move around it, and the space needed for normal household activities. We were then able to adapt this approach to arrive at a suitable set of standards for today.[28]

There was an extensive consultation process involving different interested parties, public-sector investment partners, key external stakeholders, registered social landlords, private house builders, expert consultants, and a core group of respected housing architects and other industry experts. There were meetings, working groups, workshops and building visits; there was formal and informal feedback, as well as a public consultation on the draft document.

St Andrews, Bow: live project research

St Andrews, an LDA-owned site in Bromley-by-Bow, East London, was an ideal opportunity to test some of the emerging ideas in a live project. The tender for the project to build housing on the nine-acre former hospital site was won by Barratt. Mark Brearley explained:

> There was a good relationship between the LDA and Design for London and a sense that there was a great opportunity for live project research. We steered the LDA towards the process of upfront specification parameters and an offer was made to Barratt on that basis. We made an agreement to use the project to test some of the key requirements that were being considered.[29]

As Peter Bishop commented:

> This was the first LDA project that the team was able to influence at the procurement stage. Barratt came in with the best financial bid but a poor scheme. We worked behind the scenes at the LDA to persuade them to accept Barratt's offer only if they changed their architects. This they duly did.[30,31]

Allies and Morrison were appointed as the new masterplanners. Hendrik Heyns of that practice later commented:

> St Andrews changed the way residential units were built in London. The typology of units changed. Daylight requirements and the move towards dual-aspect dwellings meant the proportions of units changed. There was also a move away from the two-bed-unit dominant scheme to a more interesting mix of tenures and types. At St Andrews, 50 per cent of homes were affordable and 30 per cent family housing.[32]

Parker Boris?

In 2008, progress on the LHDG was stalled by the pre-election purdah. Ken Livingstone was standing for re-election against the Conservative candidate Boris Johnson. A Conservative win would have significant consequences for the future of the LHDG but we knew nothing of Johnson's view on housing quality. After Johnson's win in May 2008, we seized every opportunity to promote the work of DfL and pitched as many projects and ideas as we could. The opportunities were more formal and orchestrated than they had been under Ken Livingstone. They were also heavily vetted by the mayor's advisors, who would often require pre-presentation. Guessing that housing standards were not very high up on the mayor's agenda, we knew it was crucial that we pitch an irresistible, compelling case to get the new mayor on board. Mark Brearley was adept at making arguments and had mastered an engaging, seemingly off-the-cuff style of delivery. He used this skill to make the case for a host of projects and ideas: public space, high streets, regeneration spending, streetscapes, opening up procurement and, of course, housing standards.

As Brearley said later:

> We managed to get through to the mayor and he supported it. I gave a structured PowerPoint making the argument for the LHDG to the

mayor. We were surprised by his response, with words something like 'I want this to happen, I think this is right'. After that, Boris publicly stated his belief that we shouldn't be building what he referred to as 'hobbit homes', and success became possible. The fragile initiative was sustained because of support based on belief, from the mayor, at odds with the doom-mongering of the house builders. A huge amount of luck allowed this venture to succeed. We were well aware that our team's existence was itself a lucky occurrence, resulting from the earlier one-off coincidence of Richard Rogers' support and input, and Ken Livingstone's way of handling politics and interests. But that unique alignment during Ken's years never fully empowered us; in fact we were kept at arm's length. We were surprised by Johnson's enthusiasm for the introduction of new housing standards.[33]

Like most new mayors, Johnson was looking for quick wins when he came to power; the LHDG was well progressed, but not yet public, so 'up for grabs' in many ways. However, it did (and still does) seem unlikely that a Conservative mayor would champion a project that seemed so against the thrust of traditional Conservative neoliberal ideology. Housing standards clearly was an area that Johnson was interested in. Peter Bishop believed that it chimed with a nineteenth-century Conservative ideology:

> When briefing Johnson on anything, you had to find a turn of phrase or an obscure historic reference if you were to have even a remote chance of engaging his interest. In this case it was referencing the [Conservative] Disraeli government's reforms in the latter part of the nineteenth century. He loved the turn of phrase of 'the Artisans' Dwellings Act' and kept repeating it. Referencing the LHDG back to nineteenth-century ideals of 'Tory democracy' got him genuinely excited. Even so, it was a complete surprise when he wanted the LHDG to be incorporated as the standard in the London Plan.[34]

A conversation with Kieran Long revealed a similar speculation:

> There are lots of ways to be conservative. There is a way to be conservative which is about deregulating markets; there is also a way to be conservative which is about preserving things – conserving a certain quality of life or understanding London as

> having a certain character that housing contributed to. It became a conversation about architecture which transcended the clichéd ideological camps. It didn't work under a radical mayor but it worked under a conservative mayor.[35]

Although 'Boris got the bit between his teeth'[36] on the housing quality issue, we soon learnt that he relied heavily on his advisors to deal with the content. Sir Simon Milton had a detailed knowledge of planning policy and was comfortable in signing off the detail. Without a sympathetic mayoral advisor, we would probably not have been able to withstand the fervent campaign from the house builders. The happenchance of a supportive mayoral team just when the LHDG was emerging meant that, for the first time, London-wide cross-tenure design guidance for all new homes was a real possibility.

Draft LHDG and consultation

Officially, the guidance was still focused just on publicly funded projects, but the introduction indicated that there was an ambition to level the playing field between public and private housing delivery and therefore the guide would be considered as part of the London Plan review. In July 2008, the draft LHDG was published for consultation (Figure 4.3). We knew there would be protest from the house builders and others in the industry, but we were bold with the content and ready to test the waters on some of the more contentious issues, rather than reining back for fear of causing controversy. Again, being at arm's length from the GLA and having a 'licence to generate ideas and upset people' enabled us to be more radical than conventional policy-makers. As Rowan Moore commented, 'You wouldn't have had the same outcome without Design for London being involved. The GLA is run by civil servants – they are administrative, not proactive. The mayor has to have a vision, but the civil service is, by nature, cautious.'[37]

The formal consultation on the draft ended in September 2008. A team at the LDA trawled through the feedback and produced a comprehensive review of comments. A new team began work on refining the document in response. The consultant team was led by Emily Greeves and supported by Kieran Long and by Julia Park from Levitt Bernstein and Alex Ely from Mae Architects. As project manager and editor, I was supported by Fenna Wagenaar. A new phase of collaboration with the GLA and the London board of the Homes and Communities Agency

Figure 4.3 Cover, *London Housing Design Guide*, consultation draft, 2008. Source: GLA.

(HCA London) then began. There was now momentum for the final set of standards to be included in the mayor's Housing Supplementary Planning Guidance (SPG), as well as forming the basis of the HCA London design standards (for publicly funded projects). Effectively this would mean that the standards might eventually apply to private development and publicly funded projects.

Complexities and compromises

Although we were closer to the goal of cross-tenure application, there were still many obstacles to overcome. There was the complexity of dealing with so many stakeholders with varying political agendas. There was also the bureaucracy involved in trying to make anything happen in local government: briefings, sign-off procedures, board approvals and so on. These were cumbersome but necessary procedural hurdles, and the project required us to keep track of approval processes for all three agencies. Cross-agency working was challenging, but there was an underlying collaborative attitude among many of the players involved, born from a realisation that the downward trend in housing quality had to be stemmed. The officers involved seemed willing to push aside the usual party lines; architects and specialists attended meetings pro bono in return for a seat at the table, realising that this was something that needed to happen.

HCA London needed the standards to be precise and prescriptive because their funding process was about demonstrating strict adherence to requirements. However, the GLA was concerned with planning and housing outputs so was keen to ensure that there was flexibility and room for negotiation. Key allies such as John Lett (Strategic Planning Manager at the GLA) facilitated negotiations with City Hall. The solution was to have a two-tier system of standards where Priority 1 standards were the baseline and Priority 2 the best practice. This meant that standards were flexible enough to be included in planning policy,[38] while the entire suite of standards could potentially be prescribed for publicly funded projects. It was a compromise, but crucially enabled a cross-tenure set of standards.

The consultation and subsequent lobbying efforts also had a significant impact. Some of the most fiercely debated issues concerned studio flats, ceiling heights, dual-aspect dwellings, minimum space standards and private outdoor space. There were many compromises (for example, the ceiling height standard was lowered from 2.6 m to 2.5 m, the dual-aspect standard was watered down, and studio flats were permitted in certain scenarios), but the core principles of private outdoor space and minimum space standards were protected.

Cost and delivery

To address concerns about the impact of the standards, a Cost and Delivery Impact Assessment study was commissioned jointly by the LDA, GLA and HCA London. GVA Grimley and Sheppard Robson produced a report that concluded:

> Overall, it is not believed that introduction of the Guide will lead to the delivery of fewer dwellings on any given site other than in those locations where constraints are so strong that it is likely to be difficult to accommodate as many dwellings as might previously have been the case in the absence of the Guide.[39]

The report did speculate that an increase in build costs might occur (of 1–5 per cent by 2013 for developments where sale values did not drop below the London average). There were also warnings about the viability of some schemes, but the counterargument was that clear rules become priced into land values rather than build costs, so the costs would fall on the landowner, not the developer.

We believed that any cost implication would be outweighed by the certainty and simplicity that a single set of design standards for all new housing would bring. There was nothing too bold in the LHDG: indeed, the standards were mostly a reminder of what had previously been required, and any extra demands were cautious and well chosen. Some of the new standards, such as those for private outdoor space, would add a cost, but they would also add value and might enable properties to be sold more rapidly.[40]

Fundamentally, we did not think we were asking for very much. For example, we wanted a bedroom to have enough space for items such as a bed, wardrobe and chest of drawers, and to have sufficient circulation space and the most basic provision for wheelchair access. These are reasonable, basic ergonomic requirements that are as relevant in Hackney as they are in Kensington. They are not place-specific but concern ordinary furniture and equipment and the everyday things people need to do to live in a dwelling.

Crafting the document

We realised that the clarity of the content, the quality of the writing and the graphic design were all crucial to the success of the document. We were lucky to have a like-minded core group of contributors at this stage. Emily Greeves led the writing, with Julia Park and Kieran Long reworking sections, while I incorporated the various markups into the final version. The process involved countless edits, with every word, sentence and implication pored over. We were determined that the content should be straightforward and concise.

Again, our engagement with the industry meant we were able to find the right people for tasks. Engaging Kieran Long, a journalist, was key to making the content more accessible, and he also helped us craft a confident voice:

> I was switching lots of language around – asking, 'Can we say this in a clear way using active verbs, using subject–verb–object grammar?'

Bringing something of a journalistic sensibility to it, I hoped, ensured you are immediately in the topic. One of the reasons it was easy to do that was that the guide was built on very high-quality research, a thoughtful sensibility, and officers felt confident with the material. When I asked, 'Can we put this in an active verb? Can we be less vague about this – can we be more specific?', you [Richa] would say, 'Yes, of course we can, because we know that this works. We are totally committed to this conclusion.' Our intention was, therefore, not to hide behind a passive voice but to make conclusions and draw these conclusions out. It would be lovely to imagine this is one of the reasons why it feels as if it has a relevance today, because it ended up very serious but very readable.[41]

Julia Park, Head of Housing Research at Levitt Bernstein, noted: 'The final narrative and phrasing really struck a chord with people – for example, "Home as place of retreat", "From street to front door".'[42]

We made a conscious decision at an early stage not to get bogged down in trying to illustrate the document. However, as with all DfL documents, the graphic quality was very important. The interim LHDG (Figure 4.4) marked a departure from Richard Rogers' preferred

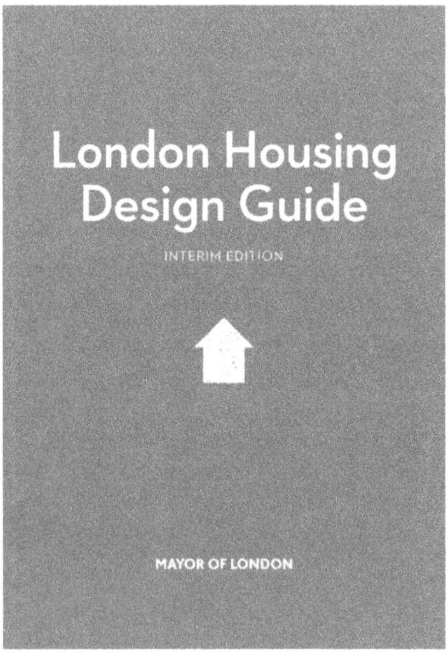

Figure 4.4 Cover, *London Housing Design Guide*, interim edition, 2010: clear, austere and easy to navigate. Source: GLA.

neon as used in most of the previous publications. We were well aware of the risk that the standards might not make it to the final policy stage, so we were keen that the document be taken seriously immediately on publication.

The graphic designers Atwork were given a brief to design the document to be as austere, sombre and clear as possible. Many users appreciated the 'Swissness' and 'austerity chic' of the final grey document. As Kieran Long noted later:

> Design for London were skilled at making documents that cut through, felt of their time but felt aspirational. If designers are not in the room, these documents take a completely different form and would be received and used differently as a result. You simply can't imagine the LDA coming up with it. It wouldn't have happened.[43]

The PR bluff

At the time of publication in August 2010, the interim LHDG had no material weight outside LDA developments and projects on mayoral land. In truth there was very little development that it applied to. Our months of compromise and close working with the GLA and HCA meant that we were hopeful (but not certain) that the standards would find a larger audience. The spectre of the Examination in Public on the draft Replacement London Plan (dRLP) loomed large as the forum in which the wider applicability of the standards would be decided.

We realised that a successful launch was important if the industry was to accept the LHDG as the future for housing in London. As with most DfL projects, we had very little budget and no press team to support us. We fought hard to get 1,000 copies printed and there was no scope for a big launch. Instead we listed everyone we wanted to influence – planners, policy-makers, those in the GLA 'family', house builders, developers, contributors and architects – and posted copies to all of them on the same day (personally stuffing copies in envelopes). Even though it was not policy, it helped that a copy of the document landed on the desks of key decision-makers, that it had 'Mayor of London' on the cover and that it contained very accessible and engaging content. The immediate uptake by the industry implies that the strategy worked. According to Hendrik Heyns, 'People have a copy on their desk and use it all the time. People take it as the bible.'[44]

Judgement Day: Examination in Public

The space standards were in the dRLP so were part of the Examination in Public process. On the day of the examination, the house builders' lobby was not as fierce as anticipated. Some of the concessions seemed to have pacified them, and the Home Builders Federation even conceded that the standards might bring greater clarity to the planning process. Subsequently the dRLP was adopted and a Housing SPG published containing the full suite of standards.

According to Julia Park:

> Opposition to the GLA standards (including the space standard) soon weakened and the vast majority of designers and developers quickly conceded that having a single set of rules was better than having different requirements in every borough. Because dwelling 'footprints' were interchangeable in terms of tenure, it also meant that designs could remain fluid for longer.[45]

We were braced for a negative reaction from the press but surprisingly this did not materialise. Much of the reporting was in fact jubilant and congratulatory. Headlines included: 'Boris is Brave to Think Bigger',[46] 'Room to Change the Way We Live'[47] and 'Standards Can See Off the Sharks'.[48]

London vernacular

The LHDG was deliberately agnostic on design aesthetics. The external characteristics of this new 'vernacular' are widely acknowledged to be brick cladding, deep reveals and recessed balconies, described by critics as 'Weetabix architecture'. Some detractors feel that the emergence of this typology has stifled creativity and narrowed the spectrum for designers. During the drafting process, there was a conscious effort to avoid entering into discussions about aesthetics and style. A conversation between Peter Bishop and Boris Johnson did touch on the question of appearance and vernacular:

> At one meeting the mayor suddenly became surprisingly excited about architecture, in particular ornamentation. He declared that all great architecture had used ornamentation and he wanted a new vernacular for London that reflected this [self-evident truth]. Apart from being wrong, this was not the purpose of the LHDG.

> In the ensuing conversation, I referenced the simplicity of the Georgian terraces of Islington [where he lived] as examples of a vernacular that grew out of the available materials, technology, and cultural and social values of the time. I also reminded him of the Artisans' Dwellings Act and the lasting importance of standards over style. The idea of a London vernacular was never mentioned again.[49]

Following this debate, we included in the interim LHDG a brief narrative about 'a new London vernacular', promoting the view that the 'best housing comes from robust guidelines in planning and regulation' and that 'London's housing should not be striving for "iconic" architecture, but should focus on great background architecture made of durable materials that weather well.'[50] As it happened, the publication of the guidance coincided with the revival of brickwork – coincidence rather than design. It is true that some of the standards had an impact on forms and massing. For instance, dual-aspect guidance affected configuration, and guidance on private outdoor space affected the proportions and arrangements of windows, apertures and so on. There was no intention to instigate a new stylistic trend; rather, there was an acknowledgement that, historically, where there have been clear ideas and thinking about how cities should develop, this has often seeded a vernacular. For example, various Housing Acts gave rise to Victorian housing in the UK, and zoning laws shaped the development of New York City. Mark Brearley recently commented:

> I think of a vernacular as something positive. A vernacular is understood, it's copied, not appraised afresh with each project. It's a way of doing something because it is obvious that it's the best way. A strong vernacular reflects a period of maturity, of running in a line, whereas we are currently going through a shift, a time of immaturity, of type invention, and such periods are usually filled with mistakes and uncertainties, until they find the way ahead that best fits with needs.
>
> London is clearly in a shift moment, figuring out challenges afresh, so it makes the emergence of a vernacular difficult. We would like there to be a London vernacular, but we aren't there yet. If people just carry on for another few decades, building in a confident way to house the city, if they do mix in the right way, configured use in the right way, then we could talk with pride of a vernacular. Worries

get raised about sameness, but even if all was built in exactly the same brick with exactly the same windows, it wouldn't trouble me, particularly as you don't have to live very long to realise that ways of building don't last forever. There is no need to worry about the world all becoming the same, it just doesn't happen like that.

Those wonderful chunks of eighteenth-century city, for example, that have worked so well through all kinds of evolutions and changes, that today we understand as finite and precious, admiring their long-forgotten confident vernacular – those were not seen in the same way in the nineteenth century. They saw what had been inherited as loathsome, plain and substandard, hating the Georgian city, just as in the sixties and seventies people loathed the Victorian city, because they were too close to it. My headline on this matter is: 'If you can get to a vernacular then you're laughing!' – laughing because a vernacular indicates a confident and easily growing city.[51]

Influence of the LHDG

The London mayor's London Housing Design Guide has arguably been the single most influential piece of design for housing in the capital so far this century.

– Finn Williams[52]

The reach and influence of the LHDG surpassed all expectations. From Scotland to Brighton, the interim LHDG has had a direct and far-reaching effect on local and regional policy. Many boroughs across the country adopted the standards immediately (for example, Ashford Borough Council adopted the standards in October 2011). In particular, the space standards have been incorporated into the Nationally Described Space Standard (NDSS) published in 2015. This too was a keenly fought battle and an unlikely outcome for a government-led Housing Standards Review which initially focused on reducing regulation. Julia Park later commented:

The government's review of housing standards was all about reining in over-zealous planning authorities – those who set high standards in local policy and guidance. It began in 2010, just two years after the global financial crisis that had seen house building stall across the UK, and the new Conservative/Lib Dem coalition government was desperate to 'get Britain building again'. The

> mantra from ministers was deregulation, removing the barriers that developers claimed were holding them back.
>
> London hadn't experienced quite the same setback in terms of falling supply, sales and demand as the rest of the country, and having published the ambitious and comprehensive LHDG just the year before, the GLA was in no mood to give it up, or even compromise. Boris Johnson had been Mayor of London since 2008, and nervous about rocking that particular boat, the DCLG [the Department for Communities and Local Government, later renamed as the Ministry of Housing, Communities and Local Government] was minded to leave London out altogether. But you can't simply delete the capital city from a nationwide review, and many of us knew that London's involvement would be vital if we were to prevent the 'race to the bottom' which seemed to be the implication of the exercise.
>
> So the GLA was invited to join the industry-wide working groups tasked with 'streamlining local standards', albeit a little late. The review took five years in total and there is absolutely no doubt that the quality, clarity and almost universal popularity of the LHDG, coupled with the GLA's steadfast refusal to give way, prevented the national review from becoming a national disaster, in terms of housing quality.[53]

Critics and supporters alike agree that the LHDG has been hugely influential. Some of its achievements concern championing an ideological shift in how we as a society think about housing. In terms of the cross-tenure debate, government standards have historically only applied to publicly funded housing. Andrew Drury of HATC recently commented:

> There was a deep-rooted cultural feeling until the mid-2000s that there should be space standards for publicly funded housing but not for private housing. The reasons given were that publicly funded housing is more intensely lived in; that private housing is more loosely lived in, with a lower household density. But this is not the case over the life of the dwelling. Often, over the decades, existing housing stock is converted to offices, houses in multiple occupation, shops and vice versa. We don't know now what the use of the dwelling is going to be in 50, 70, 90 years' time. People exercising their 'right to buy' and then selling on means that publicly funded housing becomes market housing. Housing associations

and others buying up street properties and refurbishing them turns privately owned housing into 'public' housing. Tenure and use ebbs and flows over the decades.

> How can we use rules for something as fundamental to the dwelling as space, but tailored only to one household type, when all we know with any certainty is that over the life of the building it will have more than one household type in it? We made that case strongly in our 2006 report, and the GLA accepted it. The LHDG space requirements applied to all housing and it was the first time this position was adopted by an organisation that affected national thinking and behaviour. Well done, the GLA.[54]

In addition, the guidance took a clear position that the 'design of buildings should be "tenure blind" whereby homes for affordable rent, intermediate forms of tenure and private sale are indistinguishable from one another'.[55] As Mark Brearley commented, 'It is what we hoped for, but we weren't expecting it. Why was cross-tenure application important? Because it is fairer. If something is desirable, it is desirable to all.'[56]

Other achievements are more tangible. According to Hendrik Heyns, 'The LHDG has changed the way the industry approaches housing in London. Beyond the dwelling and housing block, it fundamentally changes the way streets work.'[57] There is also now a requirement for new dwellings to have private outdoor space. For Rowan Moore:

> It's a good thing to have more balcony space, but I like the fact that you can walk down the street with a new housing development on it and it has balconies facing the street whereas before it wouldn't – it probably would have had Juliet balconies if anything. Even if there is nobody on the balcony, it creates a sense of connection between the interior and exterior, between the public and private sphere, which is a modestly good thing to have in a city.[58]

Of course, with the positives come the negatives. Minimums fast become maximums and there is always the risk that rules will be applied doggedly even when not appropriate. We are aware that the document was not all-encompassing and there is plenty of room for improvement. There have been lots of compromises during its development and since then. Although the space standards have endured, many other key requirements have been watered down or lost over time. For example, the original standard for ceiling heights to be 2.5 m has been superseded by the NDSS requirement for 2.3 m, and the requirement to include furnished layouts is under threat as the GLA may be forced by the DCLG to remove this standard. At the time of writing (2019), the current Housing SPG is weaker on quality than the 2012 Housing SPG, with most of the 'best practice' standards having been removed.

Conclusion

Some important lessons were learnt during the process of developing the LHDG:

- *You need champions.* Not every project has a political champion from the outset. The DfL team worked hard to build a compelling case and craft an irresistible argument to deliver to the mayor and his advisors. We played the long game, building support and momentum for the project among politicians and officers.
- *Ask for less, end up with more.* It is often best to get something half-decent on the table and then build up from there. This might go against the accepted rules of bargaining in business, but pushing through change in the risk-averse public sector requires a different approach. You can gain trust with a modest but compelling pitch and build on this once people are on board.
- *Do the homework and you win.* This is a spin on Mark Brearley's adage 'Do the drawings and you win'. With policy work, it was about having robust and credible research that we could defend in the face of fierce opposition.
- *Create shortcuts to the politicians.* The more hierarchical structure under Boris Johnson's administration meant that we lost some of our 'shortcuts' to the mayor, which directly impacted on some projects. It is important that the people doing the thinking are able to communicate with the politicians.
- *It helps to be transparent.* Much policy-making is shrouded in secrecy. We sustained an open dialogue with the industry and stakeholders. It meant that the emerging policy was fully informed by their feedback, so that there were no big surprises when it was finally published.
- *If you are developing policy about design, then you need designers in the room.* Clearly, it makes a huge difference to the output of policy development if the designers who will use the policy are involved from the outset.

History teaches us that these types of endeavour take a long time and considerable effort to develop and put in place, and that they are always under threat and can easily be eroded by changes in leadership and ideology. As Julia Park commented:

> Previous major standards (including those produced after the First and Second World Wars, and the Parker Morris standards) were all lost due to new political ideology. … Housing standards, particularly space standards, will remain vulnerable. We'll always need advocates to defend them.[59]

Others, such as Rowan Moore, are more hopeful: 'It's always easy for politicians to kill off policy. However, the headline "I want to lower housing standards" is not a good one.'[60]

Kieran Long shared some interesting views on this topic:

> Maybe space standards are only political if, as a society, you haven't thought it through. … Of course, a group of housing developers could come and say this is limiting our freedom of choice, our action and our output. I would hope that it is possible to get to a point where some of these topics are no longer political, to get to a point where they are accepted as the tool we have to preserve quality in the most important building type we have in our city, which is housing.
>
> Any statement of quality is always vulnerable. Anything that stands for quality is always vulnerable to the banal critique that 'this is constraining my capitalist rights'. Housing cannot only be left to capitalism. This doesn't mean you have to have a command economy or even social housing, but it does mean we need some set of values around which we can agree. Housing is the primary tool we can use to build the city. If it's just left to the market, it will not provide decent homes for the widest range of people to live in.[61]

I hope the optimists are right – that there is now acceptance of the idea that something as important as housing should benefit from having some modest standards and that these standards can improve quality. Implementation has proved that the policy has not reduced housing output, which means that the prevailing argument pre-LHDG is no longer as compelling. Recent changes to permitted development rights (PDRs) that allow office-to-residential conversions provide all the proof we need that without London's housing standards, new homes could be much smaller than they were before the LHDG was introduced. Where the SPG cannot be applied because of PDRs, we are now seeing new flats of 13 m^2 and others without windows.

The legacy is visible throughout London. It is easy to spot a post-LHDG building. On a personal level, I feel proud to observe a new development being built with balconies and usable private outdoor spaces. Once residents have moved in, with plant pots and outdoor furniture, I can be confident that similar positive outcomes exist internally as well. It is good to know that we had a hand in achieving that.

The project proves that thoughtful policy work can shape a city for the better. The LHDG has delivered a better standard of housing for the average Londoner. Let us hope the politicians can see the value of this work, protect the hard-won victories from the wolves at the door and build on the legacy for future generations.

Notes

1 Moore 2016, p. 265.
2 Design for London 2010.
3 Ministry of Housing and Local Government 1961, p. iv.
4 Ministry of Housing and Local Government 1961, p. 2.
5 Conversation with David Birkbeck, Design for Homes, March 2019.
6 Conversation with Rowan Moore, journalist, January 2019.
7 Urban Task Force 2005, p. 6.
8 Whitehead 2012, p. 12.
9 Architecture and Urbanism Unit 2003.
10 Anon, CABE blog.
11 Sheridan, Visscher and Meijer 2003.
12 Sheridan 2004.
13 Commission for Architecture and the Built Environment 2010, p. 7.
14 HATC 2006, p. 5.
15 Conversation with Andrew Drury, HATC, 4 February 2019.
16 Conversation with Mark Brearley, 26 February 2019.
17 Conversation with Peter Bishop and Rowan Moore, 16 January 2019.
18 Conversation with Mark Brearley, 26 February 2019.
19 Deborah Mathieson worked at the A+UU and DfL on housing policy and design.
20 Conversation with Deborah Mathieson, 27 March 2019.
21 Conversation with Kieran Long, journalist, ex-DfL, now Director of ArkDes, Stockholm, 16 January 2019.
22 Design for Homes 2007.
23 Conversation with David Birkbeck, Design for Homes, March 2019.
24 Conversation with Peter Bishop, November 2019. The HCA was the Homes and Communities Agency.
25 Marcus and Sarkissian 1986.
26 Smithson and Smithson 1970.
27 Conversation with Alex Ely, Alex Ely Architects, 8 March 2019.
28 Conversation with Alex Ely, Alex Ely Architects, 8 March 2019.
29 Conversation with Mark Brearley, 26 February 2019.
30 Conversation with Peter Bishop, November 2019.
31 For further discussion on DfL's use of procurement to get better design results, see Chapter 7.
32 Conversation with Hendrik Heyns, partner, Allies and Morrison, 13 February 2019.
33 Conversation with Mark Brearley, 26 February 2019.

34 Conversation with Peter Bishop, January 2019.
35 Conversation with Kieran Long, 16 January 2019.
36 Conversation with John Lett, Senior Planner, GLA, 5 February 2019.
37 Conversation with Rowan Moore, journalist, 16 January 2019.
38 Mayor of London 2012.
39 GVA Grimley et al. 2010, p. 4.
40 In a conversation at the time with Peter Bishop, the London Director of Barratt Homes reported that the St Andrews Hospital site at Bromley-by-Bow (discussed earlier in the chapter) was one of the group's best-selling schemes. He recognised that the design quality that had been insisted upon by DfL as part of the procurement process was paying dividends. Barratt London became an ally and advocate of good design on later schemes.
41 Conversation with Kieran Long, journalist, ex-DfL, now Director of ArkDes, Stockholm, 16 January 2019.
42 Conversation with Julia Park, Levitt Bernstein, 16 January 2019...
43 Conversation with Kieran Long, 16 January 2019.
44 Conversation with Hendrik Heyns, partner, Allies and Morrison, 13 February 2019.
45 Park 2017, p. 42.
46 Woodman 2010.
47 Long 2010.
48 Glancey 2010.
49 Conversation with Peter Bishop, November 2019.
50 Design for London 2010, pp. 5 and 6.
51 Conversation with Mark Brearley, 26 February 2019.
52 Comment by Finn Williams, Regeneration Area Manager, GLA.
53 Conversation with Julia Park, 16 January 2019.
54 Conversation with Andrew Drury, HATC, 4 February 2019.
55 Design for London 2010, p. 30.
56 Conversation with Mark Brearley, 26 February 2019.
57 Conversation with Hendrik Heyns, partner, Allies and Morrison, 13 February 2019.
58 Conversation with Rowan Moore, 16 January 2019.
59 Conversation with Julia Park, 16 January 2019.
60 Conversation with Rowan Moore, 16 January 2019.
61 Conversation with Kieran Long, 16 January 2019.

Bibliography

Architecture and Urbanism Unit, *Housing for a Compact City*, London: Greater London Authority, 2003.

Commission for Architecture and the Built Environment, *Improving the Design of New Housing: What Role for Standards?*, London: Commission for Architecture and the Built Environment, 2010.

Design for Homes, *Recommendations for Living at Superdensity*, London: Design for Homes, 2007.

Design for London, *London Housing Design Guide*, interim edn, London: London Development Agency, 2010. https://www.london.gov.uk/sites/default/files/interim_london_housing_design_guide.pdf (accessed 27 July 2020).

Glancey, Jonathan, 'Standards Can See Off the Sharks', *Building Design*, 3 September 2010.

GVA Grimley et al. 'Draft London Housing Design Guide: Cost and Delivery Impact Assessment', pre-publication draft, London Development Agency, 2010. https://files.cambridge.gov.uk/public/ldf/coredocs/RD-H/RD-H-180.pdf (accessed 7 October 2020).

HATC, *Housing Space Standards: A Report by HATC Limited for the Greater London Authority*, London: Greater London Authority, 2006. https://www.hatc.co.uk/wp-content/uploads/GLA_Space_Standards_Report.pdf (accessed 29 July 2020).

Long, Kieran, 'Room to Change the Way We Live', *Evening Standard*, 18 August 2010.

Marcus, Clare Cooper, and Sarkissian, Wendy, *Housing as if People Mattered: Site Design Guidelines for Medium-Density Family Housing*, Berkeley, CA: University of California Press, 1986.

Mayor of London, *London Housing SPG*, London: Greater London Authority, 2012.

Ministry of Housing and Local Government, *Homes for Today and Tomorrow* (Report of the Parker Morris Committee), London: HMSO, 1961.
Moore, Rowan, *Slow Burn City: London in the Twenty-First Century*, London: Pan Macmillan, 2016.
Park, Julia, *One Hundred Years of Housing Space Standards: What Now?*, [n.p.]: housingspace standards.co.uk, 2017. https://levittbernstein.co.uk/site/assets/files/2682/one_hundred_years_of_housing_space_standards.pdf (accessed 29 July 2020).
Sheridan, Linda, *Comparative Study of the Control and Promotion of Quality in Housing in Europe*, London: Office of the Deputy Prime Minister, 2004.
Sheridan, Linda, Visscher, Henk J., and Meijer, Frits M., *Building Regulations in Europe, Part II: A Comparison of the Technical Requirements in Eight European Countries*, Delft, The Netherlands: University of Delft, 2003.
Smithson, Alison, and Smithson, Peter, *Ordinariness and Light: Urban Theories 1952–1960 and Their Application in a Building Project 1963–1970*, Cambridge, MA: MIT Press, 1970.
Urban Task Force, *Towards a Strong Urban Renaissance: An Independent Report by Members of the Urban Task Force Chaired by Lord Rogers of Riverside*, London: HMSO, 2005. http://image.guardian.co.uk/sys-files/Society/documents/2005/11/22/UTF_final_report.pdf (accessed 24 February 2020).
Whitehead, Christine, *The Density Debate: A Personal View* [London: London School of Economics and Political Science, Geography and Environment, 2012]. http://eprints.lse.ac.uk/63375/1/whitehead_the_density_debate_author.pdf (accessed 27 July 2020).
Woodman, Ellis, 'Boris is Brave to Think Bigger', *Building Design*, 27 August 2010.

5
Peopled landscapes

Peter Bishop

Chapter 1 identifies the importance of the Urban Task Force report[1] in setting in place a framework for urban practice – one that was heavily influenced by European models of thinking, in particular by Barcelona. One of the fundamental rationales for the city is human interaction and this is greatly reduced in a city based on the automobile. Public spaces, parks, streets and squares are the mainstay of civic life. They are places for exchange, encounter and protest. In a good city they are also places to linger, relax and gossip. In many ways one can judge a city by its streets and public spaces.

In the foreword for the *Global Public Space Toolkit* for UN-Habitat,[2] Joan Clos writes: 'Public spaces contribute to defining the cultural, social, economic and political functions of cities. They continue to be the first element to mark the status of a place from a chaotic and unplanned settlement to a well-established town or city.'[3] It is valuable to understand and evaluate public spaces through the lens of their social, civic and environmental importance.

The Urban Task Force report was based on a set of values that included environmental responsibility and social wellbeing. Long before the present focus on climate change, it identified 'the ecological imperative' as one of the key drivers for changes to urban thinking. Public space was seen as not only a 'good thing' but also an essential ingredient of urban strategy if the city was to be both environmentally responsible and resilient. In a century where global temperatures are set to rise by at least two degrees and where extreme climate events will become more frequent, the importance of public space is heightened. In denser and more compact cities, open spaces provide vital places for relaxation and recreation for the urban population. The relationship between the city and nature needed to be redefined in new city policies. The report identified urban spaces as a key element of civic life and community cohesion. It described the importance of public space: 'Safe, well managed and uncluttered public spaces provide the vital "glue" between buildings and play a crucial role in strengthening communities.'[4] It recommended that local authorities establish public realm strategies to set out a clear hierarchy of open space provision, management and maintenance. This was turned into practice in some of the early programmes of the Architecture and Urbanism Unit (A+UU) and then Design for London (DfL).

This chapter briefly explores the theories of public space and landscape urbanism and examines some of the ways in which these were applied in London. In particular, it looks at how the ideas from best practice were brought in and applied in London through the team's public realm and regional landscape projects.

The importance of public space

The Task Force's ideas were not new. There had been extensive interest in the public realm and urban landscape from various practitioners going back to the 1970s at least. In the European context, much older traditions – the square, the piazza, the common and the municipal park – had been staples of urban design before the advent of mass car ownership. Although mass car ownership had only really been a factor in European cities in the immediate postwar period, the car had distorted urban strategies, dominated the agenda and led to the virtual destruction of large swathes of the fabric of many cities. In London, attempts to build inner-city 'motorway boxes' had caused such visible destruction to historic areas that it had led to widespread protest and had been abandoned by the end of the 1970s.[5]

Jane Jacobs' work in New York focused on the then radical idea that the centres of cities should be designed around the needs of people, with streets that were walkable and safe and had a mix of uses. Jacobs had organised local opposition to protect neighbourhoods from comprehensive 'slum' clearance programmes, in particular attempts by Robert Moses to drive major roads through inner-city neighbourhoods. She was instrumental in the eventual cancellation of the Lower Manhattan Expressway, which would have passed directly through SoHo and Little Italy.

Jan Gehl's work in Copenhagen is another example of a reaction against the car, but this time driven by someone in the city administration rather than by activists. His studies of public space in 1968 underlined their popularity and value. A programme of pedestrianisation had already commenced in 1962 with the main shopping street, Strøget. Gehl defined the functions of public space in cities as: *Necessary* – to move, *Optional* – to stop, and *Great* – to enjoy.[6] The number of car-free streets in the city centre increased sixfold from 1962 to 2000.[7] Importantly, the programme, its impacts and public reactions were monitored over the years by the School of Architecture at the Royal Danish Academy of Fine Arts. This provided an objective research basis to support the continuation of the initiative.[8] Parking was reduced by 2–3 per cent per year as city streets and spaces were progressively turned over to cyclists and pedestrians.[9] Gehl later applied his methodology in Australia to Melbourne city centre, which in the middle of the 1980s was in decline. New housing was built, and streets were pedestrianised. Between 1994 and 2004 there was a 39 per cent increase in pedestrian activity in the city centre and the night-time economy doubled.[10]

The importance of good public space is now accepted by most urban practitioners. Public space comprises those areas of the city that are commonly owned, publicly managed and accessible to all. It provides places where citizens meet, exchange goods and ideas, debate, linger, play and celebrate. It is the place for protest and in the last resort a place of refuge for the homeless. It is where the civic life of a democratic society takes place. Public space also includes streets which are the arteries of movement in the city. This conflict has ushered in a debate about the relative importance of vehicular traffic against pedestrian movement. Highways offer the greatest latent resource for new public spaces in the city.

Increasingly, however, the simple division between public space and private space is being blurred by intermediate spaces or 'privileged' space[11] where the public has access under particular terms including payment. Under this definition cinemas, shopping malls, theme parks, hotel lobbies, bookshops and cafes have become important intermediate spaces that also harbour civic life. Oldenburg talks about 'third places' that can 'host the regular, voluntary, informal, and happily anticipated gatherings of individuals beyond the realms of home and work'.[12] These places are neutral ground and have no formal membership requirements. They are in essence convivial and comfortable spaces. In contrast, 'corporate' spaces, where public access is allowed under certain conditions (including dress code and social background), offer another aspect of urban life. They include the plazas and street networks of office complexes, gated housing and shopping precincts that are becoming a ubiquitous part of city life. Restrictions on the use of such spaces are essentially undemocratic. That said, the threat to public space in the city is not restricted to private developments. The monetarisation of public space by city authorities and the growing restrictions posed by security, policing and bylaws also present growing threats. In this respect, the planning system has an important responsibility in maintaining open access in our cities.

Public space in London

The ideas of car restraint have been embedded in London's planning since the 1960s, when parking enforcement was first established across the city and planning policy started to restrict parking in new commercial developments. More recently Transport for London (TfL) made the transition from a highway to a transport authority, with highway space being reallocated to buses and pedestrians. Congestion charging was introduced in central London in 2002, resulting in a 15 per cent reduction in traffic. These measures, which were a direct result of mayoral policy, created the opportunity for programmes to improve public spaces.

The other problem facing London was serious underinvestment in the public realm. Following the abolition of the Greater London Council (GLC), there had been no city government between 1986 and 2000. Moreover, their opposition to the Thatcher government, where they had borrowed money to maintain their spending programmes, had left many central London boroughs so severely strapped for cash that basic services, including street maintenance and cleaning, had come close to collapse. While the boroughs were beginning to recover by 2000, there was still a significant backlog of maintenance work on London's streets and no money for new investment in public space. In any event, the capacity for new design initiatives for the public realm had been lost with the staff whose jobs had disappeared.

By 2000, when the Greater London Authority (GLA) was established, it was clear that London was well behind other European cities such as Copenhagen, Paris, Lyon and Berlin in terms of the quality of its streets and public spaces. The World Squares for All programme was an early initiative to redress this imbalance. It aimed to transform Leicester Square, Trafalgar Square and Parliament Square into attractive city spaces.[13] Norman Foster's scheme remodelled Trafalgar Square and closed the road in front of the National Gallery. It was opened in 2003 to much public acclaim and set the scene for further projects.[14]

100 Public Spaces: brokering and financing a public realm programme

One of the earliest programmes launched by the A+UU was the Mayor's 100 Public Spaces programme. This was inspired by Jean Clos's public space programme in Barcelona, which had received international acclaim. The 100 Public Spaces programme sought to identify opportunities to create new public space, especially in poorer areas where it was lacking. There was no funding for the programme, nor were there ever 100 public spaces – the name was simply a brand designed to engender public interest and political support.

New public spaces, particularly where road closures are required and inter-agency partnerships brokered, take time and are not well suited to a marketing approach that seeks to capture the public imagination without fully explaining the complexities of the processes involved. This was an early lesson for DfL and it adapted its approach to other programmes accordingly. One of the successes of the programme was that it built relationships with other agencies, in particular TfL. The new commissioner of TfL, Bob Kiley, was a personal friend of Richard Rogers, the mayor's architecture advisor, and this contact had given the A+UU unprecedented access to TfL project staff. This access began to influence the procurement and management of design teams, leading to a culture change in some parts of TfL.

When the A+UU set up the 100 Public Spaces initiative, it had no funding of its own and had to rely on others to come forward with projects and money. The aims of the programme were:

- the improvement of pedestrian mobility (providing the space to move around)
- the promotion of good design
- the creation of social value
- the cultural activation of spaces.

The A+UU could offer support and an ability to work with other organisations to broker partnerships and access money. The programme was launched with a call for project ideas from TfL and the boroughs. The bids had to identify funding sources and include a commitment to the long-term management of the new space. Despite the shortage of public money, there were still some funding pots that could be accessed. Regeneration programmes such as the Single Regeneration Budget (1994–2003) had made small amounts of money available to local authorities; the London Development Agency (LDA) had capital funds that could be directed to local initiatives, including public space projects; and TfL had significant resources. TfL was a particularly useful starting point for resources as many of the early schemes were on the public highway. With TfL's move away from highway construction, money was available if one knew where to look. 'Road safety' budgets were particularly flexible, as were the annual transport grants to the boroughs. At the borough level, there was often scope to use maintenance budgets to part-fund new works, and Section 106 monies[15] could be used to top up project budgets.

Some of the boroughs had already started to manipulate budgets creatively to fund new public-realm works. Camden had instigated a 'Boulevard Project' – a rolling programme to renew all pavements in the borough to a very high-standard specification that allowed mechanical washing and cleaning.[16] Peter Bishop at Camden, with University College London and Terry Farrell, developed this into an integrated plan for Bloomsbury. The theory behind the project was that over a 50-year period there would be numerous incremental and random decisions on street design, parking, bus stops, street trees and paving. These, by their very nature, were piecemeal and would therefore fail to optimise either movement or streetscape quality. Camden recognised that over a 25-year period it would renew most of the streetscape in the Bloomsbury area. If this was to be directed by a rational plan and with a standard specification, then a high-quality public realm could be pieced together using day-to-day budgets (effectively for nothing). In later projects in Camden, the Bedford and Shaftesbury estates contributed capital funding to top up highway maintenance programmes in order to achieve a comprehensive and high-quality streetscape.

In Kensington and Chelsea, Councillor Daniel Moylan had experimented with the concept of shared space that he had seen in other countries. He championed the renewal of Kensington High Street with high-quality paving and simple street furniture. In defiance of the advice of his professional staff, guard railings around pedestrian crossings were removed and bicycle racks were placed on the central reservation. The effect over two years was a 44 per cent reduction in accidents compared to a London average of 17 per cent.

The 100 Public Spaces programme commenced with 10 schemes:

1. Lewisham town centre (Lewisham)
2. Windrush Square, Brixton (Lambeth)
3. Gillett Square (Hackney)

4. Coulsdon High Street (Croydon)
5. Euston underpass (Camden)
6. Rainham village centre (Havering)
7. Embankment Gardens (Westminster)
8. Sloane Square (Kensington & Chelsea)
9. Lower Marsh (Lambeth)
10. Exhibition Road (Kensington & Chelsea).

Those boroughs that responded did so for the kudos of involvement in a programme that was championed by the new mayor and his advisor Richard Rogers, and on the understanding that help and money might be leveraged in from other organisations. The borough would take the responsibility for project delivery using architects appointed with help from the A+UU.

The establishment of DfL added weight and impetus to the scheme. When the third round of the programme was launched, 34 new spaces (Figure 5.1) had been identified. New projects were added to the programme, including the following:

11. Southall (Ealing)
12. Harrow on the Hill (Harrow)
13. Tottenham Hale (Haringey)
14. A4 Green Corridor (Kensington & Chelsea)
15. Barking town centre (Barking & Dagenham)
16. Grahame Park, Colindale (Barnet)
17. Aldgate roundabout (Tower Hamlets)
18. Gallions (Newham)
19. Mitcham Fair Green (Merton)
20. Little Wormwood Scrubs (Hammersmith)
21. Dagenham Heathway to the Thames (Barking)
22. Acton Town Square (Ealing)
23. Canning Town (Newham)
24. Ealing Broadway (Ealing)
25. Wembley Stadium Spaces (Brent)
26. Bow Church (Tower Hamlets)
27. Gants Hill (Redbridge)
28. North Street, Romford (Havering)
29. Pontoon Dock (Newham)
30. Highbury Corner (Islington)
31. Potters Fields (Southwark)
32. Kender Triangle, New Cross (Lewisham)
33. Erith town centre (Bexley)
34. West India Quay (Tower Hamlets).

Figure 5.1 The Mayor's 100 Public Spaces programme. Source: DfL/GLA.

These were opportunities to create public space from the fabric of the city by closing roads, as in Brixton and Woolwich (Figures 5.2 and 5.3), and discovering small areas of leftover space, as in Dagenham (Figure 5.4). The spaces would be well designed and have in place robust management regimes that would guarantee their future. Many were in deprived neighbourhoods that were deficient in public spaces, such as Windrush Square in Brixton (designed by Gross Max). Others, such as the shared surfaces in Exhibition Road (designed by Dixon Jones), were in areas of central London that had a high footfall. In some cases, such as in Union Street, Southwark, a simple intervention to reconfigure a road junction offered an opportunity for a new civic space. This project also involved the owner of the local cafe and paid for the pink chairs and tables that allowed him to activate the space (Figure 5.5). These were not *grands projets*. They were tactical and opportunistic interventions. The work was publicised in the Civilising Spaces exhibition that was held at the National Theatre in 2010. Alongside this programme there were other complementary initiatives, including the Streetscape Design Manual (Chapter 1) and Every Detail, which highlighted the importance of attention to detail and finish.

Figure 5.2 New public space in Brixton. Source: DfL/GLA.

Figure 5.3 New public space in Woolwich. Source: DfL/GLA.

The absence of a dedicated funding stream did mean that the projects took a long time to broker. The A+UU and DfL had to fight numerous battles, especially over the use of restricted highway widths and shared surfaces. The team learnt the importance of seeing urban design from the perspective of highway engineers. Most of the schemes were

Figure 5.4 Dagenham Heathway to the Thames. Source: DfL/GLA.

Figure 5.5 Union Street, Southwark. Source: DfL/GLA.

implemented.[17] The schemes that failed did so due to lack of money or insuperable difficulties on the ground. However, the most common cause of failure was political change. A public-realm scheme that involves significant highway changes can take up to three years to brief, design, obtain consents for and then procure. It might also take nine months to construct and might entail considerable disruption. Programmes might be championed by an individual politician, but a degree of continuity is required to see them through. Opposition, particularly from motorists, can sway a faint-hearted politician. That said, eight out of the first ten schemes were implemented, as have been the majority of other schemes.[18]

An approach to public space provision that provides an interesting contrast to London was that pioneered by Janette Sadik-Khan, New York's Transportation Commissioner (2007–13). Sadik-Khan closed sections of Broadway to create new public spaces at Herald Square and Times Square. The difference was that these highways were closed overnight, the surfaces were painted, and pot plants and tables and chairs were put out. New Yorkers woke up to find that their city had changed and by midday most liked it. This was a brave and brilliant project[19] that impressed DfL staff when they heard about it. There were regrets that they had not thought of taking the same approach.

London's Great Outdoors: a new mayor but the same old programme

The biggest challenge to established DfL programmes came with the election of a new mayor in 2008. London government was ill-prepared for political change. Richard Rogers resigned as mayoral advisor and the support for DfL ebbed away. An early casualty was the plan to part-pedestrianise Parliament Square – the third and undoubtedly most difficult of the World Squares for All programme. The project had been commenced late in Livingstone's second term as mayor (with the expectation of a third term). It was always going to be contentious. As the square represents the centre of government, every MP and member of the House of Lords was likely to have an opinion on its future, as were those involved in the Supreme Court and Westminster Abbey. The project needed to incorporate appropriate security measures and cater for ceremonial events such as the State Opening of Parliament, royal weddings, funerals and coronations. The 1950s design by George Grey Wornum was protected as a historic landscape and the politics involved in moving any of the statues would be Byzantine. Finally, it was located in the borough of Westminster, which saw little reason to change the existing scheme (particularly as any diverted traffic would almost certainly go into streets where some of their councillors lived). Any government team concerned for their future careers would have steered well clear of it. DfL saw this as a brilliant opportunity to do something radical.

Fosters had already produced an outline scheme. The working proposal was to close the arm of the square next to Westminster Abbey, thus connecting the abbey precinct to the square. There were three immediate problems. The first was that the abbey boundary railings were listed, so any attempt to fully integrate the two domains was a non-starter. The second was the displacement of traffic. TfL had modelled this and concluded that part-closure was achievable, but that traffic would be displaced into other boroughs. The third problem was that an accessible square would attract up to 36 million people a year. Clearly the use of grass would not be an option in the design.

The project started with a long battle between DfL and TfL, who had already appointed an architect from their approved list. DfL's argument was that a scheme of this importance required a specialist landscape architect and a good one. Eventually, the architects who had been appointed were removed from the contract and Günther Vogt, a top landscape practice from Switzerland, were appointed. The symbolism of the square dominated the discussions. Parliament Square was seen to represent the heart of democratic government in the UK. How could this be represented while dealing with security and the anticipated increase in tourism? Could the statues be re-curated, what would happen to the mature trees and to what extent could the historic landscape be incorporated? The outline Vogt scheme retained little of the Wornum scheme, arguing that the surfaces were worn out and beyond repair, that grass would not survive and that in any case the 1950s scheme had been a response (albeit a good one) to the creation of a traffic gyratory that was no longer required. Vogt proposed using Scottish sandstone, slightly elevated in the centre where there would be a lightly defined circular sitting area. Most of the trees would be retained, but some of the statues would have to be moved and a specialist curator would be brought in to advise on this.

The proposals were presented to Ken Livingstone, who was unconvinced and reluctant to push the scheme forward with a mayoral election coming up.[20] The upshot was that the scheme was deferred until after the election. Johnson, as the new incoming mayor, rejected the whole notion of touching Parliament Square. The scheme was scrapped at that point and there have been no attempts to bring back any new proposals.

Contractual and funding commitments required the public space programme to continue, albeit with a much lower profile. With the transfer of DfL to the LDA (see Chapter 2), a long-term future seemed to have been secured. The team also had access to LDA funding. Stripped of its role on the Olympics and under pressure from the new mayoral administration, the LDA had a new board and was looking for new ideas.

Figure 5.6 The Mayor's Great Spaces programme. Source: DfL/GLA.

With many of the LDA's programmes discredited, DfL was able to resuscitate the programme as London's Great Outdoors – a manifesto for 'Great Spaces' (Figure 5.6). In this, it found a new ally and champion in Daniel Moylan, an enthusiast of urban design and public spaces and now the de facto chair of TfL.

'London's Great Outdoors' was deliberately written as a mayoral manifesto in the first person, with headings such as 'My ambition for London's public space'. The language was clear and readable. The document was more than a repackaging of the 100 Public Spaces programme. It specifically brought in objectives concerning climate change, carbon emissions, health and wellbeing, and reaffirmed the importance of public space as an essential ingredient of London as a global city. It was subdivided into Better Streets, and Better Green and Water Spaces. The programme also developed concepts related to use and the promotion of public space for informal activities and for events such as marathons and festivals. This included a clear political commitment to close streets and host car-free days and other temporary events. For existing parks, it challenged the long-accepted views on night-time closures. Finally, it set out existing and proposed projects with identified lead authorities, budgets and timescales. Subtitled 'Practical Steps', it was liked by the new mayoral administration, and also by TfL and the LDA, who were tasked with delivery.

Signed by the mayor, the document was published in November 2009. It committed the mayor to procuring good architects to design public-realm schemes and to continuing the East London Green Grid and the Street Tree programme. The mayor also publicly pledged to fund public space over a three-year period. The new programme also gave DfL licence to work with the Olympics and Crossrail to create new opportunities to connect neighbourhoods. The document spelled out the mayor's desire to invest in outer London boroughs and set out a series of criteria for determining investment priorities. These had been written by DfL (with the full agreement of Daniel Moylan) and were designed to change the budgetary allocation criteria of both the LDA and TfL to its advantage.

As a result, the importance of public space was re-established as a mayoral priority and this gave access to new funding, albeit through official channels and bidding processes. The Mayor's Great Spaces programme was published in 2009 and identified a new list of 36 projects. Many of these were in outer London (Kingston, Bromley, Enfield, Barnet, Havering and Sutton), where DfL had not previously had access. The extension of the programme to outer London posed new challenges concerning low-density suburbs that often had failing local centres. In many respects the new direction of the programme suited the interests of the team. These were the difficult everyday places where many Londoners lived and worked. At this period the public spaces programme became part of the broader strategies to reinvigorate high streets and town centres (Chapter 3). Finally, it should be recognised that the change in emphasis to outer London did not preclude work and investment in central London or Labour-controlled areas. In this respect the mayor's team were generally open to ideas rather than focused on pursuing an overtly political programme of investment redistribution. The single biggest change was that the programme was to be driven by opportunity (the leverage of funds and inward investment) rather than by need and indices of deprivation.

Peopled landscapes and green grids

London is unlike other European cities in the interrelationship between its built and unbuilt forms – its urban landscapes. This is a product of its history. The rapid growth of London, no longer bounded by defensive walls, incorporated open parklands and other hard-to-develop, leftover spaces. Its patterns of landownership and its postwar industrial decline also left industrial wastelands where nature could regain a foothold. Open space constitutes 40 per cent of London's area (compared, for example, to 1.5 per cent of the area of Istanbul), and Londoners enjoy around 27 square metres of open space per person (in Buenos Aires it is

Figure 5.7 London as a garden city. Source: London Plan, 2016, GLA.

1.9 square metres). Adding in private spaces – mainly from residential gardens, agricultural land and other land such as allotments – shows that almost 80 per cent of London's area is not built on. London is the true garden city (Figure 5.7).

Open space comes in many forms: the Royal Parks, football pitches on places such as Hackney Marshes, the great commons of south London and the many municipal parks. The nomenclature of London spaces explains the many subtle distinctions in their history and use. There are commons, greens, fields, downs, marshes, heaths, forests, gardens and squares. London's open spaces form an open patchwork within the city. Added to this are London's *terrains vagues* – the leftover areas of land under flyovers, along the sides of railway lines and in cemeteries, disused gravel and chalk pits and areas reclaimed by nature on industrial sites. This rich network offered an opportunity to restructure and tie back together parts of the city, in particular in east London.

The late nineteenth century saw the establishment of municipal parks for the urban population and the early twentieth century saw a new exploration of the relationship between the city and its landscape. Raymond Unwin had pioneered the concept of green belts and proposed a green girdle from the Chilterns to the North Downs, connected by ‘green spokes’ to central London. Abercrombie in the 1944 Greater London Plan proposed establishing a far wider green belt around London, designating the Lea Valley as a regional park and protecting London’s parks and metropolitan green spaces. However, Abercrombie’s plan also recognised that ‘little has, so far, been done to knit the whole together into a continuous system by footpaths, park strips, riverside walks, bridle-ways and green lanes’.[21] The protection of the green belt and Metropolitan Open Land was incorporated within the Greater London Development Plan in the 1970s and in subsequent London Plans. Protection is one thing, but since the 1970s very little new open space had been formally planned in London despite its population growth.

Architects and urban planners were already exploring urban landscapes, partly in response to the decline, depopulation and deindustrialisation taking place in European and North American cities. In 1977, Oswald Mathias Ungers joined Rem Koolhaas at the Berlin Summer Academy for Architecture, and their collaboration led to the publication of *The City Within the City: Berlin as Green Archipelago*.[22] This proposed reconfiguring Berlin as a set of ‘islands-in-the-city’. This idea of a green archipelago sought to exploit urban depopulation as an opportunity to rethink the nature of urban life. Ungers proposed a set of ‘urban islands’ in Berlin – centres where the urban character might be reinforced while the rest of the city returned to open nature, becoming a ‘natural lagoon’. The urban environment would thus become a series of interconnected fragments surrounded by open and accessible countryside.[23]

Interest in urban landscapes in London had been taken up by David Goode at the GLC, who in the early 1980s mapped the ecological significance of large areas of London. His work was continued by the London Ecology Unit (LEU), until it was incorporated into the GLA in 2000.[24] The LEU developed the concept of ‘ecological deficiency units’ – areas of the city that were more than a kilometre from areas of ecological value. Ken Livingstone was personally interested in ecology and this became a theme within the 2004 London Plan. Others shared this interest in the strategic nature of public spaces in London. Mark Brearley had taught with Peter Beard and was part of a group of thinkers at the Architectural Association that included Liza Fior, Florian Beigel and Julian Lewis. They were interested in the ‘grittiness’ of urban landscapes, in leftover spaces – *terrains vagues* – that hosted the ordinary experiences of people’s everyday lives. The green belt and its associated metropolitan landscapes were ‘a great conceptual space without density’. These spaces were also a necessary counterpoint to Richard Rogers’ notion of the compact city. They were ‘places of slackness, wildness and escape'.[25] This perspective encouraged them to explore these largely neglected urban spaces, and one outcome was the conceptual piece *Picnics in the Green Belt* by East with Marianne Christiansen.[26] This saw the green belt as a neglected space, in many ways a void around the city. It postulated that access to, and use of, the green belt offered an opportunity to incorporate it into the spatial and social life of the city.

Alongside the thinking of Brearley, Beard and their circle, one of the early influences on the project was the work of Peter Latz in northern Germany. His strategic landscape plans for Duisburg-Nord and Emscher Park had transformed the postindustrial landscapes of the Ruhr into a regional park crisscrossed by walking and cycling routes. The land had been decontaminated and replanted to form a regional forest, but the blast furnaces and pit heads had been retained as colossal monuments to the industrial age, towering above the new forest like Mayan ruins. It was the incorporation and celebration of the area's industrial past that attracted the DfL team.

The East London Green Grid

Jamie Dean at the A+UU developed these ideas into a major project, the East London Green Grid. The City East work (Chapter 1) had analysed the eastward growth of London and the opportunity for this area to accommodate a large percentage of London's future growth. For this growth to be accommodated in the Thames Gateway and in order to attract the necessary inward investment, significant structural improvements would be required. East London had few of the topographical advantages of other parts of the capital. It also lacked historic settlements – places like Harrow, Dulwich and Hampstead – and the well-heeled suburbs that nestle into the folds of the hills and ridges of the London basin. East London, by contrast, was mainly flat, much of it had been occupied by industry, and its extensive river network was polluted and had been largely culverted. Despite this it had some important open spaces, parks and rivers. To the north-east it adjoined areas of green belt like Epping Forest, while the lower reaches of the Thames had a unique landscape of tidal flats and marshes. The East London Green Grid (ELGG) was devised to map these landscapes, join them up, and enhance and manage them so that they might become a 'dialogue between the city and its countryside'. In many ways it was the realisation of Unwin's and Abercrombie's visions of London being linked to its countryside by a network of publicly accessible green spaces (Figure 5.8).

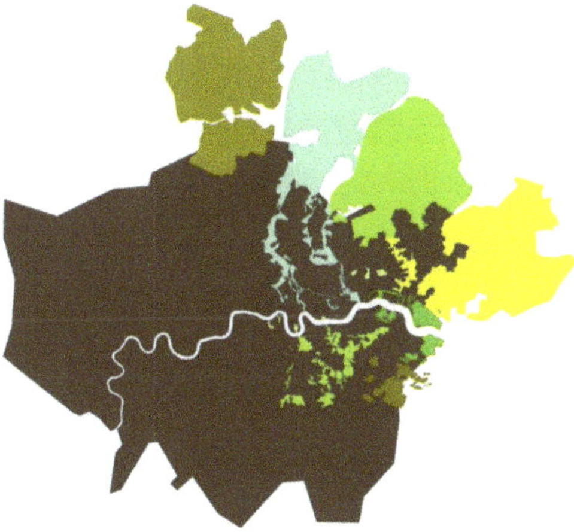

Figure 5.8 Connecting landscapes in east London. Source: *East London Green Grid Primer*, DfL/GLA.

The ELGG also created a strong environmental and ecological framework that was based on detailed mapping and analysis for the densification of east London (Figure 5.9 and 5.10). It linked the spatial distribution of existing open space with policies for healthy living, ecology, walking and cycling. Green landscapes offered a way to ameliorate rising temperatures resulting from climate change. Another key driver, also arising from climate change, was flood risk in London. Significant new housing developments were planned in the Thames Gateway, many of which were on land susceptible to flooding. In the foreword to the *East London Green Grid Primer*, Clive Coley, the Thames area regional manager for the Environment Agency, wrote, 'By opening up river corridors and creating green space in new developments the Green Grid will create a far more flexible and holistic approach to flood risk … there are also other advantages of opening up river corridors: increasing wildlife biodiversity, social benefits and improved aesthetics'.[27] The objectives of the ELGG were to:

- change the identity of the area
- remove flood risk from residential areas through sustainable drainage measures
- create a joined-up network of recreational spaces
- celebrate the heritage and culture of the area, including the folklore of its landscapes
- ameliorate urban heat island effects.

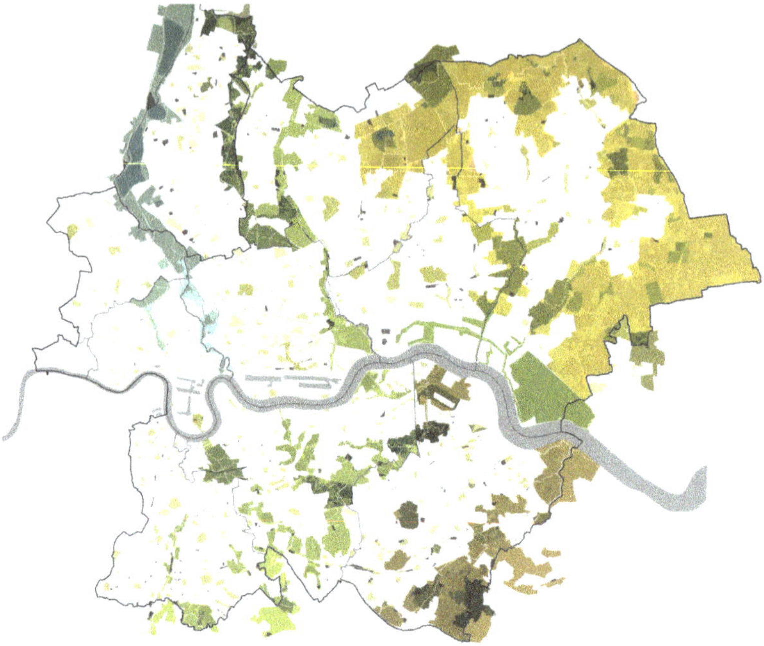

Figure 5.9 The East London Green Grid: a lattice of connected landscapes. Source: *East London Green Grid Primer*, DfL/GLA.

The starting concept for a 'grid' came from the topography of east London. Rivers such as the Roding and Ravensbourne ran north to south. If their corridors were upgraded, they could link the green belt around London to the Thames. Missing from the jigsaw were east-to-west corridors. The open spaces were largely in place; they needed to be linked and upgraded. This would then create a functional and publicly accessible green belt *within* London. Small-scale interventions would link areas to create habitat corridors and walking and cycling routes (Figures 5.11 and 5.12). The *East London Green Grid Primer* was published in 2006. It presented the results of a baseline study that had been commissioned by the LDA in 2003. This had mapped access to parks, open space deficiency areas, areas susceptible to flood risk (Figure 5.13) and areas with nature conservation value. The *Primer* set out policies for improving, upgrading and linking these 'residual' spaces. It divided east London into six local partnership bodies that were charged with implementation and management; this was later extended in 2011 to cover the whole of London in the All London Green Grid (Figure 5.14). Each area had a consultant architect, specific plans for each site, the interventions

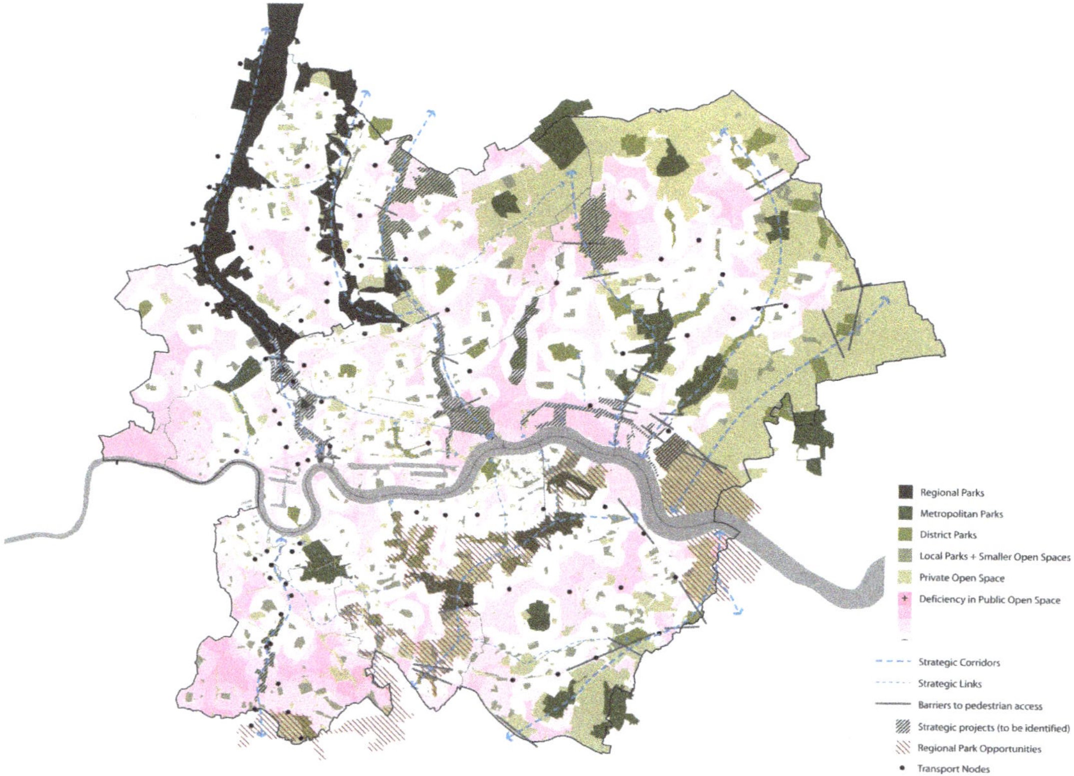

Figure 5.10 The East London Green Grid: open space deficiency. Source: *East London Green Grid Primer*, DfL/GLA.

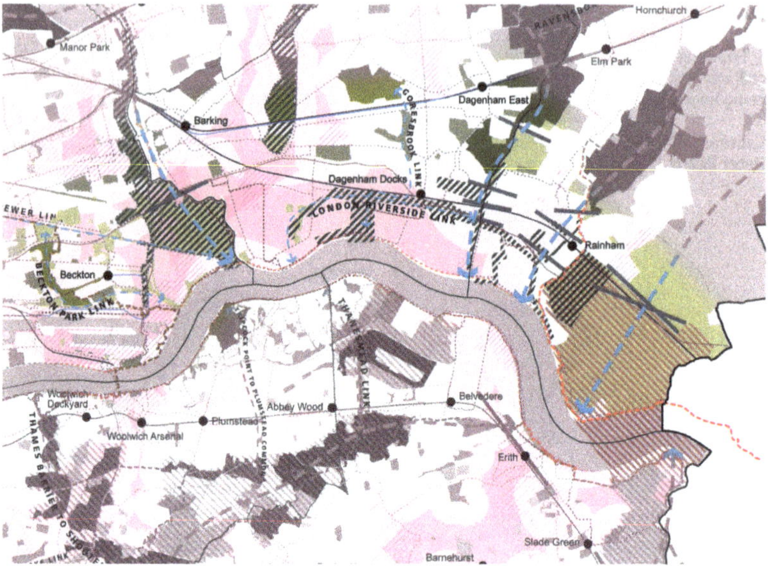

Figure 5.11 The East London Green Grid: a series of small projects. Source: *East London Green Grid Primer*, DfL/GLA.

required to link them together and plans for their eventual management. The separately constituted partnership bodies gave the project ownership at local level and a resilience that could, if necessary, outlast DfL.

The second part of the *Primer* set out a series of essays that explored aspects of landscape and its importance as a resource within the urban area. Essayists included the photographer Jason Orton, the writers Ken Worpole and Bob Gilbert, the architect Peter Beard, the broadcaster Chris Baines, and Dave Wardle from the Environment Agency. Together this eclectic group of individuals set out the economic, environmental, ecological, and access and movement rationale for the Green Grid, while Jason Orton's photographs presented a haunting picture of the places and landscapes of east London. This made the *Primer* more than just a policy document. It was an evocation of place – or what that place might become if nurtured carefully.

The delivery mechanism for the ELGG, devised by Jamie Dean, was one of its principal innovations. The project was 'sold' to powerful agencies including Thames Water, the Environment Agency, Natural England, the Homes and Communities Agency (HCA) and the Department for Environment, Food and Rural Affairs as a dispersed model for the realisation of *their* objectives. In Dean's words, 'we took their objectives and made them ours. This incorporated state agencies into a practical

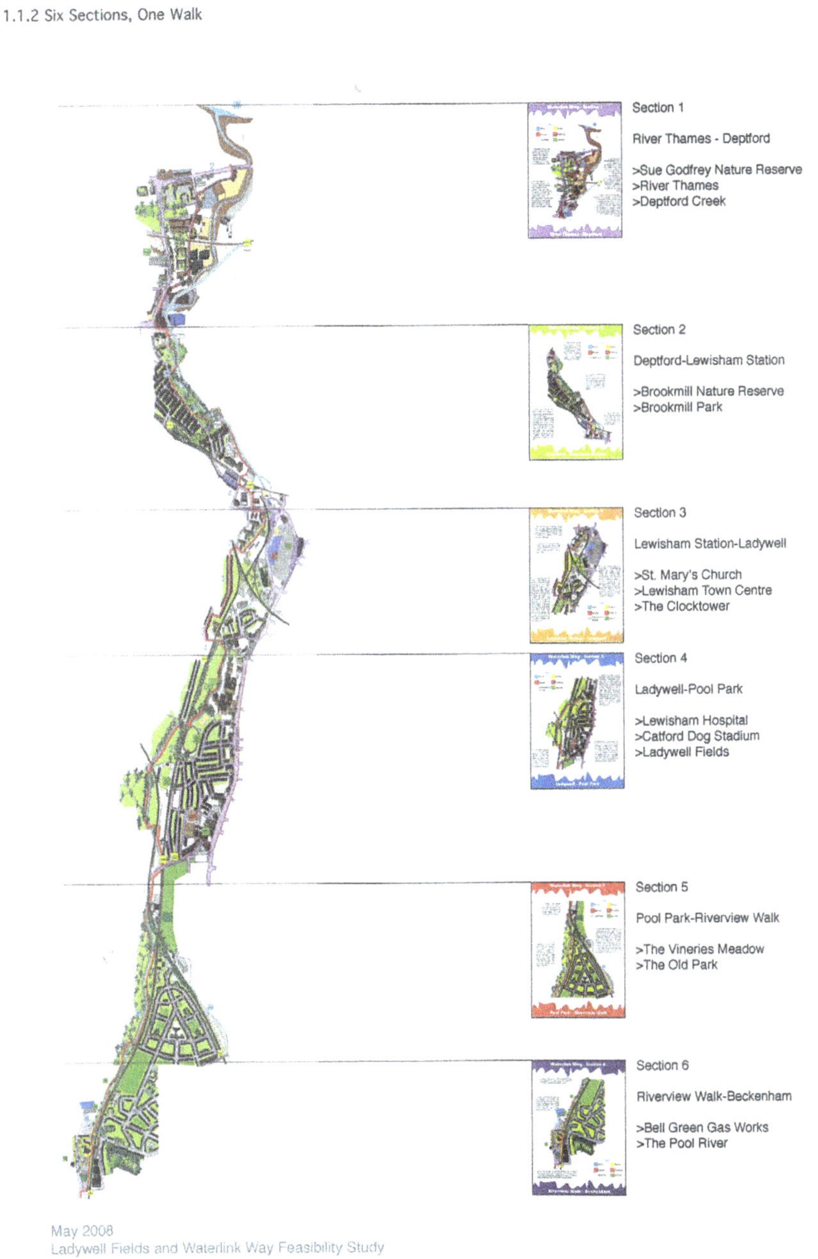

Figure 5.12 The East London Green Grid: small projects in south-east London. Source: Ladywell Fields and Waterlink Way: Feasibility Study Penultimate Report, East Architecture, Landscape Urban Design/DfL/GLA, May 2008.

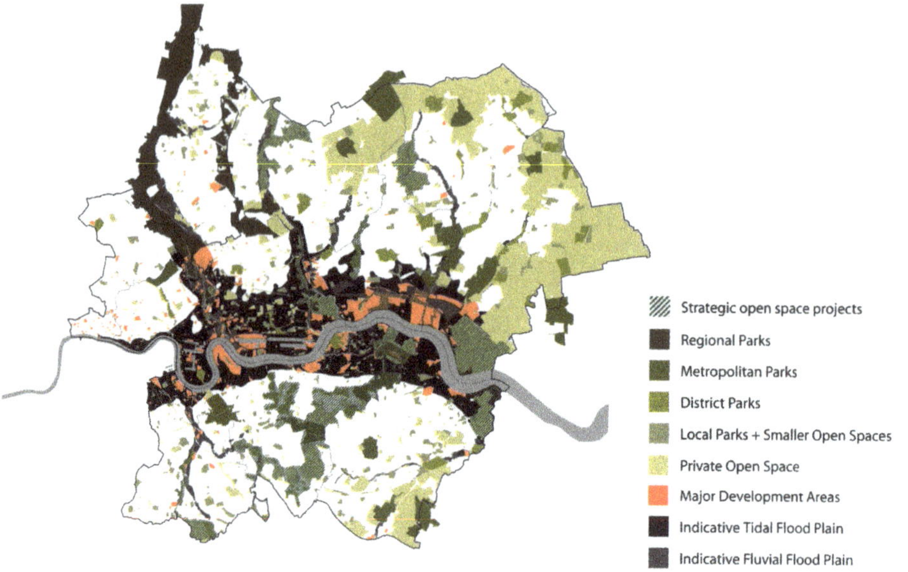

Figure 5.13 East London, showing the correlation of flood risk, major development projects and the East London Green Grid. Source: *East London Green Grid Primer*, DfL/GLA.

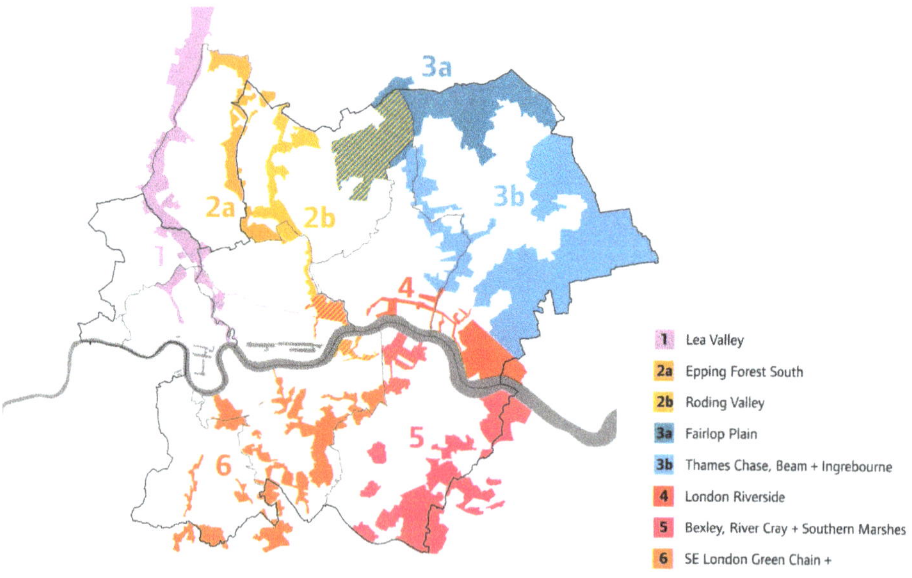

Figure 5.14 East London Green Grid partnership bodies. Source: *East London Green Grid Primer*, DfL/GLA.

implementation model that would deliver their objectives at a fraction of the cost of alternative programmes.'[28] These agencies each contributed to the introduction to the *Primer* and put their logos on the cover. Between them they made £30 million available for the first phases of the project.

One of the early projects was Rainham Marshes, which was designed by Peter Beard. Rainham Marshes is almost twice the size of Hampstead Heath. It was largely an artificial landscape, created after the seventeenth century, and had been used by the Port of London Authority as a dump for material dredged from the Thames, by the Ministry of Defence (MOD) as a rifle range, and later as a landfill site. Plans for housing and industrial development in the 1960s and 1970s had never come to fruition, and in the 1980s large parts of it were then designated as a Site of Special Scientific Interest (SSSI) in recognition of its importance, particularly for migratory birds. Beard's plans were sensitive to the marshes' landscape history and did not seek to displace the grazing or remove the remnants of its industrial heritage. The marshes were reconnected to the village of Rainham (a link which had long since been lost) by constructing a pedestrian bridge over the A13 and the high-speed rail lines. The plans for the marshes included paths connecting the bridge to the Thames, as well as boardwalks and pavilions for observing the birdlife. The Royal Society for the Protection of Birds (RSPB), which had purchased the land from the MOD in 2002, was a key partner in developing and managing the project.

Beard's designs for the marshes were influenced by the work of Georges Descombes, whose Voie Suisse scheme on the edge of Lake Uri had created a path that was discreet and minimal. Irene Scalbert describes the approaches of Beard and Descombes as concentrating 'on the most ordinary aspects that are commonly brushed aside'.[29] The ELGG captures the essence of Descombes's approach, using the found elements of the landscape and minimal intervention, rather than tidying up and sanitising the landscape. This fitted well with the DfL methodology and its aim to 'value what is there, define what is missing'.

In March 2012, the ELGG became part of the All London Green Grid and was incorporated into the London Plan. The idea was also taken up and developed by Terry Farrell in his work on the Thames Gateway Parklands (November 2009). This project, which involved DfL, was a rare collaboration between London, Essex and Kent, and extended the idea of the ELGG into the neglected and degraded landscapes of the Thames Estuary (Figure 5.15). It was also supported by the HCA as a mechanism to attract investment into the Thames Gateway and create a framework for sustainable growth. Terry Farrell championed the extension of the

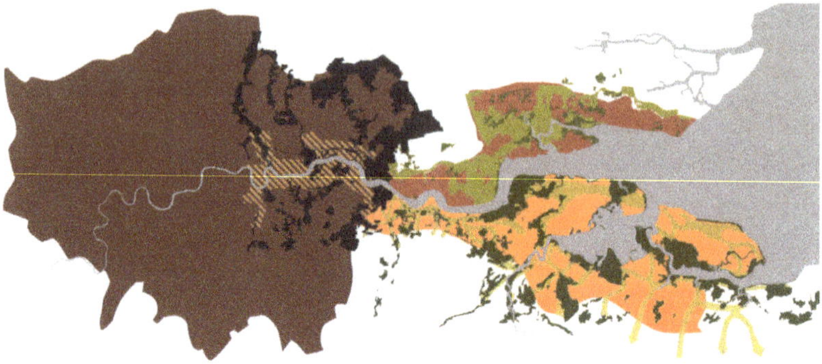

Figure 5.15 Thames Gateway Parklands: a regional green grid. Source: DfL/GLA/Terry Farrell.

ELGG into the Thames Estuary area, describing the proposed landscape network as 'the picture on the jigsaw box' that would create a regional landscape within which new settlements could be sited. In the Parklands document Farrell states, 'A high quality of life is needed to attract people to want to live here, work here, visit here, and for existing residents to want to build their futures here.'[30] The concept was that people would *choose* to move to the Thames Gateway. Although it was based on the ELGG, it effectively inverted the concept by seeing the regional landscape as a national park within which new high-quality residential settlements could be created and existing ones expanded. The HCA pledged £32 million to the Parklands project, and 15 major growth sites were identified, from the Lea Valley to Canvey Island and the Isle of Sheppey. Using the ELGG methodology, each had a plan, a lead partner and an initial funding stream that would attract matching funding. A new Thames Estuary Path led by Sustrans linked the areas together.

Conclusions

The work of the A+UU and DfL on public space and urban landscapes borrowed heavily from the theoretical and practical work of others. Interest in public space had re-emerged in the 1970s, although it is true to say that cities like London, New York, Berlin, Barcelona and Paris had always valued their landscapes, parks and squares. The difference was that from the 1980s onwards new public space was not being created in London and some existing parks were falling into neglect. The Urban Task Force created a platform whereby design strategies for public space became an essential ingredient of the compact and human city and central to urban policy. The 100 Public Spaces programme had an impact on thinking and public perceptions, and demonstrated that London could do what Paris had been doing so much better for the previous 30 years. DfL broadened the agenda to encompass health, wellbeing and climate change.

The programme was not easy to run, and initially the team was inexperienced in dealing with highway engineers, in particular. Public space provision is resource-consuming, especially when the aim is to provide high-quality and lasting spaces. Whether New York's 'pop-up' public space programmes could have been done in London is debatable, given the political risks and the fact that DfL never had the full clout of a transport commissioner behind it. However, such an approach could possibly have provided 100 public spaces quickly and at minimal cost. This might be a missed opportunity but in retrospect the 100 Public Spaces and subsequent programmes did produce a large number of well-designed and durable new civic spaces in parts of London that were in great need. These have management regimes in place to look after them and they will become a lasting contribution to London's urban fabric. This in itself is a very significant legacy. The work of the A+UU and DfL also introduced best practice to London, shifted the debate on public space and provided a firm footing for the many schemes that have been implemented in the city since. In 2020, London can boast a public realm that is commensurate with its status as a global city.

The ELGG and All London Green Grid project continues to this day, due principally to the tenacity of Jamie Dean, who is still associated with the project at the GLA. The urban landscape debate has matured, with a growing acceptance that cities need to adapt to catastrophic climate change and be resilient to events such as extreme summer temperatures and flooding. The health agenda, from air quality to obesity, is now also central to urban policy-making. Both the ELGG and the 100 Public Spaces/Great Outdoors programmes demonstrated a key move from planning as a regulatory function to protect open space, to a proactive design-led process that intervened to redress imbalances in provision, particularly in the poorer neighbourhoods. If cities are to adapt to climate change (and assist in slowing it), the relationship between built form and open space will remain at the centre of the agenda. Landscape urbanism will develop these programmes, conceptualising and planning the city and its hinterland as a single entity. Increasingly, considerations relating to food, resources, energy water and resilience will drive future thinking.

Notes

1 Urban Task Force 1999.
2 UN-Habitat 2016, pp. iv–v.
3 UN-Habitat 2016, p. 6.
4 Urban Task Force 1999, pp. 57–9.
5 Parts of the planned network are still visible today in Westway, Old Street roundabout, the Euston underpass and stretches of urban dual carriageway in Wandsworth. The plan had been to connect these elements into an inner ring, similar in function to Birmingham's Bullring (now being dismantled). This in turn would have connected to the national motorway network, destroying any community in its path.
6 Gehl 2010.
7 Gehl and Gemzøe 2000.
8 This is another example of the importance of empirical research in making the case for design, as was employed by DfL (see Chapters 1 and 2).
9 Gehl and Gemzøe 2000.
10 Gehl 2010.
11 Term coined by John Worthington of DEGW.
12 Oldenburg 1999.
13 In fact this goes back to plans in the 1970s that also included the part-pedestrianisation of Piccadilly Circus. These plans, however, included the construction of new roads that would have diverted traffic around Leicester Square and Trafalgar Square, causing widespread damage to parts of Soho.
14 Leicester Square was redesigned by Westminster Council in time for the 2012 London Olympics as part of DfL's Great Outdoors programme. Parliament Square was abandoned early in Johnson's mayoralty and is covered later in this chapter.
15 Often referred to as 'planning gain', these were negotiated benefits in kind to offset negative impacts of development.
16 Peter Bishop was Director of Environmental Services at Camden, 2001–6.
17 The Regeneration team at the GLA have confirmed that 80 per cent of the identified projects have been implemented in one form or another.
18 As at 2019 more than 100 public spaces have been delivered under this and subsequent programmes across London.
19 Sadik-Khan carried out this programme using her powers to paint traffic control measures on the public highway (i.e. white lines). This is an excellent example of the 'creative distortion' of powers to achieve public benefit.
20 Livingstone's main concerns were political. Proposals that would divert traffic across the Thames into Lambeth would have been a difficult sell before a mayoral election, creating opposition in addition to any reaction from Westminster, English Heritage and the Houses of Parliament. DfL recognised that this scheme would entail a fight. Livingstone's political instinct told him that this was the wrong time.
21 Scalbert 2013.
22 Ungers and Koolhaas 2013 (originally published 1977).
23 Schrijver 2008.
24 Although disbanded in 2003, its work informed the 2004 and subsequent London Plans.
25 Scalbert 2013.
26 https://www.east.uk.com/projects/urban-design/london/picnics-in-the-green-belt-2/
27 Greater London Authority 2006.
28 Interview with Jamie Dean, February 2020.
29 Scalbert 2013.
30 Farrell 2010, p. 4.

Bibliography

Farrell, Terry, *Thames Gateway Parklands: Delivering Environmental Transformation*, Greening the Gateway Kent & Medway, South Essex Green Grid, East London Green Grid, 9 November 2010. https://farrells.com/wp-content/uploads/2017/08/Thames-Gateway-Parklands.pdf (accessed 14 March 2020).

Gehl, Jan, *Cities for People*, Washington, DC: Island Press, 2010.

Gehl, Jan, and Gemzøe, Lars, *New City Spaces*, Copenhagen: Danish Architectural Press, 2000.

Greater London Authority, *East London Green Grid Primer*, Greater London Authority, 2006.

Oldenburg, Ray, *The Great Good Place: Cafes, Coffee Shops, Bookshops, Bars, Hair Salons and Other Hangouts at the Heart of a Community*, New York: Marlowe & Co., 1999.

Scalbert, Irénée, 'London After the Green Belt', *AA Files*, No. 66, 2013. https://www.thomasdanegallery.com/usr/documents/press/download_url/510/ml-aa-files-2013.pdf (accessed 14 March 2020).

Schrijver, Lara, 'OMA as Tribute to OMU: Exploring Resonances in the Work of Koolhaas and Ungers', *The Journal of Architecture*, Vol. 13, Issue 3, 2008, pp. 235–61.

Ungers, Oswald Mathias, and Koolhaas, Rem, *The City in The City – Berlin: A Green Archipelago: A Manifesto (1977) by Oswald Mathias Ungers and Rem Koolhaas [with others]*, edited by Florian Hertweck and Sébastien Marot, UAA Ungers Archives for Architectural Research, Zurich: Lars Müller Publishers, 2013.

UN-Habitat, *Global Public Space Toolkit: From Global Principles to Local Policies and Practice*, Nairobi, Kenya: UN-Habitat, February 2016. https://www.local2030.org/library/82/Global-Public-Space-Toolkit--From-Global-Principles-to-Local-Policies-and-Practice.pdf (accessed 14 March 2020).

Urban Task Force, *Towards an Urban Renaissance*, London: HMSO, 1999.

6

Opportunism on a grand scale: using the Olympics as a catalyst for change

Peter Bishop, Esther Everett and Eleanor Fawcett

In the summer of 2005, just after the announcement that London had been awarded the 2012 Olympics, a delegation from London government visited Turin to study how that city was preparing for the 2006 Winter Games. The question that members of the delegation were asked several times was why London was interested in hosting the Olympics. For Turin the answer was simple. Turin was a medium-sized city that had restructured its industrial base after the demise of car manufacturing in the 1980s. Its new economy was based on high-tech industries, research, tourism and gastronomy. The Winter Olympics was an opportunity to promote Turin and establish it as a tourism and winter sports centre. But why did a city like London want the Olympics? It was already a successful global city with an established 'brand' that attracted investment, tourists and global talent.

Ken Livingstone described the purpose of bidding for the Olympics as follows:

> The decision to bid for the 2012 Olympics was driven by a realisation that without a major project that could capture the imagination (and financial support) of Central Government, the deeply entrenched social and economic problems of east London would never be tackled. The Olympics locked in the Government to invest in the area, to help us acquire over 100 hectares of land, to decontaminate it, put in the infrastructure and improve transport in the area. It also was part of a wider strategy to promote London as the global

capital, a place that was welcoming and open to anyone to come and achieve their ambitions.[1]

The Olympic bid demonstrated how far London had come under mayoral government. There were three main reasons behind the bid. The first involved bolstering London's claim to be the leading city in the world.[2] Mayor Livingstone's strategy of promoting London had been clear since he took office in 2000. London's bid was based on the idea that London was an open and cosmopolitan city that attracted the brightest and most ambitious people from around the globe to come and realise their ambitions – and London welcomed them. The final part of the bidding process allowed each city to submit a short film to support their case. Paris, the favourite to win, presented a portrait of the city with pictures of its parks, restaurants, galleries and sports facilities along with the lifestyle of its (beautiful) inhabitants. London, by contrast, did not show a single image of itself or its inhabitants. Instead it showed a montage of stories about children from around the world, many from poor backgrounds, becoming inspired by sport. The film then cut to the future where they were winning gold medals and 'achieving their dreams and ambitions in London in 2012'.[3] It was a brave and compelling piece of marketing that identified London as the city of dreams, everyone's global capital city.

The second reason for the bid was to reinforce the strategic imperative to focus investment on brownfield land to the east of London in the Thames Gateway (Figure 6.1). The London Docklands Development Corporation had established a successful financial district at Canary Wharf, and other developments such as the London Exhibition Centre (ExCeL) and City Airport had ventured eastwards, but there was still a lack of appetite from the private sector to invest in the east. This was not surprising given levels of entrenched deprivation and low educational attainment in the area. The Lea Valley formed a barrier of local and low-grade industry, contaminated land and overhead power lines that severed communities and created a negative image for the whole area (Figures 6.2 and 6.3).

The third reason for the bid was a desire from Mayor Ken Livingstone to promote economic and social improvement in some of the poorest districts in the capital. Sir Robin Wales, the Leader of Newham Council, often stated that his ambition was for his borough to be 'average' in terms of London deprivation statistics. This, from the second-poorest borough, was a significant ambition. The Lea Valley needed to be tackled. In a rational world, government resources would have been made available

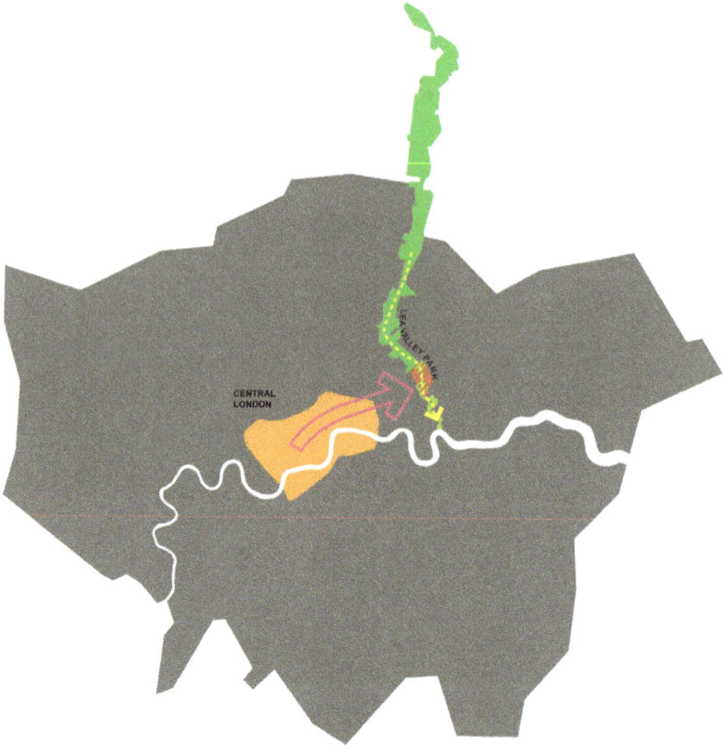

Figure 6.1 The London Olympics as a catalyst to move the city eastwards into the Thames Gateway. Source: DfL Archive, DfL/GLA.

Figure 6.2 Aerial view (looking north) of the future Olympic site in the Lower Lea Valley in 2005. Source: photo LDA; owner GLA.

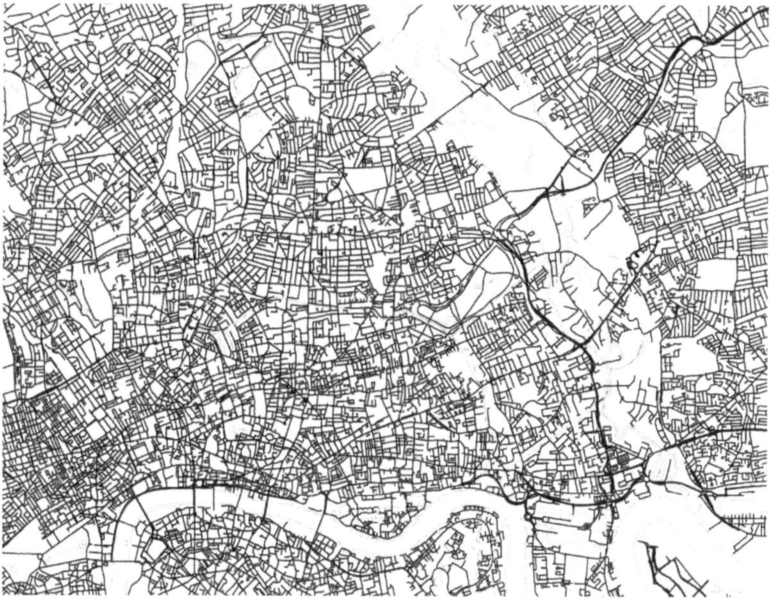

Figure 6.3 London's road network, showing the Lower Lea Valley as a 'tear' in London's fabric. Source: DfL Archive, DfL/GLA.

long before 2005. But government does not work like this and Livingstone turned to the Olympics to lever in central government commitment to do something for east London.

The strategy was sound, but the construction of a specialist sporting campus based on an exhaustive and rigid specification from the International Olympic Committee (IOC) was not necessarily the easiest way of triggering beneficial long-term regeneration. Yet it was the only option available. In 2006 the Dutch Planning Ministry established a team to consider a bid for the Amsterdam Olympics in 2028.[4] Explaining the rationale for such a long lead-in, Henk Ovink, one of the senior ministry planners, stated that 20 years was the minimum amount of time required to assess how an Olympics could be fully compatible with long-term national planning strategies.[5] The London bidding process had started in 1997 and had received ministerial approval in December 2000. London's 12-year lead-in period was still longer than that of many cities, but short when considered against the ambition of using the Games to regenerate east London. The bidding process not only had to demonstrate to the IOC that London could put on 'a great Games'; it also had to incorporate strategies for the transformation of the site into a working and sustainable piece of city.

The 2012 Games

The model for London's bid had been based on the experience of Barcelona, where the city had used the Olympics as a catalyst for structural change in the city by reconnecting the central area to the Mediterranean and revamping public spaces across the city. For London the objective was the long-term improvement of some of its poorest areas. The delivery of the Games was to be the responsibility of the London Organising Committee of the Olympic and Paralympic Games (LOCOG), which was established in October 2005. The Olympic Development Authority (ODA) was established in April 2006 with the task of building the park and all the facilities and stadia. The strategy was to develop a Games masterplan for the main park (2012) and an interim masterplan for the adaptation of the park after the Games (2012–14). The final masterplan, for the legacy, would guide the regeneration of this area of east London (2014–40). The London Development Agency (LDA) was tasked with the job of acquiring the land and relocating the existing industry to new premises elsewhere in London. The problem was that the legacy masterplan was to be commissioned some time later in the process. The focus was on delivery and on trying to contain escalating costs. Another issue was the growing cynicism of many Londoners. The legacy, initially the rationale for the bid, quickly came to be seen as a distraction.

Alongside the preparation of the 2012 bid materials for the Olympics (and because there were low expectations that London's bid would actually be successful), a parallel process had been underway. This was the process of corralling the four boroughs that overlapped in the proposed Olympic Park to work together to prepare the first-ever strategic plan for the Lower Lea Valley (LLV) as a whole. Within the Greater London Authority (GLA), the Architecture and Urbanism Unit (A+UU) led this process. A key component was to scope the opportunity that had been presented by the spotlight that had been turned on east London. In particular there was potential for serious investment in an area of London which had simply been the 'edge' since Saxon times. Ostensibly this was to be the document that would be published in July 2005, immediately after London lost the Olympic bid, to demonstrate that there were a clear vision and detailed plans for the revitalisation of the LLV without the 2012 Olympics. In the event, the document was ready for this deadline, but when London won the bid, a further year's work was then undertaken to incorporate the Olympic masterplan and update the strategy accordingly. It was finally adopted in 2007.

This document was to have been given planning status as a mayoral 'Opportunity Area Planning Framework' and was led by the GLA's planning team with the A+UU carving out a central role in coordination and as the client for the spatial and place-making aspects of the work. The A+UU also used its developing skills to graphically communicate complex spatial strategies. EDAW (now AECOM) were appointed by the GLA to produce the strategy. The considerable expertise, local knowledge and stakeholder trust that had been built up over the two years of preparing this strategy proved to be fundamental to the future success of Design for London (DfL) in shaping and delivering change in the LLV over the following decade.

The LLV strategy established five key spatial ideas (Figure 6.4a–e). These have proven lasting and effective overarching principles to guide the developments and investments across the area, including the Olympic and legacy masterplans, for over a decade.

Many of these approaches that were innovative at the time are now mainstream and included as policy in the latest London Plan. They can be summarised as follows:

- *Neighbourhoods and communities.* To ensure that successful living environments were created in the harsh environment of the LLV (and that isolated 'ghettos', either for rich or for poor people, were avoided), rules were developed to establish suitable locations for new homes. These were to be linked to public transport and in close proximity to town centres. The quality of the environment was given a high priority. The strategy also acknowledged that significant numbers of new homes could and should be delivered by ad hoc intensification of existing neighbourhoods. Workspace and infrastructure were factored into this mix.
- *The connected valley.* The LLV was impressively well connected by road and public transport to the rest of London, but was itself virtually impossible to move around in. Thanks to meticulous on-the-ground mapping by the newly established practice Witherford Watson Mann Architects, the strategy identified specific locations where dozens of new routes and bridges were required to 'stitch' from east to west across the valley and link the communities and town centres which bordered the area but were utterly cut off from one another by major infrastructure (Figure 6.5).
- *The working valley.* One of the most complex challenges was to establish a clear vision for the future of industry in the LLV. This had for centuries been a hugely important part of London's industrial

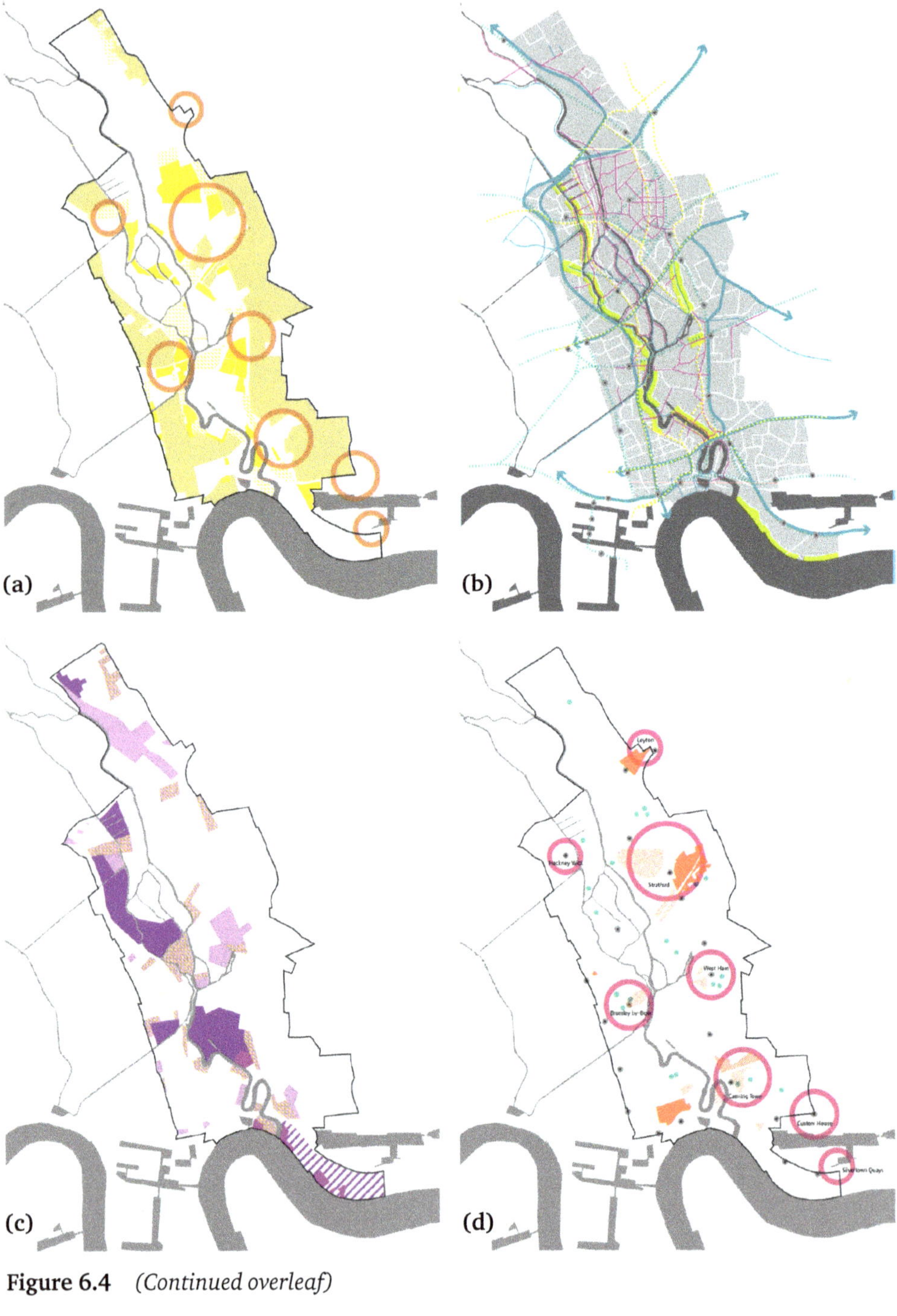

Figure 6.4 *(Continued overleaf)*

(e)

Figure 6.4 The five key spatial strategies for the Lower Lea Valley: (a) Neighbourhoods and communities; (b) The connected valley; (c) The working valley; (d) Thriving centres; (e) Water city. Source: Lower Lea Valley, Opportunity Area Planning Framework (OAPF), 2007, DfL/GLA.

story. The policy of 'industry + mix' was developed by the A+UU working with the London Plan Team. Through this framework, non-industrial uses could be added to an area, including residential uses, providing that the total industrial floorspace in the new development did not reduce. This started to establish new typologies that mixed a range of uses with lighter forms of industry that could act as successful buffers between remaining strategic industrial locations and new residential neighbourhoods. This ensured that the LLV could continue to be a place of work.

– *Thriving centres.* Learning from the fragmented, introverted high-density residential development starting to creep out from Canary Wharf, the LLV strategy strongly advocated the importance of 'proper' town centres to support the creation of successful new neighbourhoods and districts which were in London's DNA. This would require the expansion and strengthening of three existing but impoverished town centres at Stratford, Canning Town and

Figure 6.5 Mapping the connectivity of the Lower Lea Valley. Source: Witherford Watson Mann Architects, 2005, DfL/GLA.

Leyton, and, ambitiously, the creation of three new town centres around the stations at Hackney Wick, Bromley-by-Bow and West Ham. Supporting the existing town centres was a priority for achieving a successful Olympic legacy (Figure 6.6).

- *Water city.* This involved creating a new 'front' to the LLV along the waterways that thread through the area from north to south, and creating a new continuous public route and network of parks from Hackney Marshes to the River Thames – completing Abercrombie's 1944 vision for the 26-mile Lea Valley Park. This vision was central to the layout of the Olympic Park and was also a way to highlight and celebrate the special qualities of the LLV landscapes at a time when most mainstream discussion of the area focused mainly on the need to 'start again'.

The longevity and success of these principles provide a useful lesson for other major regeneration projects. Their effectiveness was partly due to a clear and compelling vision which was understood and endorsed by all involved. But they also provided a true blueprint for change because of the unusual level of specificity of the work. These were not sweeping

Figure 6.6 Integration of the Olympic legacy vision with the existing and proposed town centres. Source: DfL/GLA.

aspirational statements. They were underpinned by joint working between the GLA and stakeholders and by robust spatial propositions that worked out what the principles could mean on the ground. There was enough detail in these principles for projects to be implemented piece by piece, as individual opportunities arose, while still allowing sufficient flexibility for the specifics to evolve over time.

Working 'inside' and 'outside' the park

It is fair to say that most Londoners were surprised when the decision to award London the Games was announced, and the initial euphoria dissolved into concern about whether London could really manage to gear up and host the Games in little over seven years. The task was immense. Almost 200 hectares of land had to be acquired; the River Lea and its tributaries had to be cleaned up; most of the land had to be decontaminated; low-grade industry had to be relocated; overhead power lines had to be rerouted and buried; and a whole platform of infrastructure, including power, water and drainage, had to be put in place. Only then could work start on building the Olympic Park, the stadia and all the supporting services to host an Olympics (Figure 6.7). To make the task even more difficult, London had based its bid on hosting the most sustainable Olympics ever and on using it as a stepping stone in the longer-term regeneration of east London. Arrangements were quickly begun to establish the Olympic Development Authority (ODA) and the many other organisations and teams responsible for the multitude of activities funded by the £9.3 billion Olympic budget.

While this singular, focused, well-resourced machine cranked into life and the bright blue hoardings started to go up around the Olympic precinct, there was an almost surreal contrast with what was happening in the rest of the LLV. This was a rich and multifaceted world involving

Figure 6.7 Preparing the Olympic site, March 2008. Source: GLA.

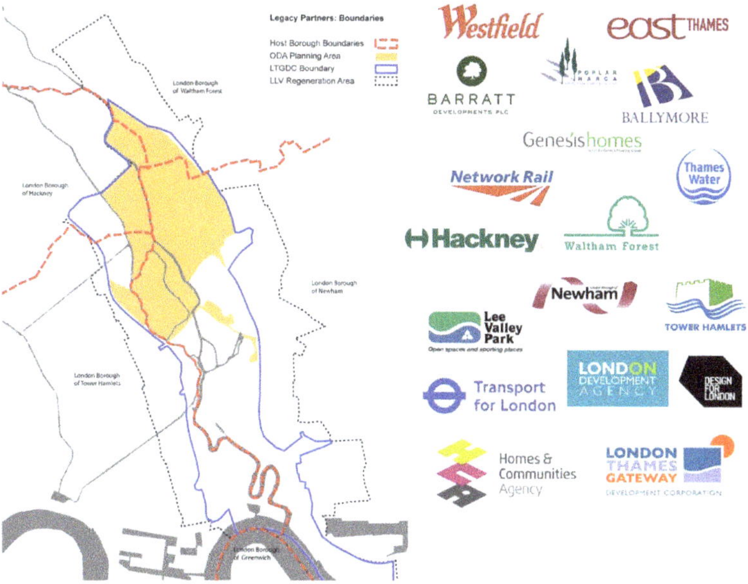

Figure 6.8 The multitude of overlapping boundaries and organisations operating across the Lower Lea Valley. Source: DfL Archive, DfL/GLA.

multiple authorities with overlapping areas of jurisdiction (Figure 6.8). These included the mayor, the Lea Valley Regional Park Authority, the four adjoining boroughs and the newly established London Thames Gateway Development Corporation (LTGDC). Alongside these were organisations ranging from Network Rail and utilities companies to developers wanting to benefit from the Olympic effect and a huge number of individual landowners surprised by their change in fortune. This free-for-all was both an opportunity and a threat. The slightly anarchistic and freewheeling spirit of change was certainly in keeping with the ungoverned feel of the LLV and held the promise of creating a rich and layered piece of city, in contrast to fears about the homogenisation of the Olympic zone. However, this period also resulted in some very poor outcomes, in particular the march of third-rate tower blocks that shot up along Stratford High Street (Figure 6.9).

In practical spatial terms, it was particularly alarming that there was virtually no joining up between the 'inside' and the 'outside' of the Olympic zone, despite the importance of the promised legacy for east London in the bid. This was the context when DfL was set up. The A+UU LLV team were working successfully outside the Olympic zone with partners at the boroughs and the LTGDC to commission a series of

Figure 6.9 Composite of schemes developed along Stratford High Street following the success of the Olympic bid. Source: GLA.

'Olympic Fringe' masterplans, as well as providing design input to all the planning applications. With the advent of DfL, this changed dramatically. DfL was for several years the only team to have clear roles both inside and outside the Olympic zone. It was in a unique position to coordinate projects and provide an underlying design ethos.

Inside the park: infiltrating the ODA to improve the legacy and design quality

Given the huge pressure on delivery within the Olympic project, there was little appetite for the involvement of an agency such as DfL. Indeed, there was little appetite for any real discussion about design in general. The task dominated; 'on time on budget' was the all-too-familiar mantra as the ODA started to erect barriers to protect itself from any outside interference. The mayor's office, worried by the spectre of late delivery, fully supported the ODA's position. The first attempts at influencing the Games focused on the design quality of the stadia and especially the design competition for the aquatics centre. Both Richard Rogers and Ricky Burdett were closely involved, as were the A+UU, and Zaha Hadid's iconic design was selected in 2004. Following criticism of their design and procurement strategies, not least by Richard Rogers, the ODA appointed Ricky Burdett as their design advisor in November 2006. This bolstered the day-to-day voice of design within the ODA, which had already appointed Nick Serota[6] to its board earlier in 2006. Serota was a highly effective design champion and he helped to establish an independent design review panel, led by the Commission for Architecture and the Built Environment (CABE), that played a key role in guiding design processes within the Olympic Park.

An opportunity to really influence the ODA came when they eventually decided to strengthen their design team. DfL offered to second in a member of staff to work within the ODA – under the ODA's full-time supervision. The idea of 'infiltration' was a strategy that DfL had always used but this had mainly been carried out by working through friendly proxies who could offer access to information about budgets and help in navigating internal decision-making arrangements. A secondment was a new departure, but an opportunity to plant a mole in the ODA. This might allow them to start to shape some aspects of the Olympic masterplan in order to ensure that the opportunities for the legacy were not compromised. Eleanor Fawcett, then an architect at DfL, duly started work at the ODA in early 2007 on a part-time basis.

Delivering real impact and influence in this role was far from easy, as the ODA was already quite advanced on key decisions about the layout of the Olympic precinct's infrastructure. Part of the role was to attend formal internal ODA 'gateway' meetings to review proposals on the 'legacy design'. Fawcett was the sole advocate of design among about 25 other heavyweight specialists in cost control, health and safety, and project delivery. In this type of setting, despite her best attempts, it proved impossible to influence some issues, such as the positioning of utilities buildings and road infrastructure around the edge of the park, especially at the southern edge. Fawcett argued that the impact of poor forward planning in these areas would seriously affect the ability of future strategies to successfully connect the communities along Stratford High Street into the park. She was right, but her voice was ignored and in consequence this problem remains today.

However, in terms of specific projects, the primary focus was on the design of the parklands. This was lagging behind schedule and a project sponsor had yet to be appointed for it. A key task became shaping the vision and approach that might be articulated in the brief for the landscape design consultants for the Olympic Park. The key contribution to this work was the introduction of a stronger appreciation of the Lower Lea Valley itself and the special qualities of its waterways and wild, intimate landscapes. This had been somewhat lacking from the more formalised proposals which EDAW had been working on, and indeed the vast majority of people who were involved in the Olympic project did not know the LLV beyond the *tabula rasa* Olympic construction site. For them the LLV was an empty and polluted wasteland (see Figure 6.10a–c, which offers differing perceptions of the area). A few months later, when John Hopkins was appointed as the park project sponsor and Hargreaves/LDA Design were appointed as the landscape consultants, this appreciation became far more integrated into the vision and future design of the park. The influence of the natural landscape on their work can be seen in the undulating, wilder northern part of the park today.

Figure 6.10 Differing perceptions of the Lower Lea Valley (2006–7): (a) Hackney Marshes; (b) Canalside, Hackney Wick; (c) Low-grade industry and pollution. Source: DfL/GLA.

(Continued overleaf)

JAYJ AUTOS
(c)

Another real success resulting from the DfL secondment was the Greenway. This project was for the landscape improvement of the neglected and vandalised embankment above one of London's main sewers. The embankment ran as a raised public pathway through the Olympic site. This was originally seen as a minor infrastructure project and had been passed to one of the big engineering firms to design and build a simple tidy-up scheme. However, following an initial review meeting Fawcett identified a missed design opportunity to create a 2.5-kilometre-long linear park – a project sufficiently noncritical to the Games programme that there might be some willingness to adopt a different approach and appoint an emerging design practice. The ODA agreed to hold an open design competition, which received 70 submissions. Adams and Sutherland won the competition with a proposal that was completely rooted in the LLV (Figure 6.11). It incorporated reused materials from the clearance of the old industrial buildings and planting that was deliberately drawn from the local postindustrial wild landscapes. Although initially somewhat nonplussed by this very

Figure 6.11 Image from the Greenway competition. Source: Adams and Sutherland, DfL/GLA.

Figure 6.12 The Greenway on completion. Source: DfL/GLA.

different design approach, the ODA delivered this rich, complex scheme and it received wide critical acclaim (Figure 6.12). It has been hugely successful and it initiated the ODA's understanding of how to celebrate the heritage of its site through design.

Appointing the legacy masterplanners

The process to finally appoint the masterplanners for the Olympic legacy was started in 2007 and was led by the LDA. This had been focused on the challenging tasks of acquiring the almost 200 landownerships within the Olympic site and relocating businesses and other groups, such as traveller communities and allotment holders. DfL had succeeded in becoming design advisors on a few of the Olympic relocation projects, which included a period where the team had to quickly develop skills in colourful decorative treatments for the many new industrial sheds that the LDA was constructing across the Thames Gateway, much to the bemusement of the relocated businesses.

As the plans for the Olympics quickly took shape, it was becoming increasingly pressing for the legacy plans to keep pace in order to ensure that decisions could be taken with the long term in mind. DfL were asked to lead the design aspects of the Olympic legacy masterplanning, so in summer 2007 Eleanor Fawcett was seconded into the LDA's Olympic legacy team. The first task was to bring the key stakeholders on board regarding the approach to the Olympic legacy masterplan. A series of major 'place-making' workshops were set up to explore priorities and establish shared objectives among the four host boroughs, the LTGDC, the GLA and central government. These essentially developed the discussions that had begun with partners through the LLV OAPF (Opportunity Area Planning Framework). The result was a 10-point set of objectives that formed part of the brief for the designers. A major open international design procurement for the legacy masterplanners was held in autumn 2007, and in January 2008 the shortlisted teams were interviewed by a panel including Peter Bishop and Nick Serota. The Dutch firm KCAP's opening slide (Figure 6.13) captured the conundrum of the legacy brief – how to turn a purpose-built (and secure) sporting campus into a living and integrated piece of city. The jury declared them clear winners.

However, KCAP had not formed the team of supporting consultants necessary for the commission. The team placed second, was led by Allies and Morrison and their partner AECOM/EDAW, and included all the necessary disciplines. This was also the team that had led the masterplanning of the Olympic site from 2003 onwards and it had a huge

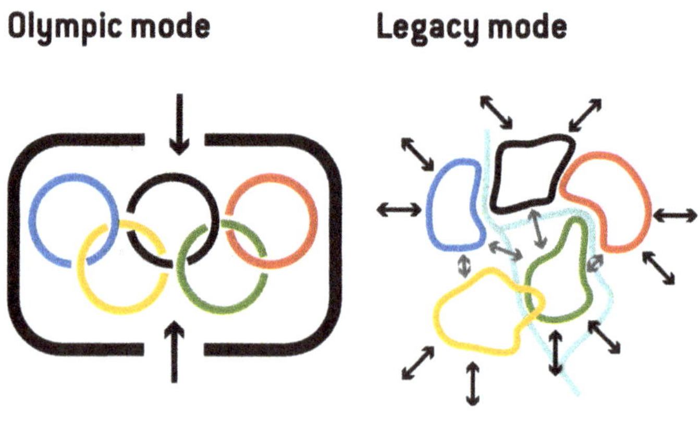

Figure 6.13 The Olympic legacy conundrum: turning a sports campus into a piece of city. Source: KCAP Olympic Legacy Masterplan Vision, KCAP, December 2007.

amount of technical knowledge about the complex site. It was considered a 'safe pair of hands' to complement and support the fresh approach of KCAP. The LDA asked KCAP to enter into dialogue with AECOM and Allies and Morrison to explore whether a joint team could be formed to take on the commission.[7] KCAP reported back that an agreement had been reached and the joint team was appointed in January 2008.

The legacy process got under way quickly, with part of the KCAP team relocating to London. A packed programme of design workshops and stakeholder meetings began. The masterplan was beginning to address the problems of transforming a games campus into a new piece of city. This was no easy task. The Olympic Park was still a relatively isolated area that was not integrated with its surrounding neighbourhoods. It was severed by mainline railways to the south and had the overground line running through its centre. Moreover, although the ODA's 'transformation' masterplan would remove many of the redundant sporting facilities and circulation spaces, the road network was still overscaled in many places, many of the public spaces were not going to be converted into usable park areas and there was considerable uncertainty concerning the long-term use of the main athletics stadium.

The legacy plan was based on a series of broad principles:

- Reconnect the surrounding neighbourhoods and connect into the surrounding existing and proposed town centres and stations.
- Retain, adapt and reuse four of the Olympic sports venues (the main stadium, the aquatics centre, the velodrome and the handball arena) and the huge media and press centre buildings.
- Consolidate the public realm to create a successful new park for east London and integrate the landscape with the existing rivers and canals.
- Build a series of mixed-income neighbourhoods to surround the park, with distinct characters, each with around 7,000–10,000 new homes.

Over the first year of work, the KCAP/Allies and Morrison masterplan elegantly incorporated these principles into a framework from which a new high-density piece of city might develop. This was supported by extensive engagement with local communities and stakeholders as part of the Legacy Now initiative. DfL's LLV team was the client of this work through Eleanor Fawcett's ongoing part-time secondment into the LDA's Olympic legacy team. As part of this work, an independent design review panel run by CABE and DfL was established.

Political leadership was shifting at this time and so too did the approach to the legacy. Shortly after the legacy masterplan was commissioned, Boris Johnson was elected mayor (May 2008). Ken Livingstone's Olympic advisor Neale Coleman was sacked, but then reinstated within the first week of the new mayoralty, so at least a degree of continuity was maintained. However, the Johnson administration decided to remove the responsibility for the legacy from the LDA and set up a new organisation to deliver the Olympic legacy. This would be under the direct control of the mayor. A limited company, the Olympic Park Legacy Company (OPLC), was set up in May 2009,[8] just as the public consultation on the legacy masterplan was commencing.

In the summer of 2009 more formal consultation on the emerging KCAP/Allies and Morrison legacy masterplan began (Figure 6.14), and some unease about the plan emerged from the mayor's advisor and key stakeholders, especially a sense that the residential densities were too high and that there were too many residential towers. There were suggestions from the Mayor of London that the legacy plan did not embody a 'London vernacular' approach to architectural design. To compound matters, the 2009 economic downturn had effectively scuppered the plan that the Treasury would recoup some of the £9.3 billion that they had put into the Games. Even residential development looked unlikely in a market that was flatlining. The challenge of being asked to plan at lower densities did not help the situation.

Figure 6.14 Legacy masterplan framework proposals at summer 2009. Source: KCAP and Allies and Morrison, GLA.

The lack of strong leadership within the newly established OPLC compounded the hiatus around the vision and proposals for the Olympic legacy throughout the second half of 2009. This continued until Andrew Altman began as the new CEO in December 2009. Altman arrived with hugely impressive credentials, having been the Deputy Mayor of Philadelphia and Planning Director for Washington DC, where he had led the delivery of the Anacostia riverfront transformation. Most importantly for DfL, Altman was a trained planner who understood the importance of place-making and design in urban regeneration and was familiar with the recent urban revitalisation of London through his participation in the London School of Economics' Urban Age programme run by Ricky Burdett. Altman quickly connected with Peter Bishop and the team at DfL and enthusiastically agreed to continue with the secondment of DfL staff to lead the Olympic legacy design client role. He also valued their wider understanding of the LLV as a place and gradually got to know the area through bike rides around the valley. Having such a strong design champion leading the Olympic legacy project transformed DfL's role and influence on the project. Ultimately in 2011, as DfL was being disbanded, it was a natural step for its LLV team to be transferred formally to the OPLC, along with all the Olympic Fringe projects and associated budgets. This led to the establishment of a new OPLC design team, which is still in existence.

Andrew Altman's first task was to address the hiatus with the Olympic legacy masterplan and get it back on track, so that it could secure formal approval in time to influence the ODA's post-Games 'transformation' plans and start to secure developer partners. It was clear that a rethink was needed in order to demonstrate to stakeholders that their criticism of the first proposals had been heard and taken on board. So, with Ricky Burdett's help, Altman bolstered the KCAP/Allies and Morrison design team with a new cohort of 'up-and-coming' architects, including Witherford Watson Mann, Caruso St John, Maccreanor Lavington, West 8, Panter Hudspith and Vogt Landscape Architects. This team was given 100 days to critique and refine the legacy vision and proposals. This process was ultimately a success and its thoughtful work started to get to grips with important questions about character, place and how the park should relate to the neighbourhoods around it. The overall densities were reduced and more recognisable typologies were introduced to differentiate neighbourhoods. Another outcome of this process was that KCAP stepped away from the team and Maccreanor Lavington and Witherford Watson Mann became part of the consultant team, led by Allies and Morrison.

The masterplan secured outline planning consent just before the opening of the 2012 Olympic and Paralympic Games and is currently being built out on site. It has subsequently been linked to a range of other DfL projects, including High Street 2012 (Chapter 3) and Olympic Fringe masterplans (Figure 6.15). Subsequently, University College London was allocated a large site in the south of the park for a new campus, and plans are being developed for a new cultural centre, East Bank, that will house

Figure 6.15 A composite suite of masterplans for east London. Source: DfL Archive, DfL/GLA.

a new Victoria and Albert museum, the London School of Fashion, the BBC, the Smithsonian and Sadler's Wells dance company. Loughborough University and University College London have set up teaching and research space in Here East, previously the Olympic media centre.

In spring 2012, the London Legacy Development Corporation (LLDC), a mayoral development corporation, was established under the powers of the 2011 Localism Act with full planning and regeneration powers and accountable directly to Londoners via the mayor.

Stitching the Fringe

Fundamental to the approach to the Olympic Fringe, and central to DfL's role in its transformation, were the six Olympic Fringe masterplans that DfL commissioned with the boroughs and the LTGDC (Figure 6.16). These were based on previous research that the team had carried out in the LLV OAPF. Although they differed in terms of timescale, brief, consultant team and client group, by 2010 they were all nearing completion and together they formed a reasonably robust strategy for investment and change in the surrounding area. These masterplans continued the theme of 'planning with plans' – a favourite DfL saying – and ensured that the tools were in place for the many parties involved to choreograph the process of change across the LLV. The masterplans were both strategies to steer future development and action plans comprising dozens of scoped individual projects. Collectively all of these projects would make a difference to the lives of local people and would integrate their neighbourhoods with the Olympic Park. These interventions ranged from playful, light-touch, 'quick-win' projects to the delivery of major infrastructural components required to 'stitch' new movement networks and connections through these new neighbourhoods. These places had always been a visible 'tear' in London's fabric but new bridges, new stations and the radical redesign of 'hostile' road arteries would make these neighbourhoods places fit for people to live in.

The area in question was covered by four different boroughs. DfL's work drew together the disparate pieces of otherwise fragmented neighbourhoods through propositional mapping that revealed how the area worked both physically and socially. The resultant plans were built on a subtle understanding of the qualities of place and the everyday – those elements of the urban landscape often obliterated by planning's constant desire to tidy things up into sanitised neighbourhoods. The team's approach brought an overarching view that helped to navigate the

Figure 6.16 The Fringe masterplans. Source: DfL archive, DfL/GLA.

quagmire of political and administrative boundaries with agility. In both process and product, it was a task of invisible mending (Figure 6.17a–c).

The six Olympic Fringe masterplans were as follows:

1. *Leyton*. Here the emphasis was on strengthening and improving an area that already had a robust character but was a neglected part of the borough and had poor links into the Olympic Park. A number of projects were developed to strengthen the High Street, improve

Figure 6.17a Improving connections: floating towpath at Bromley-by-Bow. Source: DfL/GLA.

Figure 6.17b Hackney Marshes Centre (Stanton Williams, 2012). Source: DfL/GLA.

Figure 6.17c Leyton: public realm creating new thresholds and identity (East, 2012). Source: DfL/GLA.

key underused sites and forge stronger links with the Olympic Park through identifying and opening up new routes.

2. *Hackney Marshes*. Extensive yet bleak, this is the home of Sunday league football, with more than a hundred matches played every weekend. There had historically been low levels of investment in the facilities for this. The landscape masterplan replanned the Marshes to encourage wider use, for example by introducing cricket facilities and improving amenity around the edge along the river and canal. The projects upgraded the sports facilities with two new major buildings, provided a new cafe, improved entrance points to the Marshes, introduced paths and benches and planted hundreds of trees and bulbs.
3. *Hackney Wick and Fish Island*. This gritty area was home to a high concentration of artists and creative enterprises as well as local industry. The projects sought to protect this area, improve the public realm and acquire one of the key buildings, the White Building, as a creative hub.
4. *Bromley-by-Bow*. The projects linked together a number of key development sites to forge a new centre for the area, enhance the setting of important historical sites and address the severance caused by the A12, a major urban motorway. A key challenge here was the fragmented ownership of land. Sites were brought together through a carefully brokered masterplan co-cliented with the landowners.
5. *Stratford town centre*. This was already emerging as a major shopping district on the eastern edge of the park with the construction of the Westfield shopping complex. The imperative in this area was to devise projects to revitalise the existing shopping centre and the 'old' town centre, to mitigate the fear that Westfield would prompt their demise. The plan also sought ways to reduce the impact of traffic and improve the public realm.
6. *Stratford High Street and Sugarhouse Lane*. In the heady months following London's Olympic win, local landowners were among the first to cash in. What ensued in the policy vacuum was a swathe of high-density, poor-quality residential towers along Stratford High Street. The challenge of retrofitting a strategy and coherent sense of place to this now dysfunctional corridor is an ongoing one. In contrast, the tightly knit industrial enclave of Sugarhouse Lane was the location for the first conservation area designation within the LLV. The masterplan principles continue to guide exemplary developments that have created a mixed new neighbourhood.

While it was accepted that the legacy masterplan process was on track to produce a good new piece of city, there were concerns about whether enough was being done to bring about the fundamental changes in the area that would be required if the chronic deprivation in many of the adjoining areas was to be addressed by Olympic-related investment. These concerns were already being raised by the five host boroughs[9] who had signed up to the Olympics (and had accepted its short-term disruption) in the expectation of long-term benefits for their communities. By 2010 they were beginning to put pressure on government and had drawn up a 'shopping list' of projects totalling over £150 million – money that the government (the Department for Communities and Local Government) did not have. The pressure to show concrete improvements in the Olympic Fringe neighbourhoods was compounded by the lurking threat that within a couple of years east London would be in the global spotlight and overrun by journalists seeking fresh angles on London's story. No one in government wanted to see striking examples of deprivation and degraded landscapes exposed just a stone's throw from the Olympic site (Figure 6.18).

As with many of DfL's initiatives, this presented an opportunity for involvement and to deliver benchmark projects on the ground. The

Figure 6.18 Degraded environment adjacent to the Olympic Park. Source: DfL/GLA.

political pressure from the host boroughs for funding to deliver capital improvements was reaching a stalemate. The boroughs' vast shopping list of disparate projects was too expensive and too fragmented for central government to fund. At the GLA's request, DfL began to work with the host boroughs to filter and coordinate the projects into prioritised, costed project packages, each of which had a clear rationale. The Olympic Fringe masterplans provided a ready scoped framework for these to slot into. This approach was agile and embedded in the governance structures of the area. Long-established working relationships initiated in the pre-Olympic period made it easy to sell the idea and harness enthusiastic support.

Ultimately over £100 million was secured from a range of different funds (Figure 6.19) to deliver a major programme of capital investments across the Fringe before the start of the Olympics in 2012. DfL played a central role in coordinating and providing design sign-off across these projects, including the management of a coordination group chaired by Peter Bishop. Most of this funding came from existing budgets or from generic programmes where there was underspend or where the allocation had yet to be agreed. The trick was to know where the money was located and to have a series of simple, low-risk, ready-to-go projects to soak it up. Accountancy was one of the essential urban planning skills that the team had acquired.

The projects were a typical example of the 'catch and steer' approach: a series of phased incremental interventions that are practical and realistic, and provide local solutions to local problems. The approach was well suited to DfL's work, inasmuch as it was participatory, immediate and low-risk and could yield high political rewards. As a technique it could, if handled well, leave behind more confident and resilient communities and increase social capital. This approach involved a form of curated change in neighbourhoods using a large number of small spatial interventions that individually might be insignificant, but collectively would help to stitch together the area. The benefit of this approach was that it was open-ended: the projects could emerge from community consultation and be realised through a wide range of different actors and budgets.

Making seemingly small project interventions actually happen on the ground played a powerful role in seeding and testing strategic visions, such as the proposed new town centres. It established benchmarks and a design ethos that influenced the projects and developments which would follow. In a context where there was a real risk that the Olympic Fringe masterplans would simply gather dust and be forgotten, this opportunity delivered a first phase of creative, ambitious projects utilising £12.5

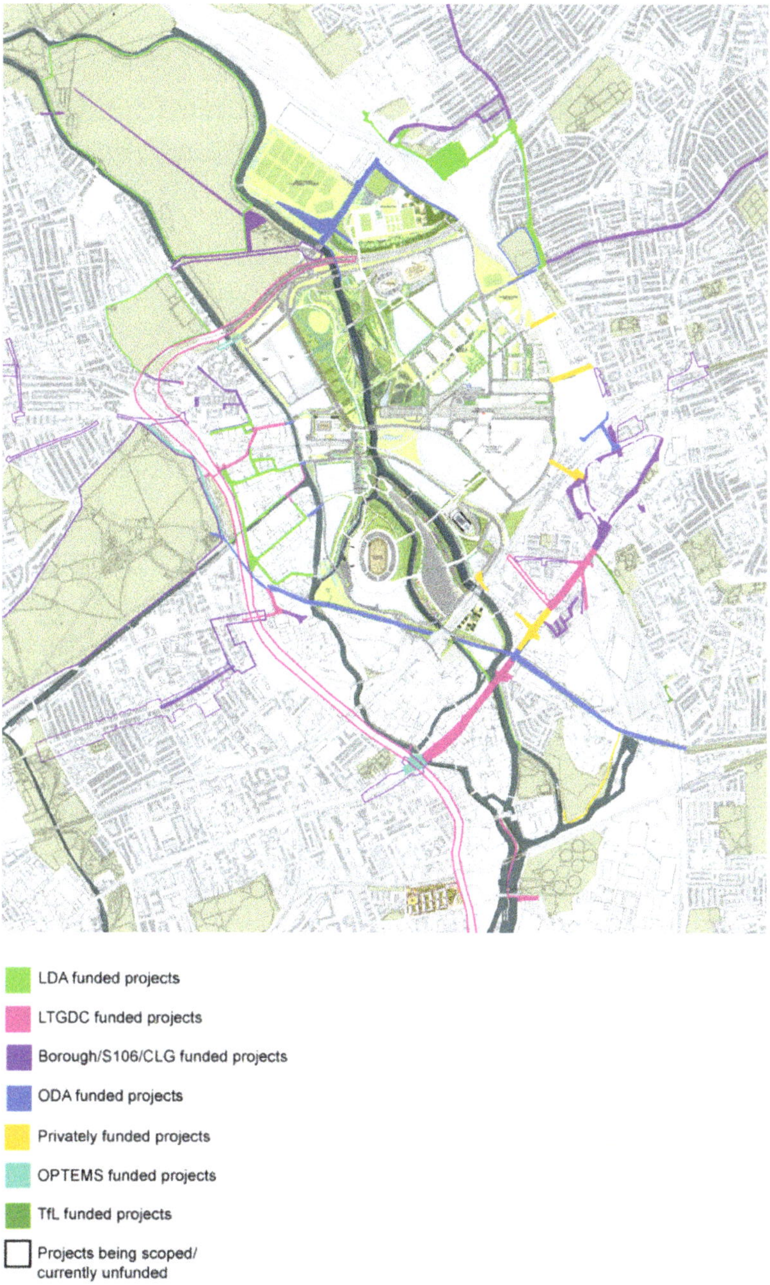

Figure 6.19 Mapping of Olympic Fringe public realm projects, showing coordination of seven different funding streams to create an integrated, strategic intervention, 2012. Source: DfL/GLA.

million secured by DfL from the LDA. These projects, and the careful approach to managing change, have profoundly influenced the areas that surround the Olympic Park, most notably Hackney Wick and Fish Island.

A key part of DfL's influence on this work was to ensure that the strategies and projects were based on an appreciation of the places and people of the LLV. The Fringe masterplans were fundamentally a celebration of the Lea Valley – an urban edge with an enduring spirit of wildness and anarchy. Here, many communities marginalised from 'mainstream' London could feel at home. The challenge was to reconcile the *tabula rasa* approach to planning unleashed on the area by the Olympic project with the LLV's fragile, special qualities. At the heart of DfL's work was a desire to understand in practical, deliverable terms how these qualities could continue to permeate the character of the future places. Accordingly, the first phase of publicly funded projects focused on protecting industrial heritage and waterway landscapes, and building new pieces of movement infrastructure.

Even to talk about 'heritage' in the LLV in the early days of the regeneration project was considered laughable. Other than hidden gems such as Bazalgette's pumping station at Abbey Mills, there was no acknowledgement of the importance of the remaining few pockets of industrial buildings and yards from the LLV's heyday as a hive of industrial innovation. DfL's emphasis on valuing the overlooked but special qualities of the areas where they worked underpinned an ambitious use of conservation area designations for these vulnerable areas. This recognised that conservation area legislation, while more typically associated with preserving 'traditional' heritage areas, was a powerful tool to control demolition and secure high-quality design. Some carefully managed change was also encouraged. Conservation areas were designated just in time to control new development and protect the quality of place. The result is that Sugarhouse Lane, Hackney Wick and Fish Island have been retained as quirky pieces of city that house a vibrant, creative local economy. The unbroken lineage of creative manufacturing which had taken place in these buildings and yards was integral to the heritage value of the area. Conservation area designation has ensured that 'making' activities still take place in the identified heritage buildings. These have been preserved against speculative residential developments that would have obliterated the character of the area.

DfL also commissioned a number of radical and creative park and public realm projects. These aimed to use the opportunities presented by landscapes that are malleable and ecologically rich, and to embody the essential qualities of the area's industrial past. They form part of a far

Figure 6.20 A linear park for the Lower Lea Valley (5th Studio). Source: DfL archive, DfL/GLA.

wider network of open spaces within east London. The East London Green Grid, devised by DfL (Chapter 5), provided a framework to integrate and upgrade disparate landscapes into a model for growth and regeneration. The Fringe plans and projects used this concept of connected landscapes to form a linear park that connects the Olympic Park to the Thames (Figure 6.20).

Hackney Wick and Fish Island (HWFI) form the western flank of the Olympic Park. This is a special area of old industrial buildings, many of which are occupied by the creative sector. The area benefited greatly from the five-year pause in development activity that was triggered by the global financial crash of 2008. This created a window of opportunity for DfL to work with the boroughs and those living and working in the area, in order to understand how to support positive change once development pressure resumed. The process of familiarisation had been developed in other successful DfL initiatives at Barking, Bankside and Dalston. It was characteristically granular and entailed spending a great deal of time on the ground exploring and talking to local residents. DfL appointed muf architecture/art (who became integral to the team's work in the area over the years) to undertake the first-ever audit and mapping of artists and businesses within the area. This revealed a huge concentration of artists. It identified 610 studios with up to five artists per studio, making it possibly the highest density of artists in Europe. This survey represented a watershed moment for the future of HWFI. Almost overnight it transformed the attitude of public-sector partners towards the area. A shared appreciation of its distinctive qualities began to emerge. To flesh this out, DfL commissioned a local architecture student, Richard Brown, to document the local vernacular of informal live–work studios which had emerged in converted industrial sheds. Typically, these were small studios clustered around large central shared spaces that hosted circus and theatre performances, radio stations, pop-up restaurants, sculptors' workshops and film festivals. Brown's resulting book, *Creative Factories* (2013), included photographs, interviews and scale drawings as well as details of rents and leases. This became a portal for local stakeholders to peek into an otherwise mysterious, hidden world (Figures 6.21 and 6.22).

The real challenge was to find the right way for DfL and the public sector to respond, to be helpful rather than inadvertently undermine the very characteristics that were being uncovered. Working with muf, DfL

Figure 6.21 Hackney Wick and Fish Island's creative communities. Source: DfL/GLA.

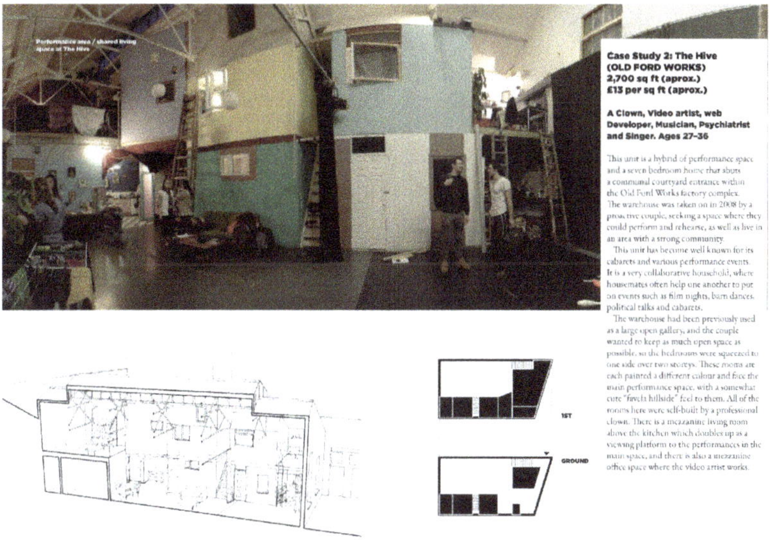

Figure 6.22 Extract from *Creative Factories* by Richard Brown, 2013. Source: London Legacy Development Corporation.

was developing an approach of 'temporary moves to influence what comes next': 'in this reversed form of masterplanning, strategy begins with the detail'.[10] DfL opened the discussions with key individuals from the HWFI creative community by asking, 'How can we help?'. Three strands of activity emerged:

- Improve the condition of streets and pavements (which was woeful at the time).
- Find ways for the creative businesses and activities to have more visibility, status and public presence, so that they would be less vulnerable when development did commence.
- Support the evolution of the creative sector in HWFI, and build its capacity to engage positively with the opportunities of the Olympic Park next door, and with future developers.

The public-realm projects that were delivered in HWFI were consciously conceived by muf architecture/art and J & L Gibbons landscape architects as a series of benchmark projects. It was an opportunity to set the tone and ethos to influence projects by others in the future. The public realm projects were 'locally sourced' in a variety of ways. These ranged from using terrazzo made from aggregate from the McGrath Bros. waste depot in Hackney Wick, to using local apprentices to build benches and walls,

Figure 6.23 The Street Interrupted project, Hackney Wick (muf architecture/art with J & L Gibbons, 2012). Source: London Legacy Development Corporation.

to commissioning a local metal workshop to fabricate a copy of a Hollywood-style 'HACKNEY WICK' sign (which a local artist had made from card and erected on a local studio building). In addition to these characterful physical projects, careful attention was given to nurturing the use of these spaces through curated programming. For example, the Street Interrupted project – which created a new public space by planting a mature tree in the middle of the road outside the Pearl cafe and See Studio gallery (the first of each to open in HWFI) – was activated by funded outdoor play sessions (Figure 6.23). This aimed to ensure that residents from the nearby housing estates felt that this new space was as much for them as for the hipsters beginning to congregate in HWFI. Similarly, the provision of new fruit- and vegetable-growing spaces, which the project delivered for Gainsborough Primary School in Hackney Wick, included funding for the chef at the Pearl cafe to run cooking sessions with the schoolchildren.

The White Building was another important DfL-led project that established a true 'hub' for the area where the many groups with local connections could meet and engage with the processes of change. These included local artists, residents from the wider area, developers scoping out the area and factory workers. The project took a lease on a derelict two-storey print workshop located on the canal at one of the future entrances to the Olympic Park. This location was significant as the project sought to act as a 'stepping stone' and ultimately to encourage local communities to connect with the legacy parklands and facilities in the Olympic Park. It also opened up the first public space on the canal. DfL ran a design competition and David Kohn Architects (shortlisted for the 2009 Young Architect of the Year award) was appointed. The project created space for the creative sector to deliver more public activities, including a studio for international artist residencies, an event space, and a cafe (including an on-site brewery). Space Studios was appointed to run the project, with the fit-out and the first five years' rent funded by the DfL Olympic Fringe budgets.

The White Building and Street Interrupted were projects that piloted and tested what the character of the proposed new town centre at Hackney Wick might be and how it could be rooted in the distinctiveness of the place. Building on the success of the White Building, further community-based pilot projects were delivered by the DfL team within the Hackney Wick town centre, for example:

- *Frontside Gardens skateboard and BMX park* – a 'meanwhile' project occupying a publicly owned site from 2012 to 2016. This hugely successful outdoor park was built by the local community, with some help and supervision, using leftover materials from the 2012 Olympics construction. The project held training sessions for girls and under-10s, as well as training local young people to help manage the park.
- *Hub 67* – a vibrant and well-used community centre built from cabins salvaged from the Olympic media centre (Figure 6.24).

Figure 6.24 Hub 67 and Frontside Gardens in the heart of Hackney Wick, 2014 (David Kohn Architects with muf architecture/art, 2012). Source: London Legacy Development Corporation.

This phase of delivering creative and experimental projects and initiatives 'on the ground' with local communities was completed with the opening of the London Olympic and Paralympic Games in 2012. The next phase was to put in place the infrastructure and statutory planning framework needed to ensure that the rapidly approaching wave of development would be of the highest calibre and would strengthen rather than diminish the qualities of HWFI. The body of work that had already been completed gave all the organisations involved, led by the LLDC, a clear vision and the confidence to be bold in setting stringent rules and demanding the best. A significant swathe of HWFI was designated as a conservation area (Figure 6.25). Planning policies set out rules regarding the replacement of all affordable workspace and height limits for new buildings, and gave guidance on the design of the public realm, including incorporating working yards into schemes. The LLDC took a lead on masterplanning and facilitating the coordinated delivery of the proposed new town centre at Hackney Wick (Figure 6.26). This included securing the funding and delivery of a new station building that was integrated into new pedestrian routes (Figure 6.27). The transformation of HWFI is now well underway, with developments at

Figure 6.25 Heritage buildings within the HWFI conservation areas, 2013. Source: London Legacy Development Corporation.

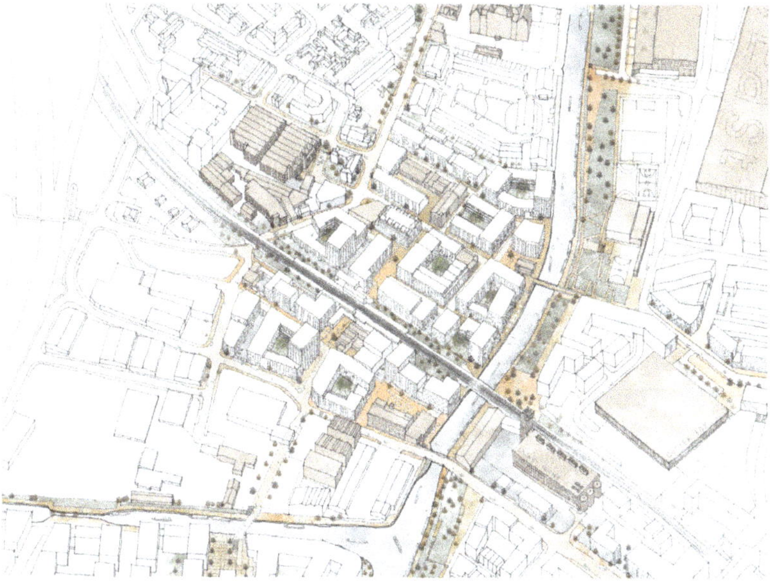

Figure 6.26 Masterplan for Hackney Wick town centre (Witherford Watson Mann and KCAP, 2017). Source: London Legacy Development Corporation.

Figure 6.27 Hackney Wick station (Landolt + Brown Architects, 2018). Source: London Legacy Development Corporation.

various stages across 22 sites. The LLDC has already approved 2,500 new homes and over 61,000 square metres of studio/workspace for the area.

The Olympic legacy has established new town centres around the Olympic Park that anchor the existing and new communities into the park. Here East, the former Olympic media and press centre, has been repurposed as a buzzing centre of academic institutions in media and design, as well as incubator spaces. East Bank will be a new cultural quarter for London, housing several internationally renowned museums and institutions. HWFI has been designated as a Creative Enterprise Zone by the Mayor of London and the workspaces and creative industries are seen as integral to its identity and value. Inevitably, a new generation of artists and businesses is now moving into the new workshops and the area is evolving. While it feels very different in places, HWFI is widely recognised as providing a benchmark of city-making with integrity and coherence.

Stretching the Fringe: strategies for the Royal Docks

Persuading developers to invest in east London was a problem that had bedevilled numerous attempts over the years to shift development eastwards where there was a surplus of brownfield land and areas of social deprivation. The Olympics provided a major new plank in this strategy and there was little doubt that it would regenerate the Lea Valley around Stratford. The LLDC was charged with spreading benefits out into the immediate surroundings including Hackney Wick, Leyton and the Lower Lea Valley. The Fringe masterplans were a vehicle to achieve this. However, the central problem remained: why was the market not responding to development opportunities on sites that were close to the financial centres of the City and Canary Wharf, were in public ownership and well served by public transport? Part of the problem was branding, and the concept of the Green Enterprise Zone (Chapter 2) had been used, with some success, to address this. The east London Green Enterprise District was not a plan, but a conceptual narrative that sought to answer Boris Johnson's questions about a wider Olympic legacy and the need to regenerate the Royal Docks, respond to the near-collapse of the financial sector after the Lehman Brothers crash and establish some environmental credentials for the mayor. The idea of a loose and extensive zone for the low-carbon economy was easy to grasp and within two weeks an enthusiastic mayor was presenting it to the prime minister.[11]

The next stage was to detail it for the Royal Docks. Clive Dutton had just been appointed as Director of Regeneration at Newham.[12] He knew

Peter Bishop and they shared a common approach to regeneration. They agreed that the current regeneration strategy needed to be rethought. First, they concluded that Newham's planning powers and the LDA's land effectively made them a two-man development corporation. Second, they counted more than 70 plans that had been drawn up for the area since the 1970s. What was *not* needed was another plan! Third, none of the plans had succeeded in articulating the area's unique characteristics. Promoting opportunities for 'mixed-use development' just did not capture the public imagination. Fourth, Dutton worked for a Labour mayor, Sir Robin Wales, and Bishop worked for a Conservative mayor, Boris Johnson. Although the mayors were not that far apart in their approaches to regeneration, for investors it represented a potential political minefield that was best avoided. The final problem was one of momentum. East London had always developed through a series of eastward 'lurches'. Canary Wharf, ExCeL London[13] and London City Airport had all been successful but had not triggered further development. The concern was that the Olympics would be the same.

A compelling narrative was required – one that would bridge the divide between residents' and developers' interests as well as the perceived political divide. A new narrative was brainstormed over a (very extended) Friday lunch with Isabel Allen (DfL's press and publications manager). As Peter Bishop and Philip Singleton (Clive Dutton's deputy) discussed the issues and a way forward, Allen took notes. By Monday she had worked these up into a strategy document that was presented to Robin Wales and Simon Milton (Boris Johnson's chief of staff at the GLA) the following week. The strategy set out a simple, clear vision for the area as a business logistics support area for London based on City Airport and ExCeL. One could fly in and out for business from almost any major European city. The Royal Docks would provide a location for headquarters and regional offices, logistics centres and hotels (Figure 6.28). There would be local jobs and a range of housing, including affordable units, and a high-quality and environmentally sustainable environment. Both mayors were convinced by the vision[14] and signed the foreword, thus giving it the instant seal of approval. The entire process took less than a month[15] and the strategy was launched in March 2010 at the MIPIM international property conference in Cannes. A joint delivery board was set up between the GLA and Newham to detail a programme of action and a site was found for Siemens to build a new European research and development centre.[16] Momentum was maintained through a series of temporary projects: Meanwhile London (Figure 6.29). Other projects included the London cable car[17] and a major new business centre

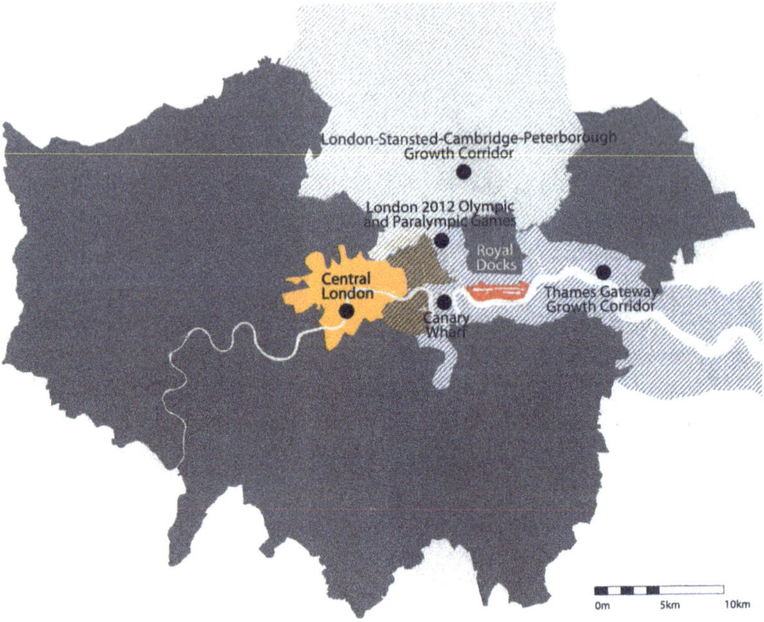

Figure 6.28 Central London and the Royal Docks: strategy context. Source: Royal Docks Strategy, February 2010. DfL/GLA.

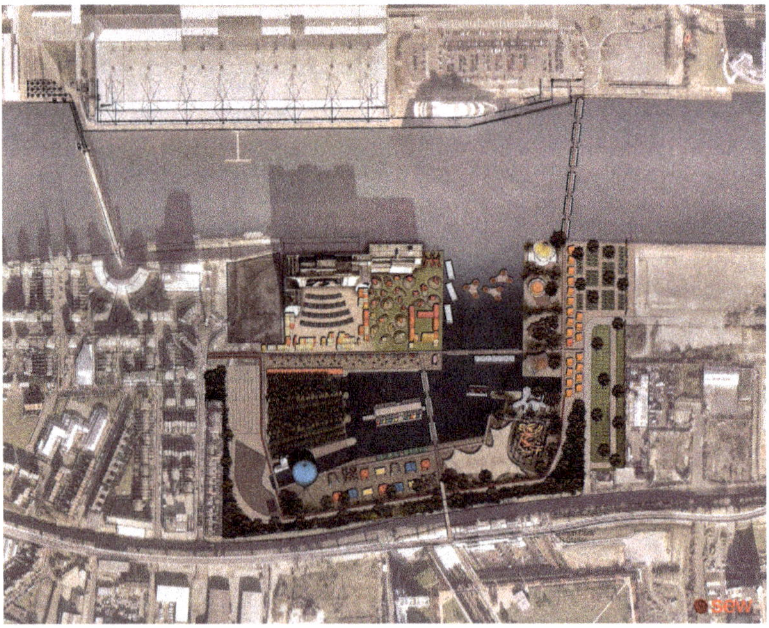

Figure 6.29 Temporary use proposals for Silvertown Quay. Source: Meanwhile Uses in the Royal Docks, March 2010, DfL/GLA.

developed by ABP of Beijing.[18] This was the first major move into the London market by a Chinese developer. The two-man development corporation model had achieved results.

Conclusions and lessons

The period of the run-up to the London Olympics was extraordinary. From 2000, London had a mayoral government that was capable of fashioning a global vision for the metropolis, and there was a national government that was forward-looking and ambitious for the UK to punch above its weight on the global stage. London government had been re-established, was becoming operationally mature and had developed influence with central government. The economy was booming and this seemed destined to continue into the far-distant future. The award of the Olympic Games to London in July 2005 perhaps marked the high point of the period. DfL was very much a product of this period.

Later came the 2008 Lehman Brothers crash, recession in the London economy, a change of mayor, a national government that imposed austerity measures, and street riots in London in 2011. London did, however, put on an Olympics that many would recognise as one of the most successful ever. London had proved its resilience. Notwithstanding a set of false starts, there is no doubt that the legacy is being delivered in a way that no other city has yet managed. Whether it is meeting the original aspirations is debatable. A new district is emerging in east London, fulfilling the overall promise of the original bid, but many of the elements, such as high streets, town centres and a wide mix of different housing tenures and workplaces, have not yet been delivered.

From a design perspective, one of the lessons is that projects of this size and scale do represent unique opportunities to reshape cities. The problem is that the stakes are so high that operational conservatism is likely to take hold early on. The mantra 'on time and on budget' might sound compelling when repeated often enough, but it ignores the obvious question, 'Is it any good?' More often than not, it is an excuse for sloppy thinking and lazy mediocrity. Good design is often seen as largely irrelevant by those in power; promoting it therefore requires a degree of political acumen and stubbornness. It also requires guile and stamina.

DfL could be described as the 'guerrilla warfare' wing of London architecture. In its role on the Olympics, it operated behind the scenes to shape some of the key components of the project and round off many of the blunt edges of the original Olympic masterplan. By encouraging an appreciation of the special qualities of existing places, DfL promoted a richer design approach. This has ultimately added value to the schemes and created places with real character and integrity. DfL worked within the political and institutional context of London to exert influence, assemble alliances of like-minded individuals and agencies, and ensure that good design and sophisticated urban strategies were embedded in the process. In doing this it used strategies of infiltration, alliance-building and incremental urbanism to improve the outcomes.

The regeneration of the Lower Lea Valley grappled with many issues common to other major urban redevelopments: integrating new with existing communities; delivering the right infrastructure, amenity and connectivity; and ensuring that private schemes deliver the big vision. But, due to the 2012 Olympics, it did so at a vastly accelerated pace. The changes that occurred in just a decade in the LLV would ordinarily take a generation or more to unfold. The strategies and projects that have now been delivered in the LLV therefore provide an excellent opportunity for learning. It was a time of ambition and experimentation, where DfL played a central role. The projects are showing all kinds of outcomes – good and bad, expected and unexpected. The evolution of the LLV continues, and the regeneration is far from 'finished'. However, the projects and initiatives now underway have learned from the earlier phase of projects and noted where opportunities were missed. The planning policies – in particular, the strategic vision and five key spatial principles

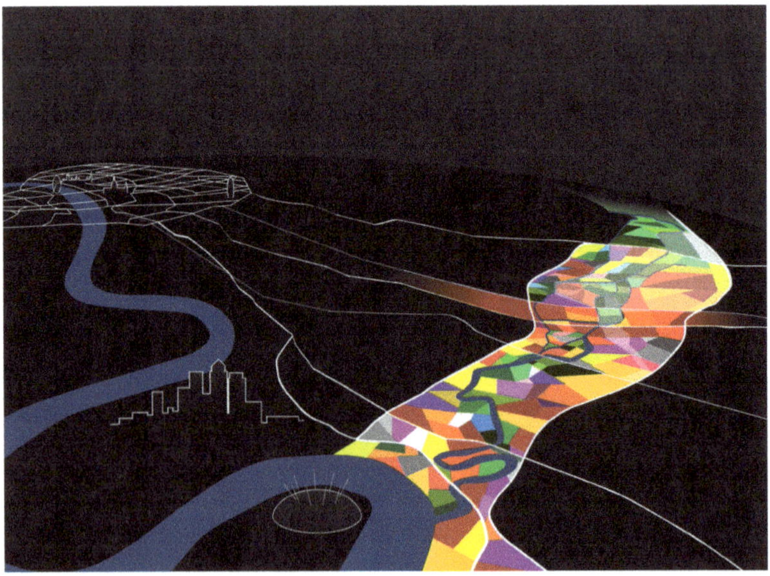

Figure 6.30 The Lower Lea Valley (KCAP, 2008). Source: DfL/GLA.

established in the LLV OAPF – have proved to be remarkably resilient and continue to act as a kind of bedrock. They still enable the many processes of change that are underway to be delivered by a multitude of actors, to create integrated and coherent places (Figure 6.30).

Notes

1 See Ken Livingstone's Introduction to this book.
2 In 2011 London overtook New York to become the top city in the global city rankings (Mori Foundation 2012).
3 *Inspiration*, the 2012 London Olympics bid film, Miros Films International, 2005.
4 Amsterdam's 2028 bid was later abandoned.
5 Conversation with Peter Bishop and Ricky Burdett in 2009.
6 Art historian and curator, who served as the Director of the Tate from 1988 to 2017. He is currently Chair of Arts Council England.
7 The panel who had interviewed all of the architects was not consulted on this change in decision.
8 In 2012 this became a mayoral development corporation, the London Legacy Development Corporation.
9 The main Olympic Park was shared by the four boroughs of Newham, Tower Hamlets, Hackney, and Waltham Forest, while the fifth borough was Greenwich, where equestrian events were held.
10 muf architecture/art, 2009.
11 The concept led to Siemens investing in their European research centre (the Crystal) and ultimately to investment from Chinese firms in a business park.
12 Clive Dutton had been Director of Regeneration in Birmingham, where he had been instrumental in some of the projects that had transformed the city.
13 The London Exhibition Centre.
14 The compromise was an interesting one. Both supported the idea of employment, and the role of the area did not threaten any established business areas. For Newham it removed the risk of extensive housing development, much of which would be private, and which could have the potential to change the political composition of the (Labour-voting) south of the borough.
15 A statutory Local Plan would have taken three years.
16 From first meeting with Siemens to the start on site took 10 months, including site acquisition, planning approval, procurement, design and construction contracts.
17 The cable car (Emirates Air Line) has been criticised as a Johnson 'vanity project'. Its purpose was to act as a giant billboard to advertise the opportunities in the Royal Docks on the back of the Olympics. It also has a carrying capacity that is the equivalent of 40 buses an hour. The majority of funding came from the EU and from sponsorship (naming) rights. All developers under the 'flight path' donated their air rights free of charge.
18 The ABP Albert Dock business centre was on an LDA site that was sold to them following an open tender. The new centre will be occupied by a large number of Chinese firms operating out of self-contained small offices. This could be one of the most significant new commercial developments in London. According to Peter Bishop, 'this is China's version of what Hong Kong was for the British in the nineteenth century'.

Bibliography

Brown, Richard, *Creative Factories: Hackney Wick and Fish Island*, London: London Legacy Development Corporation, 2013.

London Thames Gateway Development Corporation, London Development Agency and Greater London Authority, *Vision for the Lower Lea Valley*, 2006. http://www.london.gov.uk/sites/default/files/archive (accessed December 2019).

Mayor of London/Design for London, *Stitching the Fringe: Working around the Olympic Park*, 2012. queenelizabetholympicpark.co.uk/public/publications (accessed December 2019).
Miros Films International, *Inspiration* (the 2012 London Olympics bid film), Cape Town, South Africa: Miros, 2005.
Mori Foundation, *Global Power City Index, 2012*, [n.p.]: Mori Foundation, 2012. http://mori-m-foundation.or.jp/pdf/GPCI2019_summary.pdf (accessed 20 March 2020).
muf architecture/art, *Adding Value: The Role of Public Space, Open Space and Space for Culture in HWFI*, London: muf architecture/art, 2009.
Shepheard, Paul, 'Going for Green', *Building Design*, 26 August 2001, pp. 10–13.

7

Selling the story: promotion, publicity and procurement

Isabel Allen, Peter Bishop and Eva Herr

Good design is never a given. Many of the people who are involved in city planning, politics or development are not trained in any of the design disciplines and are likely to see architecture as either an impenetrable (and elitist) discipline or worse, a purely subjective field where their personal opinions are worthy contributions to the debate. It is surprising how many politicians deduce that because they may not like a building, it is per se a bad piece of architecture. The same individuals would probably not apply the same logic to the work of an artist or musician – whether one likes or dislikes Wagner, for instance, has no bearing on his standing as a composer. In addition, there are people who view architects with active suspicion – as a group of impractical individuals who are likely to cost the public purse a great deal of extra money.

Design for London (DfL) was fortunate to be working in a period when there was an interest in design quality. The Blair government had set up the Commission for Architecture and the Built Environment (CABE) and was promoting a forward-looking vision of Britain that embraced the creative sector. The National Lottery had funded major Millennium projects that included the Great Court at the British Museum and the new Tate Modern. These important new buildings were undoubtedly popular with the public. Finally, a buoyant economy had fuelled a mood of optimism in a development sector that was consequently more likely to take a degree of risk with contemporary design. The mood spilled over into society and many more people were spending their rising incomes on fashion, music, entertainment and consumer products. Design was cool and it was arriving in the city.

The political context

The two London mayors who covered the period of the Architecture and Urbanism Unit (A+UU) and DfL had contrasting approaches to design. Whether Ken Livingstone had any deep interest in architecture is debatable, but he did appreciate its role in a wider vision for London on the world stage. He also recognised that London had lagged behind cities like Paris, Berlin and Amsterdam in terms of the public realm and public spaces. His appointment of Richard Rogers as architectural advisor was as much a political act as an appreciation of his architectural skills.[1] Consequently, the A+UU was seen as a vehicle to push an urban agenda based on the recommendations of the Urban Task Force.[2] Livingstone rarely expressed any views about architecture or design. When he made interventions, it was from a political perspective. He was generally supportive, but if he saw adverse political consequences, he would stamp down hard.

In contrast, Boris Johnson expressed some interest in architecture and design, but from a perspective that was largely based on personal preferences. He was interested in grand gestures[3] and 'vernacular' styles of design, and viewed 'ornamentation' as a desirable attribute of any new building. This meant that his relationship with Richard Rogers, whom he inherited from the Livingstone administration, was destined to be short. Planning matters were largely left in the hands of his main advisor, Sir Simon Milton, an experienced politician and ex-leader of Westminster Council. He was brought into the Greater London Authority (GLA) as a 'safe pair of hands'. He showed little interest in design but understood that good design was worth promoting and that the abolition of DfL would send the wrong message. He was therefore prepared to tolerate the team, even agreeing to set up a Mayoral Design Advisory Group.

Creating a profile

The essential difference between the A+UU and DfL was their profiles. The A+UU worked within the GLA to produce ideas and influence programmes and policy. Although it did not seek publicity, it had in fact been targeted by *Building Design* magazine and accused of manipulating public procurement in favour of a small coterie of favoured practices. Although this was not correct, it was a damaging campaign; it is covered in greater detail in the section on procurement later in this chapter. The creation of DfL featured prominently in the architectural press with much speculation as to who would be appointed to lead the team. As a profile had been created, DfL decided from the outset to exploit this.

A high-press profile is a dangerous strategy for any public body, particularly as bad news has greater currency than positive stories. The reasoning, however, was that for a team with no defined role within the structure of London government, no budgets and no powers, profile would be a positive asset. This would allow it to deploy the soft power that it had by virtue of its (perceived) direct access to the mayor in order to influence and persuade those in the public and private sectors to divert resources to support its own agenda. It is very unusual for an institution within government to be allowed a public profile and to use this to campaign. It is interesting to note that CABE took a similar approach. This is possibly a reflection of the unique times in which both organisations operated. A second reason for a high profile was that DfL intended to be propositional and not to become an institutionalised part of government. It was given considerable licence by Livingstone to challenge existing practices and promote new ideas. In exercising this role DfL was operating within a broad political context that had been set by the mayor and reasoned that a positive press could be a conduit for disseminating new ideas, engendering public debate and building new alliances. A high press profile would make it easier to promote big ideas for London and to influence others to carry them through. A high profile, however, is always likely to create enemies and at times this turned out to be the case for DfL.

One of DfL's first actions was to create an International Advisory Group. This was loosely based on the experience of Barcelona. With Richard Rogers as the mayoral advisor, it was easy to attract a high-profile group that included Spencer de Grey, Peter St John, Hanif Kara, Martha Schwartz and Kees Christiaanse. Other members brought in expertise from housing, property and environmental sustainability. The creation of the group coincided with DfL's official launch party and attracted considerable press interest, thus maintaining momentum behind the new team. The advisory group's purpose was to extend DfL's networks and to use them as a conduit to find new ideas and approaches that could be applied to London. The team met four times a year and many members put in a considerable amount of their own time to champion individual projects and act as expert advisors in their own fields. At times when DfL's future was in the balance, they acted as powerful advocates in its support.

The consequence of a high-profile strategy was that the team was constantly exposed to media scrutiny. The stories of the A+UU's alleged bias against certain architectural practices continued to circulate, particularly in *Building Design* magazine. Isabel Allen, who had just stepped down as editor of *The Architects' Journal*, was taken on as Communications Director with a brief to manage the press and promote the work of the team through publications, events and exhibitions. In the paragraphs below Isabel reflects on her experience in this role.

The communications game – by Isabel Allen

As DfL's Communications Director I was faced with a conundrum. The work, by its very nature, was tricky to capture, let alone to communicate. We were operating in the run-up to the Olympics and the press was awash with controversial soundbites about bold, expensive buildings, along with an endless stream of glossy, computer-generated images. DfL was developing and implementing strategies that were long-term, subtle and rather more elusive. It was concerned with routes and connections and patterns of use, with spaces that were underused or overlooked or impossible to define. Its drawings were often at district or city scale and, however thoughtful the content, however beautiful the execution, it is hard to get people excited about a map. It is harder still to create any kind of stir around the intricacies of policy or procurement, however crucial they may be to the city.

Yet DfL's Director, Peter Bishop, was absolutely clear about the responsibilities of running an organisation that was funded by taxpayers' money and whose very existence was dependent on the mayor's personal support. We had an obligation not just to our city, but to our citizens. Our job was not simply to guide and prompt and nudge our way towards a better city, but to explain ourselves as well – to make it plain to the electorate that the city was in good hands. 'You are only as good as what you communicate' was a recurring refrain.

So, we set about the task of finding ways to make our work engaging and exciting not just to the architectural and political cognoscenti but to a wider audience. Our first major exhibition, London: Open City, at London's Somerset House (Figure 7.1), sought to communicate both the range and diversity of London's public spaces and the complexity of its governance.[4]

The mood was set by a series of tourist telescopes in the entrance hall. Instead of offering a magnified view of the prospect immediately across the Thames, they revealed film footage of unexpected and little-known corners of the city: a riding school underneath the Westway,

Figure 7.1 London: Open City at Somerset House, 2008. Source: Isabel Allen/DfL/GLA.

Hackney Marshes – where teams from a wide range of ethnic and cultural backgrounds gather to play football against each other at weekends – and panoramas of the Thames at Rainham. An entire wall of the first exhibition room was given over to a complex diagram charting the countless organisations and interest groups involved in shaping London's public realm (see Figure 0.1 on p. 1). The idea was not to explain how the city was designed but to communicate the complexity of the process – that design was rooted in political brokerage. Another room was wallpapered in life-size photographs of trees in Epping Forest, as a reminder of the extraordinary diversity of London's public spaces. It was also furnished with a giant postcard rack offering free postcards of each of the spaces included in London's Green Grid and a stack of maps showing how to find each space. The hope was that visitors would be inspired to see London from a different perspective and explore corners of the city they had never visited before. The exhibition proved both popular and surprisingly adaptable. London: Open City was quickly followed by Open City Bucharest, where we reworked the content for an international audience, and Open City in the Park,[5] where we reworked the content to be weather-proof, vandal-proof and entirely devoid of walls.

While the exhibitions worked hard to communicate the breadth and depth of DfL's work, their primary aim was to engage and entertain.

Our next exhibition at Somerset House, 'If I Could …', was more direct in its intent. DfL had been accused by its detractors of being opaque in its dealings, particularly with regard to the way architects were commissioned for public-sector projects.[6] The response was to face this criticism head on and to establish a new Architectural and Design Framework Panel for London government to use.[7] In addition to standard questions about their financial resilience and experience, applicants for the panel were posed an additional question that had been devised to explore their creativity and design ability. The question was: 'If I could design London I would … '. Applicants were asked to submit a single A1 board to illustrate their idea and this was given a weighting of 50 per cent of the total points in the appointment process (Figures 7.2 and 7.3). This was an entirely legitimate way of selecting architects' practices, but no one had ever done this before. After much internal debate, the London Development Agency (LDA) agreed to proceed. In the spirit of transparency, open advertisements were placed in the architectural press (including *Building Design*) and we took the decision to make all of the responses part of an exhibition, inviting visitors to make up their own minds as to the relative merits of the entries and to add their own ideas to the mix.

The response from the public was overwhelming. People came, not only to the exhibitions, but also to the accompanying programme of lectures and debates. They signed up for our newsletters and read our publications. It seemed that we had tapped into a genuine enthusiasm for architecture's more prosaic allies: urban design, planning, development and public space. More wonderful still, it seemed that the public shared our conviction that spaces shape our culture, that buildings can soothe our souls – that we could design our way to prosperity, to stability, to radical social change.

It was too good to last. It is possible to pinpoint the beginning of the end to one particular day: Friday, 20 June 2008 – the launch of London's Architecture Week. We had been working round the clock to transform the courtyard of Somerset House into a fitting backdrop for the launch party. The installation aimed to reflect the Livingstone agenda loud and clear and give the message that London's most hallowed public spaces were being reclaimed by Londoners – that informality and accessibility were the order of the day. We had decked out the courtyard as London's Largest Living Room: a place for lounging on the sofa, an invitation to ordinary people – 'whole new audiences' – to linger in the courtyard, curl up on a sofa, eat a takeaway and feel at home. This being a civic gesture, a celebration of the civic realm, we had gone for civic scale. Everything

Figure 7.2 Images from 'If I could design London I would … ': a series of design propositions for London. Source: Isabel Allen/DfL/GLA.

was outsize. We had installed a chequered rug of car-park-like proportions, and gargantuan chairs and sofas. There was space to clamber, climb and party (Figure 7.4). This was a cheery domestic counterpart to Sir William Chambers' classical façades – a sign that standing-up-and-making-stilted-conversation had been consigned to history. It was photogenic, punchy, populist: the kind of quick-hit one-liner that Livingstone excelled at, that politicians like.

Figure 7.3 'If I could design London I would … ': Trumpets on the Thames. Source: Design for London archive, DfL/GLA.

But Ken was out, Boris was in. Boris would now launch the exhibition and make the opening speech. Suddenly the installation did not seem so clever after all. I was due to meet him at the entrance and brief him on the event. We did not know his views on architecture, or on the democratisation of public space. But I had a pretty shrewd idea he'd take

Figure 7.4 London's 'Living Room': exhibition for the London Festival of Architecture, 2008. Source: Isabel Allen/DfL/GLA.

the view that rarefied classical courtyards were best left just the way they were. I did my best to brief him. He looked bemused, questioning, mildly appalled. The lines I had prepared for Livingstone felt puerile, adolescent. Clearly he was unconvinced.

As it happened, there was to be one final 'last huzzah' – the London exhibition at Shanghai Expo 2010. Plans for the exhibition had been rumbling along for years. The LDA had reviewed a succession of pitches and proposals from high-tech, high-profile, high-budget consultants. But nothing seemed to stick. Nobody could agree. There was too much bling, too little content; too many ideas, too little clarity. Time was running out. More to the point, times had changed. With the Olympics around the corner, the emphasis was on delivery, not vision – on tracking costs, cutting back, reining in, tightening belts. There were concerns about recession, unemployment and crime. The electorate (according to the media, at least) was after reassurance.

In this project, as with so many others, the LDA was failing to deliver and had blown most of the budget with nothing to show for it. Ideas that had looked ambitious and impressive now seemed leaden and mundane.[8] There was a general consensus that the emphasis should be on content as opposed to showmanship, that we should view this as an opportunity not to dazzle and compete but to communicate London's priorities and direction on an international stage – except that nobody was quite sure what they were. The transition from a Livingstone to a Johnson administration had brought a degree of confusion. No one really knew which messages or policy strands were likely to be dropped or revised. And there was a shortage of cash. The budget had been eroded by long-since-aborted schemes. The budget for packaging, transport, insurance – and a world-class exhibition – was a little over £100,000. By the time DfL was drafted in to organise the exhibition, it was starting to look like an impossible task. To compound matters, the expo was due to open in less than 11 months and London did not even have a venue.

By chance we had met Bill Dunster of ZEDfactory, who also had a problem. He had designed and built a venue but had no content. This was a marriage made in heaven. We adopted a strategy that killed two birds with one stone. The exhibition was conceived as a series of self-contained mini-exhibits, each dealing with a single message or policy issue, each contained in its own suitcase. The great British suitcase brand Globetrotter was persuaded to donate the cases at cost and we started to beg, borrow, steal and commission a series of exhibits to bring the narrative to life (Figure 7.5). Each suitcase had an airline baggage tag on it, LHR to PVG. The suitcase strategy meant that every element could be constructed in London. Each item was potentially dispensable. Concerns about sign-off and approval were brushed aside with the airy reassurance 'we can always drop it later'. In the event, all the suitcases made the final cut.

Figure 7.5 Shanghai Expo 2010: an exhibition in a suitcase. Source: Isabel Allen/DfL/GLA.

And there wasn't any need for packaging. We simply locked each suitcase as we finished it and shipped it to Shanghai.[9]

Exhibitions, promotion and campaigns

London is often described as a 'city of villages'. Although there is an element of truth in this cliché, the reality is more complex and more urban. The village is a form of settlement and social organisation that is distinct, bounded, inward-looking and often conservative in outlook. London is actually a city of unexpected juxtapositions, a patchwork of neighbourhoods, districts and places, each with its own characteristics and particular qualities. Although the historical form of parts of the metropolitan area might outwardly resemble the traditional village, in reality it is a series of urban fragments that are diverse, cosmopolitan and tied together through the connective tissue of the city and its complex economic and social structures.

One of the early debates at DfL concerned the nature of London. The team defined London as an 'Open City'.[10] This captured the essence of London and the fact that one could come to London and call oneself a Londoner, as with New York, but in stark contrast to cities like Paris or Rome, where citizenship implied birth or at least long residence. An early attempt to bring in consultants to define a comprehensive design philosophy and methodology for London failed. After much abortive drafting, it was agreed that a design philosophy could not be simply defined. In any case, the thinking of the A+UU that underpinned DfL's work was far more advanced than that of the consultants who had been brought in.

As well as the major exhibitions outlined above, DfL collaborated with other cities, including Berlin, Rotterdam, Amsterdam, Paris and Chicago, to explore similarities and differences in the approach that each was taking on similar issues. This was fertile ground for exchanging ideas. DfL exhibited work at the Rotterdam Biennale in 2007 and then in 2009 at the Pompidou Centre in Paris (as part of the Richard Rogers retrospective), and at the Bucharest Festival of Architecture in 2008. It was also one of the main participants in the London Festival of Architecture in 2008 and 2010.

The City Visions 1910–2010 exhibition was work that the team jointly carried out with their counterparts in Paris, Berlin and Chicago. The exhibition was a celebration of the 100 years since the 1909 Burnham Plan for Chicago had toured each of these cities. It was looking at a century of planning and at ways in which each of the participating cities was tackling the same pressing problems of housing, transportation, open space, urban renewal and neighbourhood centres. This was the result of the international networks that were being built, networks that allowed for an exchange of ideas and best practice.

The annual property event, MIPIM, gave DfL the opportunity to open up new dialogues with architects and developers. The New Urban Agenda which was launched at a series of events was a simple repackaging of London's urban priorities. The events were all designed to engage a wider audience and included a breakfast 'Pecha Kucha'[11] where invited participants from London and other European cities were asked to present an idea for the future of London in two minutes. It engaged and amused the audience from the property industry over breakfast, but its intent was serious. It was an open dialogue about the possibilities of a city and how they might be realised.

From the outset DfL sought to build a set of loose networks across London. These were designed partly to infiltrate other parts of London government and create points of influence, and partly to seek out and support individuals in the boroughs who were also trying (often under very difficult circumstances) to carry out their own design initiatives. Initiatives like the 100 Public Spaces and the East London Green Grid were designed to co-opt the boroughs into strategic projects, to educate and to extend DfL's reach and influence. Projects developed in partnership with other agencies were also likely to bring direct support and new funding sources, and to build the political capital of the team. London has 33 units of local government and a decision was made early on to work only with those boroughs that wanted to engage. Some boroughs remained hostile to collaboration and that was fine – there were plenty of places that wanted to work with DfL.

Along with the boroughs, there were also a number of architect practices keen to work with the team both in paid commissions and on an informal basis. Many of the team members taught part-time or held academic posts, and the debate with practitioners was mirrored by a similar dialogue with academia. The importance of these exchanges cannot be overemphasised. They refreshed both the team and the practices concerned and opened up a channel between academic research and government.

DfL's high profile allowed it to build a positive set of networks with most of the architectural press, particularly *The Architects' Journal* (*AJ*). The editor, Kieran Long, was a keen supporter and understood DfL's objective of nurturing new talent. London was full of young practices, but many were finding it almost impossible to break into the public sector due to over-complex commissioning procedures. The opening up of the Architectural and Design Framework Panel, described above, was one way to nurture and develop new talent. Another was to encourage them to work directly with the team. The *AJ*/RPS scholarship emerged from the relationship between the team and Long. This was an open competition run by the *AJ* to find three young emerging architects who would be paid to work for six months in DfL on a propositional project of their choice. The *AJ* would then feature their work. This project was designed to build a bridge with practice and to help to develop a wave of new London-based talent (the Richard Rogers and Norman Fosters of the future). The three 'scholars' were Fiona Scott (Gort Scott Architects), Joe Morris (Duggan Morris Architects) and Alicia Pivaro. The bursaries injected new ideas and energy into DfL, maintained positive press coverage, diversified expertise in practices and produced a set of radical ideas that could push the boundaries of thinking without the team necessarily taking ownership. One of these pieces of work was Fiona Scott's High Street London project (see Chapter 3).

The architectural press also helped to promote some of the team's key initiatives. DfL had worked with the London Borough of Barking and Dagenham and had completed major projects in Barking town centre. The *AJ*, under both Isabel Allen and Kieran Long, and the *Evening Standard*, under Rowan Moore, were strong supporters. Moore[12] commented as follows on the work in Barking town centre: 'A make believe ruin,[13] an arcade with chandeliers and a grove of trees – these are the ways to bring new life and homes to the Thames Gateway.' He concluded by saying: '[N]o one has tried this hard since the Second World War to bring real architectural quality to this place or to revive the old idea of civic pride.' Even *Building Design* magazine concluded: 'That a public space might accommodate such a lavish provision of bespoke design is pretty unprecedented.'[14] The Barking Abbey Green project came out of this working relationship. The final piece of the jigsaw was a joint project between the council, DfL and the *AJ* which selected Lynch Architects to redesign the 6.5-hectare Abbey Green and connect the town centre with the River Roding.

The theme of 'ideas without responsibility' was developed further with the annual student project. Each year an architectural graduate was invited to join DfL and carry out a project of their choice. The project was theirs, not the team's, and it was an opportunity to push the boundaries of the politically possible. One of the students, Oliver Wainwright,[15] produced a project that looked at the London Plan viewing corridors to St

Paul's Cathedral. It concluded that the statutory protected views correlated closely with areas of the city with high property values (Richmond, Blackheath and Hampstead). He identified a series of other viewpoints from poorer neighbourhoods, such as Norwood, Forest Hill and Fairlop, that had no protection. The conclusion that planning policy was being distorted for the amenity of wealthy neighbourhoods was obvious. The final aspect of this broad approach of using advocacy and debate to raise the profile of architecture and design was active engagement with existing festivals. For the London Festival of Architecture, DfL sponsored a programme to bring in international speakers, including Pasqual Maragall, Jaime Lerner, Majora Carter, Torange Khonsari, Lotte Child and Ruth Padel. This programme complemented the team's extensive international speaking programme as part of the promotion of London on the international stage.

Polemical debate was part of the team's approach to opening up wider dialogue on issues across London. It was relatively easy to organise, cheap and fun. Furthermore, the association with some of the world's great urban thinkers added to the profile of the team. Advocacy from within government is rare outside the circle of elected politicians. It was only possible because the team was trusted by the mayor and had the operational independence to take a position. The approach continued when the team was absorbed within the LDA. It was more dangerous to take a public position on policy matters, but as long as this was dressed up in the guise of an architectural debate, it was unlikely that anyone would notice. Like much of DfL's work, it was a case of 'continue until someone stops you'.

DfL always realised that it would be a time-limited body. It was just too different (and difficult to control) to last. At critical times, press support proved crucial to its chameleon-like transformations. It might have been abolished with the election of Boris Johnson as mayor in 2008, but instead it was allowed to move into the LDA due to its profile and a sense that it might be useful to a new administration. Many similar agencies and departments did not survive this political transition. When the LDA was itself facing abolition in 2011, it was the press that created a campaign to save it, partly orchestrated by its national and international networks. The Architecture Foundation wrote to the mayor,[16] arguing that it would be 'short sighted and detrimental' to disband DfL, and Ellis Woodman wrote a leader in *Building Design* magazine[17] entitled 'An Agency to be Cherished', stating that 'the potential abolition of this team is an extraordinarily bleak prospect not just for London but the country as a whole'. The *AJ* ran a campaign to 'Save DfL' that was endorsed by the Royal Institute of British Architects.[18] *Building Design* published a letter in February 2011 from an international group of architects that included Frank Gehry, Zaha Hadid, Renzo Piano, Daniel Libeskind and Rafael Viñoly. The letter pressed the mayor to 'secure the survival of this remarkable team. We hope that he is aware of how widely admired the efforts are of this small group of talented designers.'[19] It is difficult to assess the impact of this level of support on the decision-making within London government, but the team did survive, at least in part, with Mark Brearley taking it into the GLA to work with the mayor's new design champion, Daniel Moylan.

Narratives, not plans

Mark Brearley summarised part of the approach of the team as follows: 'do the drawings, win the argument'. He had also coined pithy phrases that described both opportunity and context, such as 'London is a city of trees', 'slack spaces' and 'small things everywhere', as part of his approach to communicate design to a wider audience.[20] To this DfL added the concept of the design narrative. This was a technique for consensus building. Design narratives were propositional frameworks within which more formal planning exercises might fit. They gave individual projects both context and rationale. Planning had become enmeshed in technicalities and legal frameworks, and, although it purported to want to engage with the public, it was largely incapable of doing so. Consulting on a set of regulatory rules is never likely to get much of a response beyond those who find rules and their infinite nuances fascinating. Although DfL was an architecture team, most of what it did was, in fact, planning. The difference was that simple, easy-to-read drawings and engaging narratives could be used to depict imagined futures that neighbourhoods could relate to, get excited by or reject if they did not like them. DfL took responsibility for defining future states that the planning process was all too willing to leave to chance and market forces.

A design narrative is essentially a description: an aspiration that stakeholders and the community can evaluate and, with negotiation, adopt. Making Space for Dalston[21] was an example of a narrative driving local area regeneration and the East London Green Grid[22] of a landscape narrative. The Green Enterprise District and the Royal Docks Strategy[23] were examples of regional strategies that combined spatial, economic and environmental ideas into a simple compelling story.

The working methodologies around incremental urbanism lend themselves very well to techniques that foster public involvement through collaborative design. As DfL gained confidence in area-based initiatives, it honed its skills and those of its collaborating practices to embrace participatory planning. Participatory planning was not new; a number of practitioners had become very skilled at opening up dialogue with local communities and then developing proposals that had broad support. The Making Space for Dalston project covered in Chapter 3 is a good example of this approach.

Another example of participatory planning is the Deptford Creekside Charrette. The Borough of Lewisham had been an active partner of DfL and invited the team's involvement in Deptford, a historic but poor riverside area that was becoming the subject of intense development pressure. A six-day charrette was held – a collaborative event part-funded by the private sector. A local shop unit was taken for the event and was open to anyone in the community. The objective was to harness the local knowledge, creative talent and energy of the community and produce feasible design options for the area (Figure 7.6). These would be a set of drawn proposals – not a final plan, but rather a starting point for further discussion with the community, landowners and the council to develop ideas further, within a spatial context. Over

Figure 7.6 Deptford design charrette. Source: DfL/GLA.

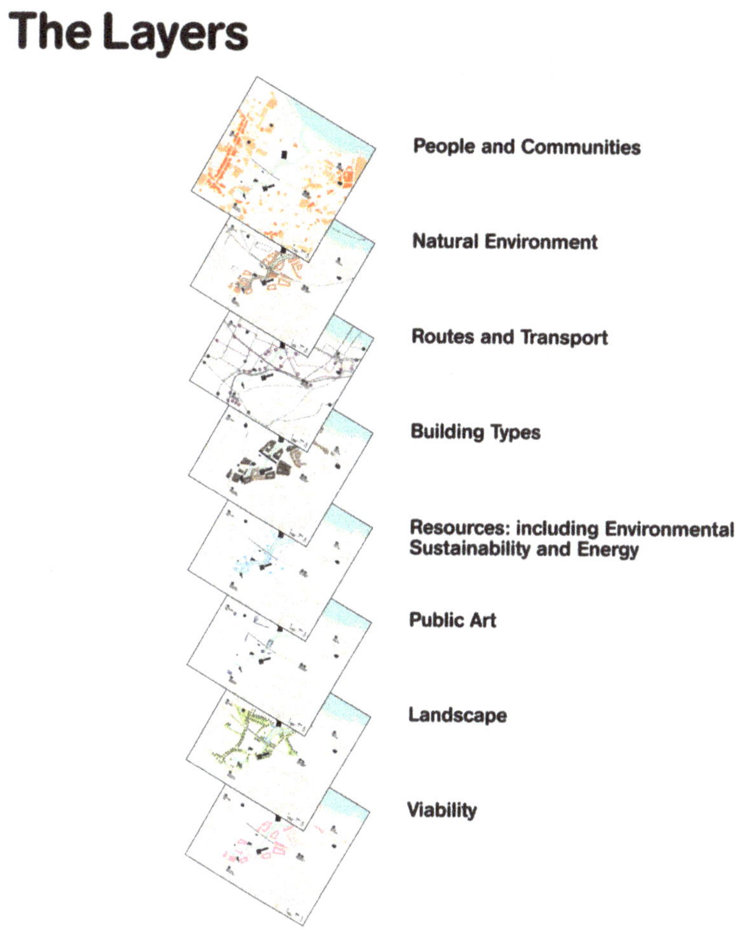

Figure 7.7 Deptford as a series of layers. Source: Deptford Creekside document, DfL/GLA.

the six-day period a multidisciplinary team of 26 architects and planners worked with more than 350 local stakeholders. The resulting proposals were grouped into 'layers, projects and rooms'. Layers (Figure 7.7) included themed strategies, for example for people and communities, routes and transport, and public art. These themes were then considered against a series of 'rooms' that represented distinct areas of Deptford such as the Creek Walk and Waterworks Park (Figure 7.8). Finally, all of the ideas were combined into an area plan (Figure 7.9).

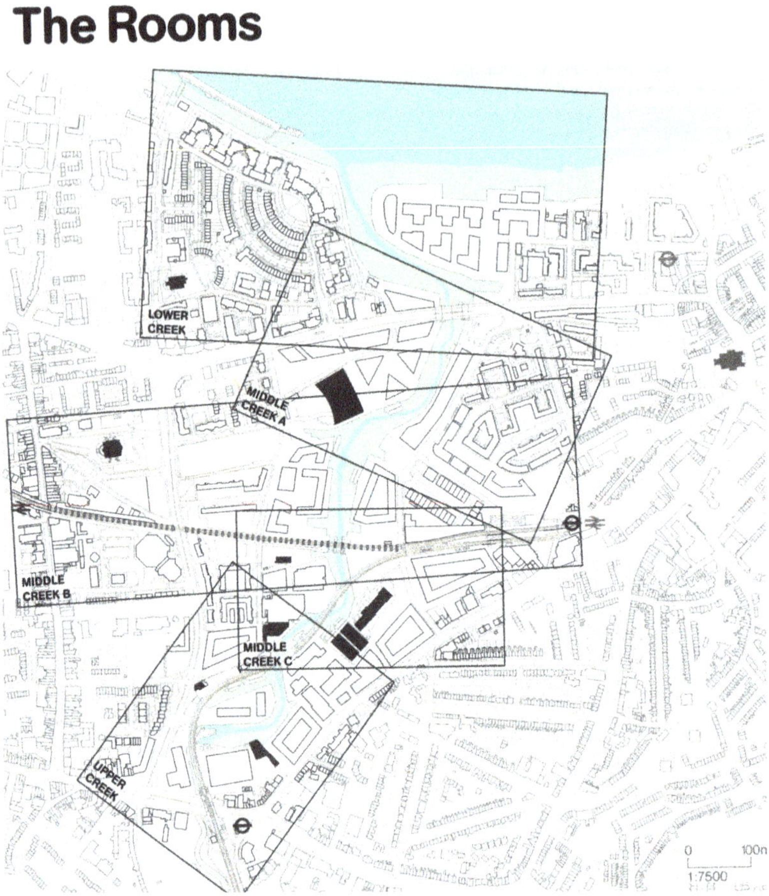

Figure 7.8 Deptford as a series of rooms. Source: Deptford Creekside document, DfL/GLA.

Procurement systems

Public expenditure is rightly carefully regulated in the UK. The notion of responsible stewardship of taxpayers' money is essential to any functioning democracy. Public contracts are often large and can be profitable, and there are too many examples from across the world where bribery and graft syphon off large sums of money. The notion that public spending needs to be transparent, fair and subject to scrutiny is essential. As a result, public procurement is a strongly regulated, stringently documented process. If appointment to public contracts is perceived to be unfair or biased, it fuels cynicism and a lack of trust in

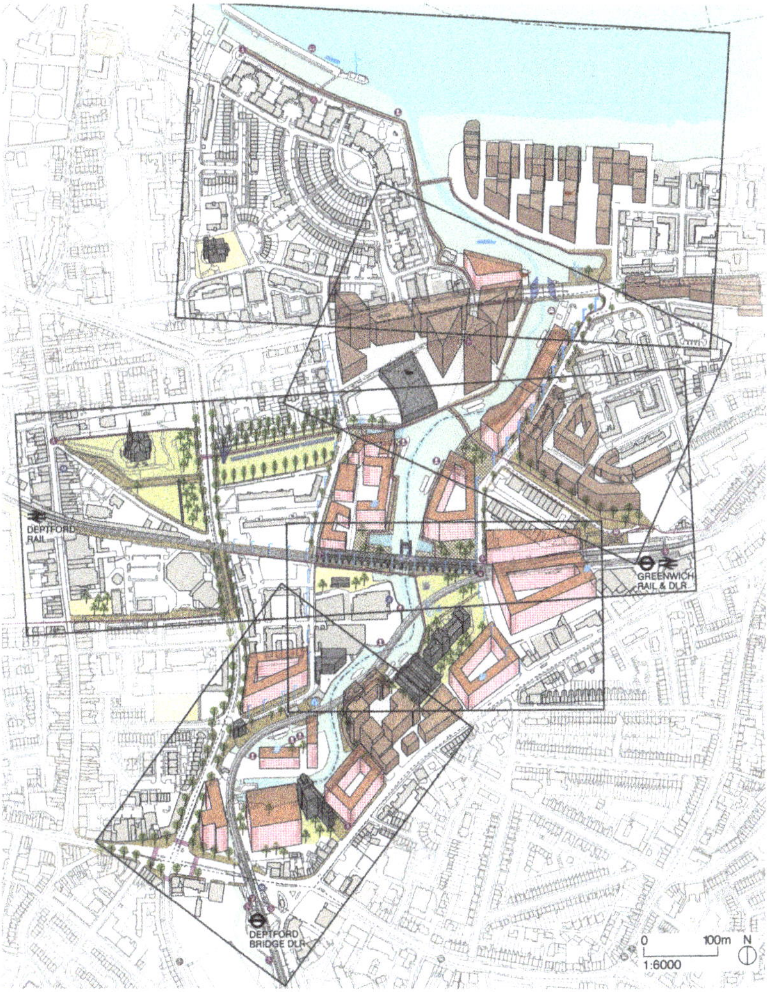

Figure 7.9 Deptford: area plan. Source: Deptford Creekside document, DfL/GLA.

public authorities. Furthermore, if procurement decisions are successfully challenged, this can have a profound and negative impact on a project's finances and delivery timescale, and the reputation of the organisation and individuals concerned.

One way to manage these risks is to systemise the process into complex sets of procedures. The risk is that the driver of the process inexorably moves from outcome to audit. As procurement processes become more elaborate and risk-averse, any focus on qualitative rather than quantitative selection criteria, such as a practice's design ability, is viewed as suspect and open to challenge. Until the end of the 1980s there had been considerable in-house architectural expertise in the public sector. As capital expenditure decreased, so did the work and effectiveness of in-house client organisations. Open competitions were rarely attempted, and most design firms were selected from a limited approved list of contractors – a list that had in itself been procured along risk-averse lines. Approved lists were often used out of laziness or under the pretext of time constraints. In fact, open procurement rarely entails more than an additional three months, which is purely a matter of good project management.

Rigorous procurement may make sense for large-scale, high-risk, high-value construction and infrastructure projects that cost tens or even hundreds of millions of pounds. The costs of running such processes are small compared to the final project cost, and the costs of participating are offset against the huge fees that can result from winning the contract. However, this approach has permeated the public sector to such an extent that even small-scale or low-risk projects go through relatively bureaucratic selection processes. Large firms have the in-house capacity to navigate the public procurement process. They have dedicated teams, standardised documentation and access to legal advice. Small firms without these advantages find participation in these processes risky, expensive and disproportionally time-consuming. For those that are seeking to build up their reputation through design excellence rather than a rigorous health and safety policy, a certified quality management system or knowledge of procurement legalities, the public sector is not always an obvious place to look for commissions.

A practice's turnover, risk exposure ratios or internal human resource policies can all be quantified. But design quality is a lot more difficult to assess. Accountants and procurement managers can rarely make value judgements on quality (and many would see this as too dangerous to entertain). The evaluation of design quality is, after all, difficult to do objectively. Consequently, a successful procurement process is more often than not judged by the fact that there was no challenge. The fact that a second-rate architect's firm was awarded the contract is rarely seen as an issue (and this is in any case a purely subjective view). As a result, public procurement has become ever more cumbersome over the past 20 years. The EU requirements under *OJEU*[24] need not necessarily be a problem, as they can be applied with a relatively light touch. The problem is that often they are not. A whole procurement industry has sprung up, run by 'procurement professionals'. While they might understand the process, they know little or nothing about architecture and design. For them a successful procurement is one that cannot be challenged, regardless of whether the firm chosen is any good.

In addition, other questions have crept into the process, such as data security systems (relevant on government defence contracts but hardly important when designing a park). More recently, local authorities have been asking firms to pay a fee to join a tendering process, or to offer social kickbacks, including the employment of local people as apprentices. These act as a form of disqualification for small firms operating on tight budgets. Similarly, requirements for excessive insurance liability (sometimes set at the capital value of the project) are in effect anti-competitive; and insistence that firms should be able to demonstrate that they have worked on similar projects in the past three years shrinks the pool of those able to compete.[25] What is essential for firms is that the client should be experienced and understand the commercial realities of bidding.[26] Most experienced firms will not bid if there are more than six firms on the tender list, and good practices will be put off if design quality is only a small part of the assessment process.

The UK system is similar to that in Canada and Australia, but as always it is the interpretation that is important. In New South Wales, for example, it is typical for government competitions to weight cost (fee proposal) at 60 per cent and quality at 40 per cent. This is not conducive to the promotion of design quality. Consequently, fees for public contracts have been driven down to very low levels. Current fee levels for government projects are often around 2–2.5 per cent. This is half the rate that is likely to produce good design thinking and execution.[27] In other places, especially in the Middle East, procurement processes can be extremely complicated, costly to take part in and opaque in their decision-making. In theory, procurement processes should be the same across Europe, but in reality, the interpretation of EU rules differs. France tends to be very procedural, while systems vary from state to state in Germany. The German process is generally design-led and offers interesting lessons that were studied by the DfL team. Eva Herr, who worked at DfL from 2007 to 2010, and later worked for the cities of Bremen and Hamburg, has continued to champion the procurement of good architects on city-led projects using many of the methodologies from DfL.

Germany has several mechanisms for including design quality as a key procurement criterion. More recently, the call for greater transparency and community participation has also enabled a degree of public involvement, in particular in urban projects and masterplans.

Well-organised public involvement has strengthened design quality and the public debate on design. Germany has a strong system of competitions, as well as regulations to ensure that independent design expertise forms a prominent part of procurement and competition juries. If competitions are held under official guidelines, architects' chambers sign off the process. Regulations state that the jury must include more qualified independent members with design expertise than members who represent the client side, cost control and so on. The jury's chair is always an independent design expert. This is a relatively established process and, while costs, deliverability and durability are taken very seriously, it is design excellence that makes the difference as to whether a project is chosen or not.

Germany makes extensive use of design advisory panels, such as the *Gestaltungsbeirat* or *Baukollegium* in Berlin. Cities including Hamburg, Berlin, Bremen and Munich have a high-ranking chief architect (*Oberbaudirektor* or *Senatsbaudirektor*) who is involved in major design decisions. Recently there has been a tendency to ensure public scrutiny and even public participation in competitions and design decisions. There are various ways of doing this. For example, members of the public may form part of the jury, either as guests or participants. The presentation of design options can be public and there may be public feedback on competition entries prior to the jury's decision. The most radical approach is to involve members of the public in the jury and ensure a public discussion and decision. Involving the public does not replace the role of independent architects. The idea is to broaden the scope of the design decision by including a wider range of viewpoints.

Using procurement as a design and publicity tool

One of the roles of government is, arguably, that of sponsor and patron. London had the ability to use its purchasing clout to provide market access to small and medium-size enterprises, and indeed the LDA saw this as one of its stated objectives. DfL sought to put this into practice and provide access for small, local and design-focused firms, where public commissions were suitable. From the outset DfL set out to influence the procurement of architects working on programmes that were managed or funded by London government, the boroughs and other public bodies. Control the procurement, be an active client and good design just might occur. This meant influencing the lottery of public procurement in order to appoint good practices that would be curious, engaged and ambitious in their work. This would greatly improve architectural quality on publicly funded projects in London. There was a mantra in the team: 'Good architects *can* design good buildings, poor architects never will.' There are good and bad teachers, doctors, builders and car mechanics. The architectural profession is no different. There are many good practices staffed by individuals with flair and talent. There are also many that are mediocre and cynical. In addition, many architects believe that they can design at the city level, but few can. Lee Mallett, writing in *Planning*, expanded this truism: 'Many clients seem happy with poor design. Many poor architects seem only too happy to supply it. Many local authorities seem happy to live with it.'[28]

The use of procurement as a tool to improve design quality is a completely reasonable approach. After all, why would one willingly select second-rate architectural practices to work on schemes? However, this raises the problem of transparency. Poor architects' practices are rarely self-aware enough to recognise their mediocrity and are ready to call foul when they are not selected for projects. Moreover, their discontent was aggravated when they saw a few relatively small and unknown practices getting the commissions that they were not. The A+UU was already viewed by some as being a small and elite unit with close links to Richard Rogers and a small coterie of practitioners.[29] It was tempting to make the leap to assume that there was a 'black list' of practices that were being deliberately excluded from public contracts. This was never the case,[30] but the rumours continued. This was a toxic and distracting news story, and when DfL was set up, a decision was taken to address it. There were two parts to the strategy. The first was to ensure that the new Advisory Board was advertised and openly recruited; the second was to revamp its whole commissioning process and to use the press to assist in this task.

Underpinning this was a belief that, although there were many excellent large practices operating in London, some of the smaller ones were hungrier and more innovative in their approach. With a smaller practice it was clear who would be doing the actual work on the project. From a project perspective, small firms were also easier to manage and more likely to produce a good scheme; they had more at stake and their reputation depended on delivering a good project. The idea was to broaden the range of potential bidders, lower the threshold for access to public commissions and help smaller firms gain knowledge of how to bid for public projects. And most importantly, the aim was to reintroduce design quality as an important procurement criterion in the selection of firms.

Influencing the selection of architects was seen as an important way to improve the quality of design projects. A number of large firms had cornered the market and were not being scrutinised hard by the client bodies. Managers took the attitude that they had been used before and, as long as there had been no problems, could be used again. Public procurement is actually quite flexible. It can occur through open competition, through design contest (open or invited), from preselected framework agreements or, on small projects, through three to six quotes against a project brief. For most projects the framework agreement was the best way of operating – but only if the framework contained a range of talented firms. Most of the existing frameworks that were being used had not tapped into the vast array of diverse talent that was available in London, the UK and the EU.

The A+UU had managed to influence procurement of design teams on LDA projects. It had already produced a best practice guide in which it stated:

> An open, transparent, competitive selection process is one of the best ways of delivering quality in design. It is not only a legal requirement when public funds are involved, it is also an effective way of getting the best for our built environment. Some of the most successful buildings and urban projects of recent years are the result of competitive selection. The award-winning Laban Centre in Deptford, the Baltic Flour Mills in Gateshead and the masterplan for the Lower Lea Valley at the centre of the Mayor's vision for the London 2012 Olympic Bid are the products of design competitions. The same is true of many of Europe's most attractive and sustainable urban developments in Barcelona, Amsterdam and Berlin.[31]

This practical guide set out the principles of good, open procurement. Architects were included on the selection panels. Ricky Burdett and Richard MacCormac acted as external advisors on some of the larger projects. The A+UU had also persuaded some managers to increase the weighting given to design ability in the assessments. In 2007, on a large housing scheme in Bromley-by-Bow, DfL had persuaded the LDA to award the development to the highest bidder (Barratt), but only if they were willing to change their architects on the scheme.[32] The LDA had already agreed to allow DfL to write the briefs, sit on selection panels and include clauses in procurement documents that the LDA could request changes to the design team when awarding contracts. As DfL was an amalgamation of design teams from the GLA, the LDA and Transport for

London (TfL), it was able to extend its influence to the appointment of designers on transport projects as well.

The opportunity for change arose when the LDA's approved list came up for renewal. Under London government procedures, any of the mayor's agencies (as well as boroughs and the Homes and Communities Agency) could access firms from each other's approved lists, which provided an opportunity to introduce new firms. Understanding the Byzantine processes of public procurement might not be interesting, but it was essential if design quality was to be raised across London. The task of understanding and restructuring the process fell to Eva Herr, an architect in DfL, who later stated:

> When the LDA's architecture, landscape und urban design framework agreement panel was procured, there was a strong internal debate as to whether design quality could or should form part of the selection process. This was partly due to intense public criticism and accusations of favouritism ahead of the procurement process. A lot of effort went into dissolving these accusations and demonstrating that design quality could be evaluated in a fair and transparent way that was up for scrutiny. The panel's EU-procurement was announced widely, not only in specialist publications, as is usually the case. The selection process for design quality was carried out with external independent advisors,[33] helping to dissolve the accusation that internal DfL staff picked firms of personal preference.[34]

The real success was to persuade the LDA to place design ability at the centre of the process and give it a weight of 60 per cent in the evaluation scoring. So that design quality and creative thinking could be evaluated, firms were required not only to submit references, but also to submit a single panel to answer the question 'If I could design London I would … '. This aimed to test their ability to think conceptually and imaginatively. All submissions were published and the panels were used to provide an instant exhibition at Somerset House (as described earlier in the chapter) that coincided with a series of international talks and the announcement of the procurement decision. The process attracted the participation of many firms that had previously doubted that public procurement processes were worth the effort and cost. They trusted that design ability would be taken seriously in the selection process. Part of the selection process, which was initially perceived as being 'secretive', became public. In the end, the decision was not challenged, and nor did it receive negative publicity. On the contrary, it was noted that the LDA had appointed young and small firms alongside some of the UK's most reputed design practices. Procurement, for once, became interesting and relevant to a wider audience. The press, for its part, covered the process and considered that the ghost of bias had been laid to rest.

Conclusions

Having a high profile can be a double-edged sword. On the one hand, it allows access to the press to promote ideas and help to recruit like-minded partners. On the other, it can open up a team to criticism. There are only so many good stories that the press will cover before it seeks to find fault. Critical stories and scandal sell more newspapers. DfL took a conscious decision to break away from the low-profile approach that the A+UU had adopted. It was created in a blaze of publicity and saw profile as a means to develop a debate around how London could be shaped. The employment of a press insider, Isabel Allen, allowed it to keep a high profile with relatively little collateral damage. The campaigns, launches, exhibitions and publications were all part of this strategy, as was the content. If the design ideas were edgy and innovative, these had to be portrayed in the images and exhibitions. They were deliberately designed to provoke a reaction and were all written and presented in a style that kicked hard against the dull approach of public-sector PR departments. The communications strategy was designed from the outset to create a new culture of interest in design, and to launch different approaches that would engage with government, practice and the general public.

The procurement of good architects to work on public projects is one of the keys to raising design quality in a city. Practice in Germany shows that when decisions are made in an open manner, with inputs from both practitioners and the public, then good design is likely to ensue. The experience from New South Wales is that processes that seek value for money purely through reducing fee levels are unlikely to produce anything worthwhile. By playing an active role in the procurement process, DfL was able to exert considerable influence and raise the profile of design across London.[35] The panel was able to nurture a new generation of practices and develop wider and more diverse expertise, particularly in urban design. One of these firms was Karakusevic Carson Architects. It was successful in joining the new LDA panel (its exhibit was a series of tape measures that recorded the ever-reducing floor-to-ceiling heights in London residential properties). Because the panel was used by the boroughs, the firm was subsequently awarded contracts in Hackney, Havering, Lewisham and Brent. Paul Karakusevic of this firm is a strong supporter of the panel system and has stated that it was a lot fairer than basing decisions on 'who you played golf with'.[36] The panel enabled many practices to grow and to become a pool of mature talent that is still shaping London. Perhaps this is one of DfL's most important legacies.

Notes

1 Rogers was a Labour peer and had been one of the participants in the 1996 London debate that had led to the establishment of the GLA and a London mayor.
2 Set up by the Blair government in 1997 and chaired by Rogers; see Chapter 1.
3 Such as the Garden Bridge (subsequently abandoned) and the ArcelorMittal *Orbit* at the Olympic Park.
4 London: Open City was curated and designed with Gerrard O'Carroll, Morag Myerscough, Luke Morgan, Jake Moulson and Lucy Sollitt.
5 An installation on the Greenwich Peninsula that was part of the London Festival of Architecture.
6 This is covered in more detail in the later section in this chapter on procurement.
7 A framework panel is an openly advertised and vetted panel of approved contractors. Once set up, it is standard practice for practices to be selected from this panel without the need for preselection. This speeds up the process considerably. Obviously, a panel is only as good as those on it, but a well-selected panel will improve design quality significantly.
8 The centrepiece would have been an interactive map of London where, as one of the consultants proudly explained, a ballet dancer would pop up when you pushed a button for Sadler's Wells. Uninspiring as this idea was, it was irrelevant as the funding had been spent on 'creative content' and there was not even a map, let alone an interactive one.
9 The exhibition was a critical success and was visited by a large number of people, including the architect Thomas Heatherwick and the chair of CABE, John Sorrell. Both left very flattering comments. After the expo closed, the suitcases disappeared, but Peter Bishop later came across them in a university near to Chongqing where a museum had been built to exhibit them!
10 This is now often used in urban parlance and an early example is the Rotterdam Biennale in 2007. Although it cannot be proved, DfL would claim to have first used the phrase, basing it on the title of the Rossellini film *Rome, Open City*.
11 This is a Japanese presentation technique where 20 images have to be presented in 6 minutes, with the presenter not being able to control the timing of the slides.
12 Moore 2007.
13 Reference to muf's folly on Town Square and AHMM's housing and library arcade.
14 Woodman 2009.
15 Now architecture correspondent for the *Guardian* newspaper.
16 17 November 2010.
17 Woodman 2010.
18 Fulcher 2010.
19 *Building Design*, February 2011.
20 Interview with Mark Brearley, January 2020.
21 See Chapter 3.
22 See Chapter 4.
23 See Chapter 6.
24 The *Official Journal of the European Union* (*OJEU*) requires all contracts above certain limits to be openly advertised.
25 Interview with Helen Logan, partner at Allies and Morrison, March 2019.
26 Typically, a medium-to-large firm will have a standing team and this will account for around 3 per cent of turnover. The cost of the average bid is likely to be around £2,500–10,000 and a successful firm would expect at least a 25 per cent success rate.

27 Bishop 2017.
28 Quoted in Bishop 2011.
29 For the record, Richard Rogers' practice never bid for, or was awarded, projects from the A+UU or the mayor.
30 In 2006 the GLA carried out an internal inquiry into alleged bias in the A+UU and concluded that there was no evidence of bias or malpractice.
31 Greater London Authority 2005.
32 Allies and Morrison, Glenn Howells and Maccreanor Lavington were subsequently selected by Barratt and approved by DfL. This was a turning point for Barratt (London) as it proved to be one of the most successful projects that they had built. They went on to do other schemes on LDA sites, including Barrier Park and Dalston Junction, always seeking DfL advice on their choice of architects.
33 This included Hanif Kara from the DfL Advisory Group.
34 Interview with Eva Herr, December 2019.
35 The GLA still operates the panel and the processes that underpin it. The typical selection criteria are now 70 per cent design quality, 20 per cent price and 5 per cent social value.
36 Interview with Paul Karakusevic, October 2019.

Bibliography

Bishop, Peter, *Bishop Review*, London: Design Council/CABE, August 2011.

Bishop, Peter, 'Review of the Government Architect for NSW', November 2017. Unpublished MS.

Fulcher, Merlin, 'Call to Arms: "Save Design for London"', *Architects' Journal*, 25 November 2010. https://www.architectsjournal.co.uk/home/call-to-arms-save-design-for-london/8608474.article (accessed 20 March 2020).

Greater London Authority, *Commissioning a Well Designed City: A Guide to Competitive Selection of Architects and Urban Designers*, London: Greater London Authority, Architecture and Urbanism Unit, July 2005.

Moore, Rowan, 'How Barking is This?', *Evening Standard*, Life and Culture, 11 September 2007, p. 39.

Woodman, Ellis, 'Square Dancing at Barking Central', *Building Design*, 27 November 2009. https://www.bdonline.co.uk/buildings/square-dancing-at-barking-central/3153931.article (accessed 20 March 2020).

Woodman, Ellis, 'An Agency to be Cherished', *Building Design*, 29 October 2010. https://www.bdonline.co.uk/opinion/an-agency-to-be-cherished/5008074.article (accessed 17 March 2020).

8
Conclusions

Peter Bishop

The immediate postwar period in the UK was dominated by the need for reconstruction. This required the creation of powerful state agencies, and architecture and planning were viewed as the realm of the professional expert. In the immediate aftermath of a war-time economy, their visions for the future were rarely debated, let alone challenged. Despite real postwar austerity, the concept of state expenditure to redress social and economic issues was broadly accepted within the political mainstream. The state had land and funds and believed it knew best how to use them. There was limited interest in preserving heritage (and the definition excluded much of the nineteenth-century fabric of cities). It was widely believed that 'slums' should be cleared and that the motor car was the future for transportation. An extended middle class that was embracing modernism and consumerism saw itself as the vanguard for a better future. In the words of Harold Macmillan, Britain had 'never had it so good'.[1]

By the 1960s a new awareness was emerging concerning the relationship between urban form and civic life that was fundamentally challenging the worst excesses of the modernist movement. Urban thinkers such as Jane Jacobs had begun to question the impact of the wholesale restructuring of cities driven by neighbourhood clearance and the construction of urban motorways. Implicit in her arguments was that 'strips of chaos' were worth valuing over the excessive ordering principles of urban planners. Jacobs established a set of principles that might have been radical at the time but have since become enshrined as some of the founding principles of present-day urban planning. These included the primacy of the street as a social place, mixed-use neighbourhoods and the notion of social capital. Through her grassroots campaigning she also established the principle of practitioner as activist.

This was carried forward by a new generation of urban planners and architects, including Design for London (DfL).

The Architecture and Urbanism Unit (A+UU) and DfL inherited a rich vein of late twentieth-century thinking about the city. Their design methodologies reflected 'careful urban renewal' and 'critical reconstruction' and incorporated principles of community participation and engagement. The city was no longer a place to be planned and rationalised. It was a complex, collaged and untidy place that was in a process of continuous adaptation and change. Its 'found' elements, its sheds, industry, wastelands and leftover spaces were parts of the richness of the city. To the designer these places offered material that could be refashioned into new urban forms and configurations. The fine-grained, mixed-use nature of the mature late-twentieth-century city provided a fertile laboratory for experimentation.

It is extremely difficult to assess good design objectively. Highway design can be measured through accident statistics, but how can the quality of urban spaces be assessed? Certain measures such as footfall, safety and crime statistics and the economic turnover of local businesses may all point to good design, but they miss those intangible elements that delight and enchant. We know good design when we see it but have difficulty in defining why we like it, or even how we could replicate it in other contexts.

The barriers to good design are complex and deeply embedded in the culture of government at all levels in the UK. Design considerations are often overtaken by operational requirements. The readiness of the media to seize on delay and overspend as examples of public-sector incompetence can turn public projects into damage limitation exercises. In addition, the experience and design expertise of public-sector architecture and planning departments has largely been lost through expenditure cuts. Subjective opinions and personal taste can often dominate the design debate, and these can be hard to resist. Local government is political by nature and its perspectives are often framed by the electoral cycle. Architectural and urban design projects might be seen as desirable but, against demands for education, housing and social care, they are rarely of high priority. The problems are compounded by the lack of design training in planning and engineering courses and the lack of planning and contextual education in architecture courses. Recent national reviews on design in the built environment have all identified shortcomings in design education, lack of local leadership, low levels of design training among politicians and the lack of resources at local level as contributory factors behind poor-quality place-making.[2]

Each chapter of this book has set out its main conclusions and there is no need to repeat them in detail here. Some broad points are worth summarising:

1. Good design is not a given. Some cities might be fortunate enough to have elected representatives who are passionate about design (*and* understand what it is and how to realise it), but these are exceptions. For most senior politicians, design is at best peripheral to their thinking. It does not win votes. Or does it? The key challenge is to demonstrate that good design is about doing things well and that *if* it can be grounded in a broad agenda of urban and social improvement then it *can* win votes.
2. The business of thinking and delivery in government is largely entrusted to a cadre of senior professionals who understand their area of expertise. They might not always be creative, but they do get things done. Educating, infiltrating and cooperating with them will move the agenda in the right direction and achieve better results.
3. Good design needs advocates who have real influence at the city level. Mayoral government has worked well in London so far (although, as power is so concentrated into the hands of a single politician, it does depend on the electorate recognising the qualitative difference between candidates' capabilities to responsibly run what is in effect a multi-million-pound institution). Good design also needs managers and fixers who understand the organisational and political environment and can shield others to produce good and thoughtful work.
4. Building networks across agencies is perhaps the most effective way to influence government. This creates allies at points of influence and allows debates to take place. These debates will eventually be manifest through better things happening on the ground.
5. Agency is essential. Designing at the city or neighbourhood level is not a neutral activity. Urban design has multiple clients and it changes the relative balance of benefits within an area. There are winners and losers in the process; architecture and planning have political outcomes. This applies to the issue of where resources are deployed in the city. Wealthy areas are usually well enough organised to protect their interests, while poorer areas are not.
6. Understanding the city is an essential component of good design. The extensive mapping and analysis that was undertaken in London set a foundation for thoughtful interventions and careful strategies. It also proved critical in winning arguments. For design teams to be

effective, it is essential they have detailed local knowledge. Local politicians and communities see through 'technical experts' pretty quickly. Positive change has to be grounded in local knowledge and understanding, in the history, culture and everyday experience of the neighbourhood. Empathy, which develops understanding, grows with exposure to the locality, its issues and the lives of its people.

7. The issues that are important in determining the quality of urban living are widely applicable. They are shared by most cities. In London, projects to provide public space (100 Public Spaces), policies to improve housing (London Housing Design Guide), programmes to improve town centres (High Street Places), plans to regenerate areas (Olympic Fringe and Royal Docks frameworks) and initiatives to address climate change (East London Green Grid) have all been resilient enough to withstand political change and are all still operating in one form or another. These pieces of work have had a very significant impact on making London a better place.
8. Urban design uses many of the tools of the planner. These include an understanding of how policy works to shape the city. Policy is not abstract. Good policy-making starts from a clearly imagined outcome and works backwards to create the framework to bring it to fruition.
9. Unlike planning (as presently practised in the UK), urban design is able to do the drawings. Plans, drawings, narratives and 'minted phrases' are more effective in fashioning change than regulatory planning frameworks.
10. An incremental, or tactical, approach to shaping the city is more likely to work in an uncertain age. There will rarely be opportunities to plan on a grand scale, so design needs to be opportunistic and agile. A design team will never be able to control a city's development, but it can shape it through 'catching and steering'. Incremental urbanism is spontaneous. Getting started on projects is important to establish momentum and demonstrate commitment. Incremental urbanism also allows networks to be formed and nurtured. It allows experimentation, feedback and adjustment. In many ways the networks formed through good interdisciplinary working at a local level can be as important as the project itself. Capacity building increases resilience.
11. Designers need to understand budgets, processes and regulations. These are the factors that make things happen. Ignore or fail to understand them and very little will ever happen.

12. Design is part of a process. It needs an understanding of how the city is managed, how space is used and how activity can be curated. Good design crosses boundaries between disciplines, and good practitioners also engage with and learn from their clients, especially the communities they work with.
13. Effective urban design works at different and contrasting scales – from the city region to the street corner. It is the intelligent interrelationship between these different scales that gives policy, programmes and projects their coherence.
14. There is a difficult choice between aiming for a high or low profile as a design team. The A+UU and DfL experimented with both approaches. Ultimately this is a matter of tactics and dependent on the circumstances of the time. Sometimes it is useful to infiltrate and give others credit; at other times it is important to be clear who did the thinking and the work. In a mature and stable environment (as certainly exists at the GLA today), campaigning is less important than in the early days of London government, when the case for design had to be made.
15. Publications, events and exhibitions are important instruments in communicating design ideas. The presentation of many public-sector documents is dull. Crisp graphics and clear writing are vital tools to engage with the public and stakeholders.
16. Good architects design good buildings; bad architects never will. Procurement and the client role are crucial tools in ensuring that good designers are given the opportunity to produce good outcomes. City government also has an important role as patron and design champion.
17. Design review is a tool that might improve particular schemes, but it will not in itself make fundamental changes to the city. It is not a substitute for proactive design agency that gets 'stuck in' to tackle the underlying issues of the city.
18. Finally, a design team is *not* a luxury. It can be embedded in the structure of city government or it can be given the freedom to operate outside formal structures. This will depend on the state and nature of a city's government. The use of 'soft power' can be a very effective methodology, but only for as long as political patronage exists. A licence to think, to question, to debate and challenge are essential attributes for any city that is ambitious for a better future.

Although DfL made a significant impact during its short life (and most of its projects came to fruition), there is inevitably regret about a number of high-profile projects that were not implemented. Some of the 'ones that got away' include the partial pedestrianisation of Parliament Square (Chapter 2), major projects that would have redesigned Marble Arch to connect Oxford Street to Hyde Park (by John McAslan) and the closure of part of Sloane Square (Stanton Williams; Figure 8.1). One of the first proposals in the 100 Public Spaces programme was Richard MacCormac's scheme to redesign the Victoria Embankment and create a 'Northbank' to complement London's South Bank. The scheme would have doubled the width of the walkway along the Thames and replanted a double avenue of trees, creating a riverside boulevard along which art would have been exhibited in a curated outdoor gallery. Sadly, the only intervention to date has been to paint part of the carriageway blue as part of the London cycle network. Perhaps a future generation of planners, designers and politicians will resuscitate some of these schemes and adapt them to present circumstances.

It is interesting to consider the design agenda for London now. In many ways it remains the same as it was 20 years ago: public space, responses to climate change, regional landscapes, high streets and town centres, streetscapes and housing standards. Indeed, all of these areas are part of the work of the present team in the GLA under the Good Growth by Design programme. The working methodology would still be similar. Design ideas would still be multi-scaled, from the city to the

Figure 8.1 Proposals for Sloane Square (by Stanton Williams) as part of the Mayor's 100 Public Spaces programme. Source: 'Civilising Spaces', DfL/GLA.

street corner. Hands-on design charrettes would still be central to all local work, as would the methodology of research, mapping and incremental urbanism. Influence would still be exercised through a complex network of partnership arrangements.

There would still be a search for the 'next big thing for London', but in reality the next big thing will be 'lots of little things'. In his foreword to this volume, Ken Livingstone proposes that the 'next Olympics' should be a programme of measures to reduce carbon emissions *and* create new jobs and that this should be at the heart of urban policy. Another fertile area for design thinking would be the places where we all live. On a day-to-day basis, many people rarely leave their neighbourhood, but almost everyone leaves their house to experience the spaces outside their front door. For some, this is an elevating experience, but for many it is not. Drab suburban streets, roads cluttered with parking, estates that are poorly maintained (or are just bleak areas of grass or tarmac) – these could all be so much better. We all know that space is a valuable commodity in the city, so why are we so unimaginative in how we use it? Why do we allow empty cars to occupy it and municipal authorities to manage it according to the lowest common denominator?

The East London Green Grid programme explored the importance of landscapes in the city and extended the concept beyond London into the Thames Gateway. This raises issues about the metropolitan limits of London and the green belt. The flaw of Mayor Johnson's Outer London Commission was that it defined outer London only in terms of its relationship with inner London. A far more interesting exploration would focus on outer London's relationship with the South East region. This would open up critical design issues such as access to the countryside, environmental resilience, resource management, and settlement and work patterns. The future extent and shape of London would be considered in such a work theme. A study of the Thames would similarly be rewarding. The A+UU carried out some initial work that looked at green spaces along the river and ways in which they might be connected together. But what if radical policy shifts could be considered? Should the Thames be designated as a conservation area[3] in order to exert greater design control over the buildings along its length (and the detritus of wharves, landing stages and run-down ships that form such an eyesore in central London)? Would changing navigation arrangements for the Port of London Authority allow the building of bridges in east London without the need for excessive clearances, costs and land take?

There are also many possibilities for subtle pieces of work that might allow the city to be seen through other lenses. Fenna Wagenaar[4] has suggested mapping sunshine and light across public spaces in the city, including church interiors, terraces, pavements, street corners, gardens, playgrounds and parks. Such a map would ensure that future development would not compromise this precious but under-documented feature. Lara Kinneir[5] has suggested that a model of computer-generated images could be produced to demonstrate how new development proposals will look in five or ten years, or when the sun is not shining on a wet February afternoon. If we are serious about building for life, addressing climate change and creating places that are qualitatively sustainable, we must include new measures to engage with these agendas through the planning process. The above are just a few of the ideas that might be developed in a city such as London, but without a dedicated design team with the licence to think and imagine, the urban debate will be the poorer.

DfL spanned an extraordinary period in both the history of London and the development of urban thinking. The case for good design, public space, city-wide landscape and proactive local renewal strategies still had to be made. The built environment professions were on a steep learning curve and so were politicians and city managers. Thinking of the city as a collage of fragments and valuing the everyday suited the condition of London. London is after all a city of fragments and its in-between spaces offered a rich canvas of possibilities for imagination and intervention (Figure 8.2). The scepticism inherent in mainstream political thinking in the UK and the lack of dedicated large-scale funding for major projects opened up 'tactical' urbanism as a clear strategy for change. This in turn forced DfL to work deep within the political structures of city government, to seek allies and alliances and to find ways of persuading other agencies to steer their programmes towards broader and more imaginative outcomes.

When the GLA was re-established in 2000, the model of a decoupled design agency was probably the only way in which a design agenda could have been incorporated into London government. DfL was more than a design agency. It was given a licence to think conceptually about the city, to be its conscience and act as a positive irritant to stimulate debate within government. This book throws some light on how it operated. Hopefully, other cities will build on some of these ideas and develop them further.

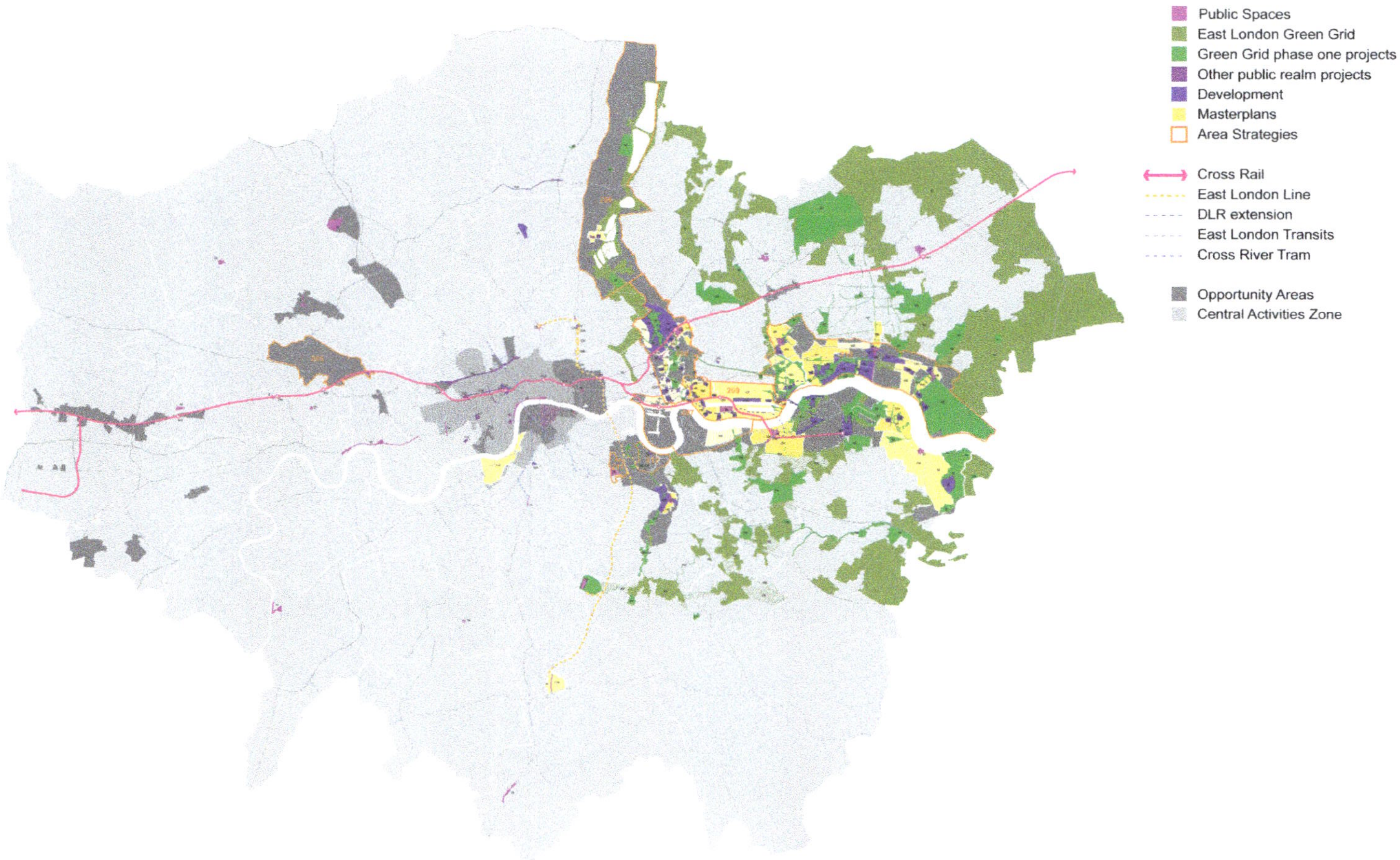

Figure 8.2 London, a collaged city: Design for London projects. Source: Lee Kuan Yew Prize submission, November 2009, DfL/GLA.

Notes

1 Harold Macmillan's famous declaration that 'most of our people have never had it so good' came in July 1957, at a time when the country was riding high on the postwar economic boom. Two years later, the country was hit by inflation and recession, and this, along with internal scandals, paved the way for a Labour government in 1964.
2 The Bishop Review 2011 for the Design Council/the Department for Communities and Local Government, the Farrell Review 2014 and the House of Lords Select Committee 2016.
3 An idea that has been mooted by the architect Graham Morrison.
4 Formerly of Design for London.
5 Formerly of Design for London.

Index

www.ingramcontent.com/pod-product-compliance
Lightning Source LLC
LaVergne TN
LVHW052016300826
846742LV00020B/76
9781787358959